# CARING FOR THE SUICIDAL

John Eldrid

# CARING FOR
# THE SUICIDAL

Constable · London

First published in Great Britain 1988
by Constable and Company Limited
10 Orange Street, London WC2H 7EG
Copyright © 1988 by John Eldrid
Set in Linotron Plantin 11pt by
Rowland Phototypesetting Limited
Bury St Edmunds, Suffolk
Printed in Great Britain by
St Edmundsbury Press Limited
Bury St Edmunds, Suffolk

British Library CIP data
Eldrid, John
Caring for the Suicidal.
1. Suicidal persons. Care
I. Title
362.2'0425

ISBN 0 09 467990 8

TO ROSALIE

# Contents

# List of diagrams

# Acknowledgements

My most grateful thanks are due to the people whom I have had the special privilege of encountering; sometimes they were known as callers, sometimes Samaritans and professionals. I am most thankful for their unique insights and sensitivity, when I was in need.

I am indebted to Pam Wilson for her patience and expertise in the preparation and to Rosalie, my wife and partner, for her continuous support and wise counsel.

We wish to make acknowledgement to the following for extracts used from their editions, publications, or where copyright permission was needed; C. J. Hogrefe, Inc., Toronto – Lewiston – Goettingen for 'Group Therapy for Survivors of Suicide', by Allen O. Battle, published in *Crisis* volume 5, issue 1 (1984), (*Crisis* is the international journal of suicide and crisis studies published under the auspices of the International Association for Suicide Prevention); Edwin S. Shneidman for *Definition of Suicide*, John Wiley & Sons, 1985; the Estate of Erwin Stengel, 1964, 1970 for *Suicide and Attempted Suicide* by Erwin Stengel reproduced by permission of Penguin Books Ltd; Martinus Nijhoff/Dr W. Junk Publishers for *Suicide in Adolescence*, edited by Diekstra and Hawton, 1987; Jonathan Cape Ltd for 'Stopping by Woods on a Snowy Evening' by Robert Frost, *Robert Frost Selected Poems*, ed. Ian Hamilton, Penguin 1973; the King's Fund Publishing office for *Professionals and Volunteers, Partners or Rivals?*, ed. Pat Gordon, 1982.                    J.E.

# Foreword

The act of suicide, attempted or completed, provokes in all of us, professional as well as lay, a riot of conflicting emotions. We are moved with compassion by the thought of someone who so despairs of life as to take the irrevocable decision to end it. We are ourselves driven to near-despair by what we see as our failure to give meaning to the life of another. We are irritated beyond patience by the apparent emotional blackmail implicit in some suicidal acts. And we are threatened by what appears to be a meaningless, a futile gesture. These emotional conflicts, as this book bears out, influence the variety of ways we have of responding to suicide, of recognising or ignoring the suicidal in our midst.

Suicide, as an act, challenges us all. For Albert Camus it was the one serious philosophical problem. Another person's suicide provokes the rest of us to reflect on just what or who it is that keeps us going, that makes life bearable, that sees us through the moments of despair and the occasional dark night of the soul. Is it so surprising, therefore, that we are so ambivalent, so contradictory in our responses to the 100,000 and more who every year in England and Wales make an unsuccessful suicide attempt and the 5,000 or so who in the same place and over the same time scale kill themselves?

Every book needs to be justified. The justification for this thorough, unsensational and sensible book is that it dispels the myths and restates the facts about suicide. It summarises simply and positively the responses we make as individuals and as a society to it and the services we have evolved to cope with its impact on families and friends. It reminds us that suicide respects no social class, no creed, no ethnic group; that while it is true that it is more frequent in the middle-aged and the elderly, suicide is rising in adolescents and young adults across North America and Western Europe.

But this book does more. As befits its title it is an eminently practical summary of the real issues facing anyone who works in a suicide prevention setting. It faces up squarely to the difficulties involved in arriving at a more precise and accurate assessment of suicidal behaviour and it examines the risks that often have to be taken by those engaged in working closely with actively suicidal individuals. Many such individuals are psychiatrically ill but by no means all are. This book adopts the view expressed by, amongst others, Voltaire who pointed out that while there are said to be occasions when a wise man chooses suicide 'generally speaking, it is not in an access of reasonableness that people kill themselves.'

It is fitting that it ends with a section devoted to the problems and the sufferings of those bereaved by suicide. Edwin Shneidman's observation about the suicide's psychological skeletons being put in the survivor's emotional closet underscores the enormity of the impact and after-effects of this most final of deeds, a deed that leaves no room for reconsideration, no opportunity for apologies, no moment for goodbye. If no man is an island, no act of suicide is truly an isolated event. How we respond to the needs of those left surviving is as much a measure of our compassion, our knowledge and our expertise as how we identify and prevent suicide itself. In re-emphasising this fact this book fulfils a pressing need.

But the ultimate test of any book devoted to a subject so seemingly irrational and pointless as self-destructive behaviour is whether it makes it just that little bit less mysterious, less threatening, more comprehensible. Read carefully, this book

meets such a test and as such it cannot be more highly recommended.

Anthony Clare
Professor of Psychological Medicine
St Bartholomew's, London

# – 1 –

# Getting to know them

The experience of being in despair, and perhaps wanting to end it all, is very much part of the drama of daily life. Those who frequently encounter troubled people soon discover that despair and suicide are no respecter of persons. The last straw which breaks the camel's back can fall on anyone irrespective of age, race, creed or social status. Suicide kills at least 1,110 people every day worldwide – that is, one every 80 seconds. In Britain, the average is 84 per week and over 150,000 attempt suicide annually.

It is a sobering thought to recognize that we all have our breaking point and, given the right circumstances, suicide is a possibility for any one of us. Today we may be one of the helpers, but next week in desperate need of help ourselves.

All of us in the course of our lives can expect to experience a number of crisis situations. A crisis is seen to occur where there is an impending new major development in one's life such as birth, adolescence, marriage and first parenthood. Many of these biological events, whilst causing very significant change, will produce positive results. There are also the crises caused by aging, bereavement, divorce; by environmental disasters, road, rail and air accidents, floods, wars; and by economic breakdown with extensive unemployment which cause shock and very negative results. Whilst there are always many contributory factors leading up to suicide crises, a common cause seems to be the pressure of unresolved emotional conflicts. These are not always easy to identify and may be the result of a gradual accumulation of emotional pressure over a long period or during a particularly stressful crisis experience.

It is not unusual for the suicidal crisis to be activated by an apparently insignificant event masking the serious emotional vulnerability of the person concerned. That is why when caring for people in distress it is most important to discover what underlying emotional traumas have been triggered off by the recent events. This requires patience and sensitivity to what is said and unsaid. Quite often the person concerned will be unaware, or confused about what has been happening to them. They need to feel reassured and accepted by the helpers. This will give them time to lower their emotional temperature and help them to explore their inner feelings more deeply. Quite often this reduces the immediate suicidal risk.

In the case of sixteen-year-old Mary, in love with a man in his early twenties, the trigger points were not noticed. She killed herself when he broke off their relationship. Yet many teenagers fall in and out of love without experiencing a major crisis. Mary was different; she was especially vulnerable as her father, to whom she was very attached, had been killed in an air crash when she was 13. Her mother, who had been having extramarital affairs for years, had little or no love for her. Mary desperately needed attention and affection. Her emotional investment in her boy-friend was out of all proportion to his response. After her father's funeral at the local Christian Mission, she began attending regularly. She then stopped going because she felt guilty about having sex. The loss of her boy-friend triggered off feelings of her unworthiness of affection caused by her mother's lack of love, and opened up the terrible unhappiness caused by her father's death. She could no longer cope with the repeated emotional losses and so succumbed to the despair they caused. She did not feel able to ask for help.

If you are feeling happy and calm it is easy to forget how hard it can be to ask for help when you are really down. This can be illustrated by reflecting on the encounters in a Samaritan context, from the caller's point of view. Both of these imaginary first-time callers, want help. David is feeling very low and suicidal, whilst Joe seems to be mentally ill and considering trying to get some professional help.

## THE ENCOUNTER WITH DAVID

1. *How do I open up?* Will I have enough courage? Will they think I am making a fuss? I feel so anxious, so stupid. Better say I'm lonely, do you know of any clubs? I feel so confused and fed up, who the hell are these Samaritan do-gooders who think they are better than me? I just do not know, but I need help – things are getting so desperate, I just cannot manage, I cannot decide anything.

**Note** The caller is expressing anxiety, lack of confidence, confusion, anger and depression.

2. *The vital step – making the call to the Samaritans.* I ask, is that the Samaritans? A friendly voice answers. I forget most of my opening gambit, so I patter on about any old thing. The Samaritan seems interested. I feel more confused. I jump from one point to another. Perhaps it is not serious enough. We play around with various things, the Samaritan seems the kind of person I could trust. Should I speak of my real worries – feelings of wanting to end it all, my inability to make friends, my sexual hang-ups, tell them I have been in mental hospitals, or just how awful I feel? The Samaritan seems rather quiet.

3. *Taking the plunge.* The Samaritan seems OK so I will take the plunge, I pour out confused feelings and facts. I just do not get on, I feel so fed up, so alone. (I am all the time worried how the voice at the end of the phone will react, perhaps he will start telling me not to be so stupid, or tell me to pull myself together, as I should, or think I am just immature with sexual hang-ups.) However, he listens and does seem interested, caring – somehow he seems to share my feelings of confusion, anger, iso-

lation, depression – dare I mention that I have thought of killing myself.

4. *Really getting together.* I begin to feel he is OK – safe, even – so I'd better go the whole way and get it off my chest. But he hasn't noticed any hint of death or suicide, and I know people think you are very weak if you even think of killing yourself. Then he does introduce it, so I feel I'll tell him the truth. Now we are really getting together. He can accept that I have thought about killing myself, accepts my frustrations, my sexual hang-ups etc. I begin to feel good, a bit more relaxed, less angry – this is good. I want to keep up the contact.

## THE ENCOUNTER WITH JOE

1. *How do I open up?* I feel so confused. God! How I wish 'they' would stop following me, bloody CIA. I wish I could know what was happening, I feel so outside myself. I feel I am changing sex, funny no-one seems to notice. I wish those voices would stop telling me what to do. Will these Samaritans try to put me away again? Dare I see a Doctor?
**Note** The caller is out of touch with reality, confused, afraid, feels alone, but is sometimes very aware of reality.

2. *The vital step – making the call to the Samaritans.* God, I must try and do something, the CIA are not going to get me. I must find out, control what is going on, someone must help me. I'd better not say anything about being in a psychiatric hospital, or about wanting to kill myself or someone else. The Samaritan seems safe enough, he listens and seems to understand about the CIA, my loss of identity etc. I wonder if it is a trap – you never know.

3. *Taking the plunge.* I'd better risk it. I can always put the phone down and he doesn't know my real name or address. So I tell him more about the CIA etc and he encourages me to come

to the Centre or meet him outside. He reassures me about confidentiality and all that – so I will try again and see if someone will understand, believe me. Better be very careful.

4. *Really getting together*. So I pour it all out, careful details about the CIA, how I can see myself, how I know I am changing sex and how I have thought of ending it all. How I was locked up in hospital and had no visitors, and how the doctors just used me for experiments. The Samaritan seems very much aware of the CIA, my loss of identity, changing sex, confusion, perhaps he is like me too. I feel I've made some kind of contact. The Samaritan seemed able to listen – in fact he didn't say very much.

Although both these illustrations were in a Samaritan context, a very similar pattern could emerge in an encounter with the neighbour, friend, bartender and so on, depending upon the sensitivity of the helper. The essential qualities are caring, patience, understanding and the ability not to become over-anxious. The more we understand about suicidal behaviour and begin to appreciate the ways people try to communicate their distress, the more confident we will feel about giving help and support.

The suicide ladder (Fig. 1) gives a simple overall introduction to those moved to despairing and suicidal behaviour. It will be helpful if we consider, in some detail, all the steps on the ladder before we begin to explore the bigger question of how we can offer more precise on-going support and help in Chapter four.

The first rung of the ladder is the point of initial encounter through which the early warning signs of suicide may be given to anybody. This person may be a relative, close friend, neighbour, workmate, shop assistant, bartender, barber, Samaritan, GP, professional helper or indeed any caring and sensitive member of the community.

It is most important to recognize that everyone in our society has a vital part to play in the work of suicide prevention. The earliest warning signals are most likely to be noticed by the

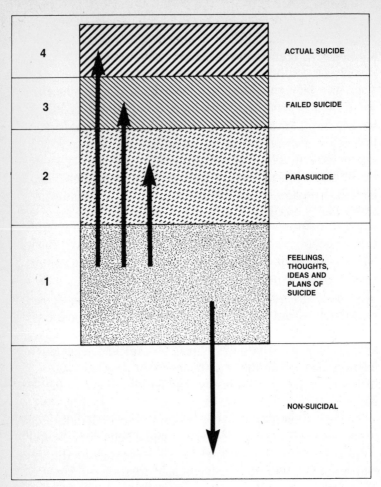

Figure 1: The suicide ladder

person who happens to be nearest at the time of crisis. Therefore, in this book, it will be assumed that those called helpers
are caring men and women. These may or may not be directly
involved as volunteers or professional helpers in suicide prevention. Yet they should all acknowledge the great benefits of
psychological medicine whilst recognizing the need for human
togetherness, because to behave like a human being may save a
life.

We need to guard against the temptation to rush in with
possible solutions and advice. It is essential to recognize that
people in acute crisis situations are very vulnerable and im-
pressionable, therefore great care and sensitivity is needed
when responding to them. Those who have encountered distressed people, as a neighbour or customer, may have been told
how they have been let down by doctors or by some voluntary
agency, when in fact their complaint is that these people did not
solve their problems. Although it is understandable for people
to want relief from emotional pain and distress, and often
professional help can be very effective, one must accept that
emotional pain is part of our daily life. At times of crisis it can be
most therapeutic to have a good listener.

Chad Varah, who founded the Samaritans in 1953, has been
most successful in developing the concept of befriending the
suicidal which is now used most effectively all over the UK and
the Republic of Ireland, and is being developed world-wide[1].
The Samaritans find that callers often say after an initial
encounter that they feel much better for talking. Although their
problems are still far from solved, the callers no longer feel so
alone in their despair and anxiety. When you are out in the cold
feeling suicidal and seeking help, the warm response of another
human being could save you from freezing to death.

Here on the first rung of the ladder we are concerned with
helping people to open up about their feelings, their thoughts
and ideas, their plans for suicide. The most determined is the
one on the left with the arrow ending at the top of the ladder
with actual death. The second arrow ends on the third rung, as a
failed suicide, in spite of definite intentions to end it all. The

third arrow ends on the second rung, because the person was more concerned with crying out for help, i.e. a temporary escape, sleep, an expression of anger and frustration, rather than a commitment to death. The downward arrow goes out into the area where life is still worth living. It is obvious that the first rung is the most important place for recognizing and assessing the degree of suicide risk. Many people very much at risk will seek the help of, or be referred to doctors, clergymen, Samaritans, social workers, relatives or friends. Many of them will not be confident enough to speak openly of their suicidal feelings and thoughts straight away. They are likely to present all kinds of other worries, because they feel ashamed and afraid to mention their need to escape, to attack themselves, to kill themselves or at least to sleep. Or perhaps they are afraid to die.

The great hope is that we will not share their fears and inhibitions, because if we do, it will be difficult for us to help them reveal their suicidal feelings, ideas and possible plans. Our failure could strengthen their wish to go on up the ladder to death or a suicide attempt.

It is as if they need permission to talk about the forbidden subjects. If we are able to help them feel that it is safe to do so, then through befriending, listening, caring and just being there, we can begin to reduce some of the shame and guilt. This will help guide them down from the ladder of despair. It is well established that talking about suicide will not put the idea into a person's head, on the contrary, it will reduce the risk.

Let us look more closely at what is happening on this first rung where we have so much to give and learn. Some may say people who are really suicidal, really intent on ending it all, would not want to talk about it. This is still the common view of the general public. Yet we know from the experience of the Samaritans how relieved many callers are when they feel it is safe to speak about their death-wish. We also know from research carried out by the Institute of Psychiatry in London, and the Suicide Prevention Centre in Los Angeles that the majority of suicides send out direct or indirect signals to friends, relatives, doctors, social workers and members of the clergy – but these are not often picked up. Professor Lader reminds us that,

> the lay belief that those who talk openly about suicide do not kill themselves is fallacious. Up to 70% of people who kill themselves communicate their ideas beforehand, often to several people, and about 40% state their intent unequivocally. It is a sobering fact that over half of patients who commit suicide were either currently or in the recent past consulting a doctor, and often a psychiatrist[2].

Ed Shneidman provides us with some penetrating psychological and sociological insights into what is happening.

*Fable:* People who talk about suicide don't commit suicide
*Fact:* Of any 10 persons who kill themselves, 8 have given definite warnings of their suicidal intentions

*Fable:* Suicide happens without warning
*Fact:* Studies reveal that the suicidal person gives many clues and warnings regarding his suicidal intentions

*Fable:* Suicidal people are fully intent on dying
*Fact:* Most suicidal people are undecided about living or dying, and they 'gamble with death', leaving it to others to save them. Almost no one commits suicide without letting others know how he is feeling

*Fable:* Once a person is suicidal, he is suicidal for ever
*Fact:* Individuals who wish to kill themselves are suicidal only for a limited period of time

*Fable:* Improvement following a suicidal crisis means that the suicidal risk is over
*Fact:* Most suicides occur within about three months following the beginning of 'improvement', when the individual has the energy to put his morbid thoughts and feelings into effect

*Fable:* Suicide strikes much more often among the rich – or conversely, it occurs almost exclusively among the poor

*Fact:* Suicide is neither the rich man's disease nor the poor man's curse. Suicide is very 'democratic' and is represented proportionately among all levels of society

*Fable:* Suicide is inherited or 'runs in the family'
*Fact:* Suicide does not run in families. It is an individual pattern

*Fable:* All suicidal individuals are mentally ill, and suicide is always the act of a psychotic person
*Fact:* Studies of hundreds of genuine suicide notes indicate that although the suicidal person is extremely unhappy, he is not necessarily mentally ill[3].

Therefore it is likely that we may encounter some who are very determined to kill themselves but for some reason are resting on the first rung – a last minute plea. It is unlikely that the very determined will appear so; they may present a very simple problem or worry about accommodation, feeling lonely, inability to pay the electricity bill, or perhaps they feel they are losing their sexual ability to get an erection, or are ashamed of their appearance. All these may be related to the onset of a depressive illness. Some disturbed people, especially committed Christians, will hint at immoral behaviour, guilt about their failings and how they have let God down. These may seem valid subjects for discussion, but they are likely to help us and the distressed person to avoid the real issues. They may lead us into a rather superficial emotional and spiritual dialogue – when the real issues are death, suicide and despair. These subjects; loneliness, unpaid electricity bills, spiritual problems and so on do present important worries and it is most unwise for us to ignore them – they could be the stepping stones to death or life, depending on how we react in our initial encounter. Do we realize that this is only the tip of the iceberg? It takes a lot of courage and inner confidence to recognise that these are the presenting problems. Below them is a cauldron of unresolved conflicts and anxieties, the beginnings of the black despair of a depressive illness. Whilst it is useful to have some education in psychological reactions and mental disturbances, it is most important to use your instinct, your hunches, your feelings, allow yourself to let go and take the risk, by assuming the person is suicidal. If you make a mistake your sincerity may be recognized or you may make a fool of yourself – if you were right you may have helped to save a life. In the care of the suicidal, clear cut assumptions are unwise; a readiness to meet every new encounter as a unique human experience is essential.

No one really knows why human beings commit suicide. Indeed, the very person who takes his own life may be least aware at the moment of decision of the essence (much less the totality) of his reasons and emotions for doing so. At the outset, it can be said that a dozen individuals can kill themselves and 'do' (or commit) twelve psychologically different deeds[4].

We have to accept that it is not always in the person's best interest to try to make him/her feel better, less sad. They may already have approached other people who may have minimized their troubles, or were so afraid they did not want to listen to the awful details. What is needed is to empathize with them, not to jolly them along, rather help them to keep going. As we know, not all suicidal people are depressed, but if you encounter the quiet, rather gentle type of person, never delay checking out all you know about depressive and suicidal signs. It is essential to appreciate that those who are suffering from a depressive illness will find it most difficult to express how awful they feel. This is not because they are playing hard to get, but because it is very difficult for them to articulate their feelings, to be logical, to make decisions, even to concentrate for long enough to explain. An awful fog or mist surrounds them and they feel lost. Indeed they are in a lost state, often aggravated by fear and anxiety.

Take Tom, for example, a solicitor in his late fifties, married with grown-up sons. A churchwarden of the local Anglican church, greatly loved by all age-groups, he killed himself by breathing the exhaust from his car. Some months before his suicide Tom seemed to his wife and friends a little moody, tired, less active than usual. He was not sleeping well, waking very early in the morning. At the last Parochial Church Council two weeks before he died, he said to the vicar, 'Don't you think you should get some new blood – I am getting old!' Yet Tom was regarded as one of the most progressive on the PCC. The young vicar, of rather liberal persuasion, was so pleased to have the support of such a lively churchwarden. Somehow no one had noticed that for some six weeks Tom had been waking very early. His concentration had not been very good – he had forgotten to follow up an enquiry about a project for a new youth centre in the parish. Several people knew about it. He used to be a very keen gardener and of late felt too tired to do anything more than was essential. If his inner secret fear had come to light it would have been discovered that he felt unworthy to be a churchwarden, for some reason God was withdrawing his support. Some sort of blackness was descending upon him – he felt so bad. Tom had all the symptoms of a severe depressive illness – not so uncommon for men at his age.

These people are very seriously ill and will need urgent psychiatric help as well as befriending. They may or may not have a history of depression, sometimes with periods of excessive elation. On the other hand they may be experiencing this depression from within for the first time in their lives. They need lots of firm support with psychiatric help, beware of being non-directive. It is no use asking someone who is acutely depressed to make decisions, it is like expecting someone with a broken leg to walk. They need immediate support without any emotional demands and this may help to reduce the awful sense of loneliness and isolation created by psychotic depression. However, it is most important to realize that in this situation loving, caring support on its own will not be enough and psychiatric treatment is most urgent. Any delays can be dangerous. Reassurance from the depressed person may be very sincere, but they are not in a position to make any promises and should not be asked to do so. It is better not to force the person to get treatment or to enter a protective environment. With such a very depressed person it is more than likely that they are desperately asking for help and will readily go along with the arrangements you can make on their behalf. An extremely high proportion of suicides are caused through psychotic depression, and many people also have a compulsion to kill their immediate relatives in order to save them from the disaster which their delusions forecast as imminent. Yet with modern psychiatric treatment this kind of depression can often be reduced in the comparatively short period of three to four weeks.

On this first rung we must watch also for those who are not suffering from psychotic depression, but are still very suicidal. If they are very depressed as a reaction to an external situation, suicide may be a logical answer for them. Dr George Day, Psychiatric Consultant to the Samaritans, prefers to describe this state as one of 'dispiritment'[5]. Many of these are the men, women and teenagers who have been taught or encouraged that it is essential to have high expectations of their performance at work, family, school, whatever. They have never had permission to fail and so can never give themselves permission to fail.

Take for example, Steve, twenty-seven, an unmarried maths teacher with excellent academic qualifications. In spite of doing well with his work Steve complains of feeling life is worthless. His girl-friend has recently broken off the relationship because he is so selfish. He feels isolated and unable to make close relationships. Seriously considering suicide, his presenting crisis is his tendency to excessive drinking causing lack of concentration. Steve is not an alcoholic and although he is very unhappy and suicidal, he is not suffering from a depressive illness. The underlying problems are about his identity and his failure to keep up with his standards of perfection. He is in a state of dispiritment. There is a great deal of anger and frustration that has built up over the years. As Steve has had little or no positive emotional experiences from either of his parents he feels cut off from those around him and the probability of suicide offers relief. Fortunately for Steve he was able to talk with a very good GP and with his help went into psychotherapy and within two years was beginning to respond more positively to all aspects of his life.

These are often rather 'cut-off' types, sometimes very intellectual people, successful businessmen or war heroes. Watch out for them, because when they get into a crisis situation this will open up many vulnerable unresolved emotional wounds of the past. Suicide or a suicide attempt is a real risk. The unsuccessful student, the high-powered businessman cannot accept the experience of failure. Their great intelligence and power drives cannot be proved wrong at this vital point. The guilty teenager must not fail his A levels. Many people in this sort of situation will respond well to the type of befriending provided by the Samaritans because they will find it less distressing to talk with a stranger. Many volunteers report this can be an ideal befriending situation, providing they can cope with the initially rather powerful and resentful reactions of the callers. Befrienders have to be very sensitive to the need for such callers to get through the crisis with their human dignity more or less intact. Once again much depends upon the early encounters. Many people who are dispirited need friends, but are too emotionally isolated to relate to them. Some are also likely to need long-term therapeutic help in the form of counselling or psychotherapy. At this point our main concern is with having positive encounters and making an assessment. Later, in Chapter five, it will be necessary to consider more deeply the social and psychological reactions of young people.

On the first rung we need to be on the alert for those who are 'setting things in order'; giving up gardening, their hobbies, etc, and for those who are bereaved, not only of husband, wife or gay partner, but also of a goldfish, dog or cat. We need to take note of those involved in shop-lifting, particularly if it is for the first time or out of character; of those in trouble with the police, especially for sexual offences; and of those in the early stages of recovery from a mental illness or clinical depression. When people who have been out of touch with reality begin to come back 'to normal' there is often a heightened anxiety level and they may now have enough energy to kill themselves. The aged and people with a terminal illness are also very much at risk if there is insufficient consistent support and professional care available for them. Many of the people in such situations will not make demands on potential helpers, so it is easy for their distress to go unnoticed.

Alcoholics and drug addicts frequently ask for help when in a crisis and have little intention of changing. They need urgent medical help and support, but be cautious when making emergency arrangements for them as they may suddenly decide not to co-operate. However, when they are motivated for change help is likely to achieve positive results.

At this stage it may be helpful to gather the situations and reactions we have discussed into more defined guidelines to help us in the process of our assessment of the suicide risk. Figure 2 shows five areas of essential enquiry. Initially, we cannot expect to answer all the questions posed in great detail, but they can serve as guidelines for helping with the most necessary assessment work. This is not an exercise in putting labels on people, psychiatric, psychological, social crisis and so on, we are seeking to discover from the distressed person, what is happening and how the emotional pains can be relieved. At the same time we need to recognize it is the quality of the personal encounters which, in the end, are the essential factors for creating positive changes. Wherever possible the distressed person needs to be helped to find their own solutions to their problems.

STAGE 1:   THE SUICIDE ENQUIRY

a. Begin with some general questions – this is a tactful and friendly approach. Encourage the person to talk about themselves and their worries for a while. They need time to feel safe with you, e.g. How do you feel? How are things going? You have had a hard time lately? Then begin to move from the general to the more specific with the idea of giving them permission to speak of their suicidal feelings.

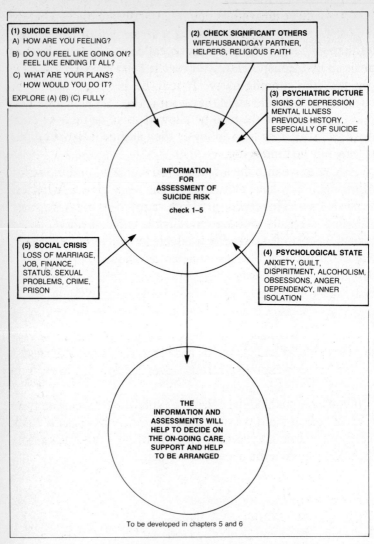

Figure 2: Gathering information for the assessment of suicide risk

b. As you move into this second stage tactfully explore whether they can see any way forward, light at the end of the tunnel? Remember people do not usually reveal their suicidal feelings or plans spontaneously. Have you ever felt like ending it all? Do you feel like running away? It may be better to tackle the question directly and ask if they want to die, or kill themselves. It is important for them to be allowed to voice their suicidal feelings. This does help to lower the emotional temperature, at least for the time being.

c. As you move into the last stage you will need to discover by what means they have thought of killing themselves and if it has been planned. This could vary from vague ideas of taking some pills to a carefully worked out, highly lethal method. If the person has planned a readily available lethal method there is a serious emergency. It is also dangerous when the person sets a deadline, an anniversary or birthday.

*Results*

If it has been established that there is a vague, moderate, or very serious risk of suicide from the answer to the enquiry in stage 1 you will need to explore carefully stages 2, 3, 4 and 5 in order to complete the whole picture.

If you have enabled the person to explore and talk about their suicidal feelings and possible plans, you may have made them feel more emotionally secure. This will make it easier to explore the other stages in the overall assessment.

STAGE 2:   THE SIGNIFICANT OTHER

There will be a need to discover who this is – if anyone. It could well be the wife/husband, the boy/girl-friend. It could be a professional helper – the social worker, doctor or therapist, or even God, Christ or their religious faith.

The person may allow you to talk to a friend or relative who may have contacted you themselves. It may be more beneficial to help the Significant Other, than the caller, as the latter may take more notice of the Other than of you, a newcomer.

It is sadly true that many Significant Others and those who are partly in this role have not had any particular help from those caring for the patient/caller. This seems to happen with those suffering from manic-depression and schizophrenia. It is true there are problems of keeping confidentiality but, in my experience, confidentiality is not the reason why the other person was not briefed or helped.

Sometimes we may have to search hard for the Significant Other, because it may not be the obvious person but the woman in the office, the secret gay partner.

It may be necessary to consider ways and means of creating a Significant Other. The big question then is who shall it be, the social worker, volunteer, etc.? We may have to cope with our own anxieties about commitment, or even a partial or limited involvement. Much may depend upon our reaction.

If there seems to be a sudden loss of Christian significance for the devout person, this could indicate the onset of a depressive illness. For others who are passing through a crisis of faith, despair and possible suicidal ideas may be linked with spiritual and psychological problems. Special care is needed in the confessional and in any spiritual counselling.

Some devout Christians become very angry with God but feel afraid and ashamed to express their anger. This results in serious dispiritment and guilt.

People who have had little or no experience of religious life sometimes seek for some special Significant Other in God. Beware of rushing in with quick solutions, especially quick conversions.

Some people, especially those of the Jewish faith, may have a need to talk of their spiritual problems, but feel ashamed to do so and so need help to explore these worries. The absence of a Significant Other or failure to provide a substitute will increase the risk factor. People who have lost a Significant Other or who do not want anyone are very much at risk. Watch out for the very angry ones, who are turning the anger on to themselves.

STAGE 3: THE PSYCHIATRIC PICTURE

Somehow we must discover whether the person is suffering from depression or not – as we know depression and suicide go hand in hand.

If there is no recent psychiatric information available or the immediate possibility of psychiatric referral is unlikely, we have to make our own assessment. Suicide risk factors cannot be assessed without careful check for the presence of clinical or reactive depression, or dispiritment. It is probably better to begin with depression as this seems more acceptable to people. Then gently check the psychiatric history; a brief account of any hospital admissions, any previous suicide attempts, and types of treatment given can be very illuminating.

Watch out for what may be called a low-key psychotic illness, where the person seems to have a history of sharp mood changes, low-key mania or depression, troublesome personal relationships, suspicion of doctors, drugs, treatment, etc.

There are also those who are out of touch with reality, those suffering from schizophrenia who may not readily disclose their suicidal feelings and plans, or orders from the voices. Peter, sixteen, recently converted to Christianity, says, 'I have special powers since my conversion to Jesus. I will die for everyone – I can save the world if they will listen to me'. Peter was regarded as a brilliant scholar at his public school and was wandering in London beginning a serious loss of contact with reality. Fortunately, in spite of his confusion he had a need to talk and phoned the Samaritans presenting these rather wild claims. He was also beginning to feel very isolated and suicidal – through immediate befriending support and psychiatric help he recovered.

We need to note that depression can appear during the recovery from schizophrenic illness. It may occur through the natural course of the illness or as a complication of long-term drug therapy. Linford Rees points out that

Treatment for depression arising during the course of prolonged phenothiazine therapy may need urgent application because sometimes the depression can be of suicidal intensity and admission to hospital may be needed[6].

It is becoming increasingly important for helpers of all kinds to be more aware of those who are mentally ill or recovering from a recent psychotic disturbance, because it is now the policy for these people to be treated outside hospital wherever possible. Many professional community workers are doing a great job in the care of these patients, but it is impossible for them to continue without effective support from the whole community. Much of the work is being developed in Day Centres and many GPs have a community psychiatric nurse on their team. Because of the more open way of care and treatment, many disturbed people become unsettled and travel from place to place. This is likely, in the long term, to be more beneficial than the incarceration in old-fashioned mental hospitals. At the same time, we have to recognize that very depressed and confused people often find it almost impossible to make a decision. One part of them is refusing help and the other part is asking to be taken into care, so the person may need someone to decide for them. However, whenever possible, it is best to allow people to make their own decisions to take voluntary treatment.

STAGE 4:   THE PSYCHOLOGICAL STAGE

Identification of suicidal risk factors in those with serious psychological problems is not at all easy. It may be the first time they have sought any help and they may have well-developed defences against opening up to the helper.

There is a considerable risk where the client is dispirited, ie. very unhappy or very sad. This is rather like depression, but is reactive to an outside event or related to some inner unresolved conflict. Sometimes anti-depressants will take the edge off the sadness, but they may have little or no effect. Unlike the clinically depressed those who are dispirited may feel happier if their immediate problems are solved or the crisis lessened.

Some will respond to the crisis intervention approach.

The cut-off personality will often be encountered and is very much at risk of suicide. It may help to discuss some of the intellectual pros and cons of suicide with them. Care has to be taken against trying to give too much support, too much emotional involvement. Some may react well to the opportunity to get into psychotherapy. They are likely to be undemanding and may see suicide as an insurance against the unbearableness of life.

People in therapy may often experience periods of quite severe emotional distress and suicide or attempted suicide are quite likely. The distress may be of short duration, a day or so, and the patient is likely to respond well to support which does not interfere with the therapy. The risk of suicide will then be reduced.

Alcoholism and drug addiction are serious factors in suicide risk. Alcoholism has been called chronic suicide by Menninger, the implication being that alcoholics are really trying to drink themselves to death[7]. Neil Kessel and Henry Walton suggest that, as there are close parallels between fluctuations in alcohol consumption and male morality from suicide, the slightest intimation of suicidal intent by an alcoholic must be taken very seriously[8]. A close watch needs to be kept upon alcoholics before, during, and after treatment so that suicidal intentions can be detected in them.

Perfectionists are especially at risk, particularly if their neurotic perfectionist drives get really out of hand. They cannot accept failure and will feel very guilty.

There may be links between the psychological state (stage 4) and social crisis (stage 5) which need to be closely considered in assessing the suicide risk.

It has been suggested that a religious faith commitment to a Christian Church or some other faith, will be a safeguard against suicide. This is not by any means so with people suffering from clinical depression. Many religious faiths are likely to increase feelings of guilt and a sense of responsibility, depression is likely to exaggerate these feelings out of all proportion and so suicide is seen as the answer. Where there is a risk of suicide related to genuine guilt, then the appropriate clergy should be involved. 'At the same time it is essential to recognise not all clergy are literate and one needs to look around for a suitable, informed, priest' (the guidance from Father Anthony Ross O.P., former Roman Catholic Chaplain to Edinburgh University, and a Samaritan leader).

Sexual problems, generally symptoms of underlying psychological difficulties, contribute a lot to suicidal feelings and ideas. These difficulties are likely to cause a lack of confidence and guilt. Many people today are still ashamed to ask for help.

*Dramatic suicide situations* There are a certain number of people who climb on to high buildings threatening to jump, or who lock themselves into a building. Some of these may be acting this way for attention, indirectly asking for help. Others may be mentally ill, paranoid and quite suicidal, so great care and patience is needed with both groups. More often than not they respond positively to help, especially from one person who stays with the situation.

STAGE 5:   THE SOCIAL CRISIS

In many ways it should be easier to help the person who is suicidal due to a social crisis. If the crisis is closely linked to psychiatric problems it will be more complex.

The social crisis and psychological state are bound to be interrelated. The crisis intervention approach may well be very helpful. The risk of suicide is going to be serious at the onset of the crisis and may decrease, as the emotional temperature is lowered with befriending and professional help. If, however, the situation does not show signs of being contained and improving, the suicide risk is very great.

Loss is going to be paramount in most of these situations. Loss of a partner, job and therefore self-esteem, loss of ability to cope financially, loss of status by being cut off by those around you because of a sexual offence or some other crime. Here quick and sustained action is needed for the crisis period – maybe only for a few weeks.

Teenagers are often seriously at risk of suicide or attempted suicide. Many young people make a tremendous emotional investment into their relationships, often out of all proportion to the response of the partner, in their search for affection and emotional support. In all age-groups it is well established that the experience of significant losses in the present trigger off emotional losses and traumatic shocks of the past. Undue distress and prolonged bereavement indicate suicide risk.

There is still a high suicide rate among the elderly and special attention needs to be given following the loss of a Significant Other, or during certain physical illness, thrombosis, high blood-pressure, etc. Many elderly people benefit from anti-depressants and it is important to recognize that being aged does not mean you have to expect to be depressed or in a state of dispiritment.

In our assessment of the suicide risk we will soon discover how frequently situations overlap and that a clearly defined picture is unusual. Therefore it is essential to keep reviewing the situation, taking into account not only the reactions of those in distress but of ourselves as well. In the majority of the suicidal there is a great deal of anger which is sometimes expressed directly or indirectly towards the helpers. We can also expect anxiety levels to be fairly high and it is most important that the helper does not become more anxious than the distressed person. It is because of these problems that continuous consultation with an experienced colleague outside the immediate encounter is so valuable for both the volunteers and professionals.

A SUMMARY OF SOME WARNING SIGNALS OF SUICIDE RISK

1. Depressive illness (especially endogenous)
2. Reactive depression or dispiritment

3. Resistance of the underlying depressed mood when person is in early stages of recovery. *Note* They now have enough initiative to try suicide
4. Normality in schizophrenics, especially in the early stages of the illness
5. Alcoholism and drug addiction
6. A history of previous suicide attempts
7. The suicide of a close relative or companion
8. The loss of the Significant Other
9. Severe personal crisis
10. Inner emotional isolation, the cut-off type of personality
11. Anti-social personalities with abnormal aggressive behaviour
12. Very inadequate personalities
13. Sleeplessness which concerns them greatly
14. Depressive effects of drug treatments for mental or physical illness
15. Sexual failures or problems
16. Post-abortion guilt feelings, depression
17. Shop-lifting, especially for the first time or when out of character
18. Non-demanding approach, often dragged into helping agencies by friends or helpers
19. Serious physical illness
20. Unemployment and financial difficulties
21. The last straw that breaks the camel's back. Those who make a lot of fuss and become very distressed about a minor mishap or loss. There could be very serious worries below the surface.

It is becoming increasingly clear that the care of people in crisis and the prevention of suicide are not the special prerogative of any one group of helpers, whether professional or voluntary. This is well illustrated by three major developments of recent years; the work of the Samaritans, the International Association of Suicide Prevention (IASP) and the Suicide Prevention and Crisis Intervention Centres.

REFERENCES

1. Varah, Chad, *The Samaritans: befriending the suicidal*, Constable, 1985
2. Lader, M. H., *Focus on Depression*, Bencard, 1981
3. Shneidman, Edwin S., Facts and Fables, from an article 'Suicide', written for the *Encyclopaedia Britannica*, 1973
4. Ibid.
5. Day, George, in *The Samaritans: befriending the suicidal*, Constable, 1985
6. Rees, Linfort, *A Short Textbook of Psychiatry*, Hodder & Stoughton, 1982, p. 179
7. Menninger, Karl A., *Man Against Himself*, Harcourt Brace & World, 1938
8. Kessel, Neil and Walton, Henry, *Alcoholism*, Penguin, 1965

# – 2 –

# Parasuicide

'The thought of suicide is a great consolation: by means of it one gets successfully through many a bad night', Nietzsche.

It is estimated that, every year, over 100,000 people try to communicate their feelings of desperation by taking an overdose of tablets. These become associated in the mind of the general public as 'attempted suicides'. For those of us who have the privilege of seeing many of them in hospital and outside, it seems that the majority do not want to die.

It is true that most of them were very upset and often had reasons for taking an overdose. If we look at Figure 1 we will see that those who overdose are coming out of the debating area and are moving up the suicide ladder, taking action towards suicidal behaviour. Many people dismiss overdosing as mere attention-seeking behaviour and do not appreciate the emotional pain and stress these people are suffering. Even some doctors and nurses have this attitude, and a patient who is taken to casualty and then admitted into hospital may have an unsympathetic reception. This is understandable as hospital staff are trained to treat those suffering from an illness of accident, not from deliberate self-harm. It is crucial to realize that overdosing is normally a symptom of underlying feelings of acute desperation, dispiritment, anxiety and sometimes even terror.

It is not easy to measure accurately our own emotional tolerance in a crisis, and some people surprise themselves when

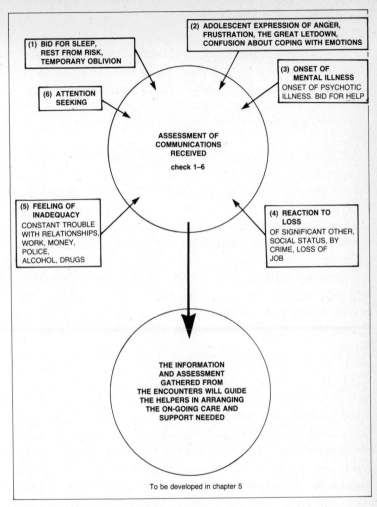

Figure 3: Assessing suicide risk from the communications received

they take an overdose. Most of us will have had some experience of reaching a breaking point and of trying to cope. We may use alcohol, soft or hard drugs, indiscriminate sexual encounters or even kick the cat to get relief from intolerable emotional tensions. A number of Samaritan callers telephoned as an alternative to taking an overdose – or took the overdose when the emergency lines were all engaged at the crucial time.

Unless we are receptive to what they are trying to communicate, we will confuse the situation, causing increased emotional pain in very distressed people and perhaps even placing them more at risk of actual suicide. On the second rung overdosing is used as a way of saying, 'I have had enough, I want help, I cannot stand this emotional pain any longer', 'I am all screwed up inside, I am feeling desperate'. Obviously there are many causes for their distress and it will be helpful if we examine some fictitious presentations of the very common backgrounds to these desperate communications which we can expect to encounter.

FIRST COMMUNICATION: A BID FOR SLEEP

Kate, aged twenty, the eldest of four, had had a very insecure family life. Her father was often violent after heavy drinking. Her mother was very responsible and tried hard to care for the family. At the age of sixteen Kate met Ted a boy two years older than her, who worked in the same factory. He had spent most of his life in local authority homes and found in Kate the ideal girl-friend cum mother. She, desperately wanting to get away from home, he needing to be loved and mothered, they married within the year. Three years later they had a boy, aged two, and a baby girl of six months. Ted was very jealous of the little boy's demands on Kate's attention. He frequently had too much to drink and hit both his wife and the boy. This became worse after the birth of the second child. Kate tried hard to cope and to meet Ted's demands for affection. One weekend both children had colds and Kate had been up most of the night with the baby. Ted, furious because she would not have sex with him, came back from the pub in a rage, very late for Sunday dinner. He told Kate that she was useless both as a wife and mother – for her this was the last straw. She picked up the half bottle of vodka which Ted had left on the kitchen table, rushed upstairs and drank a tooth-mug of water and vodka in which she had dissolved about forty soluble aspirin.

When Kate was questioned by a doctor in the local hospital, it was clear she did not want to die. She needed to sleep, to rest from the emotional torment of her husband and the demands of her two young children. She had been caring and responsible trying so hard to keep the marriage together. It seems that Kate was unaware of the intensity of the inner emotional and physical stress to which she was exposed. That is why she did not ask for help but expressed her need in a spontaneous act of overdosing. This could be described as a desperate cry for help forcing itself out from the depths of her being.

Simon, twenty-two, was adopted as a baby and had always longed for a home and family of his own. When only twenty he married seventeen-year-old Sue, an immature girl quite incapable of coping with money and the day-to-day domestic chores. After two years of marriage they had a son, Jason, now aged ten months. The number of rows was increasing. Simon did all he could to make life easier for Sue, looking after Jason when he woke in the night and playing with him for hours so that she could go out. He was tired and upset to discover that he might be taken to court over non-payment of hire-purchase premiums, in spite of the fact that he had given Sue the money for these.

Simon had always dreaded the thought of getting into debt and of losing his job. He was a loner, not used to asking for anything, and now he felt really isolated. He drank most of a bottle of sherry and took thirty paracetamol tablets and five sleeping pills left over from an old prescription. His communication was – 'I am in a panic, I cannot cope anymore, I want to sleep'. He did not want to die.

Both Kate and Simon were responsible people who did not want to make a fuss or try to be manipulative. Both had come from difficult family backgrounds, and wanted their present family life to work. In most of these cases the victims are shocked when they realize they have overdosed and respond positively to support from Samaritan befriending and help from social workers.

### SECOND COMMUNICATION: ANGER, FRUSTRATION, ANXIETY

In our second communication ages may be similar but the underlying problems are rather different.

Tony, nineteen, youngest of three brothers, is in the second year of a degree course in science at university. At school he was popular, good at work and sports, interested in drama and literature. His elder brothers, aged twenty-two, and twenty-five, had done very well – one a research chemist, the other lecturing in America. The parents were both teachers and highly intelligent but did not have the academic qualifications of their sons.

Tony's mother, deputy head of a church primary school, suddenly announced that she was going to live with the man with whom she was having an affair. At the same time, his father, a member of the Parish Council regarded with respect by everyone, disclosed that he had had a mistress for some time and wanted a divorce.

Tony was extremely shocked, all his illusions about his parents were suddenly shattered. He just could not believe it – how could they have deceived him, the family and all their friends? He had never been particularly close to his brothers, neither of whom showed much marital problems. Tony felt let down – he was a sensitive boy and had not had sex with his girl-friend because he thought he would not be able to face his parents afterwards. He could not handle the emotional turmoil created by their behaviour. He took a large overdose of codeine with whisky. By this act he was communicating anger, especially against his mother, tremendous emotional frustration and an acute sense of loss.

Tracey, almost twenty, an only child, was over-protected by her parents who were ambitious for her. Although she was attractive, she was not a good mixer and her first emotional experience with a man was short lived. At the end of her first year at college her boy-friend jilted her for another student in the same group. Tracey was very upset, then angry and fed up with studying. She was on edge and not sleeping well but no one seemed to care, even her girl-friends said that she was making too much fuss.

At home for the summer holidays, Tracey went to the family doctor who had known her all her life. She tried to explain how she felt but did not mention losing her boy-friend. The doctor assumed that she was over anxious about her studies and told her she had always worried too much. He prescribed some mild tranquillizers and encouraged her to socialize more. Tracey did try the tablets but nothing changed. She felt unable to tell her parents how miserable she was because she had lost her boy-friend. She took a large dose of aspirin but survived. Her communication was, 'I am desperate, I am a failure – help me'.

It is essential to remember that even if a young man or woman feels rejected by their parents, there is still a deep emotional bond. If there has been some instability in past relations with parents, emotional temperatures are likely to soar at a time of external crisis.

Many people in this position are hard to help and when in hospital, will express their anger by being unco-operative with doctors and nurses, pulling out the drip and trying to leave. They have been disappointed by the very people who mean so much to them. On the one hand, they experience hopelessness and feel sad, on the other, they are frustrated and angry. We have to realize that behind depression there is often a great deal of anger. A number of very emotional hurt teenagers, and some adults, show their distress by cutting or burning themselves.

In the following account, Angela aged fourteen, was not so

much angry as afraid and wanting to help. She and her brother Paul, twelve, were both doing well at the local comprehensive school. The children were happy, they seemed a close-knit family, and Angela felt very secure. Her father travelled to work every day and appeared to be successful. Her mother was a very out-going person, relating well to both children. Soon after Angela's fourteenth birthday in January things began to change at home. She noticed that her father often had to work late and her mother was irritable and impatient. As the weeks went by she became more confused, especially when their summer holiday was cancelled. Angela tried to talk to her father but he seemed remote and preoccupied. This upset her as she had always felt close to him. She asked her best-friend about it. This girl's parents were separated and she thought Angela's father was seeing another woman.

Paul went camping for two weeks with friends and in the tense atmosphere at home, feeling shut-out and afraid, Angela made her decision. She had to make her parents realize that family togetherness was important. She reasoned that if she took an overdose her father would surely see how much he was needed by her, her mother and Paul. He would understand the risk she was taking and she would arrange it so it would be he who found her. She found several kinds of tablets in the bathroom cupboard, took them on a Saturday night, and left a note saying she did not want to live if her parents were splitting up. She was communicating her deep concern and distress as she rightly believed that the family was threatened. Her world was falling apart and she was making a genuine attempt to put things right.

Like many teenagers, Angela was bright and intelligent but she still needed the support and understanding of both parents. It would be easy to misinterpret her action as over-dramatic and attention seeking. This is an adolescent girl saying, 'I want to help. I want to share your problems. When you are worried, it scares me, and I worry too because I love both of you'. It is very unwise and dangerous to underestimate the seriousness of this kind of communication, for the next one may result in death. Young people like Angela will need patient support, counselling and perhaps psychotherapy.

THIRD COMMUNICATION: ONSET OF MENTAL ILLNESS

The concern here is for people needing help at the onset of mental illness. They feel confused and may hear voices telling them how to kill themselves. They often have anxieties about a great darkness surrounding them and about sexual obscenities. They sometimes fear they are losing touch with reality.

Janet, twenty-six, had two spells in a psychiatric hospital but since the last one, nearly two years ago, managed to keep a secretarial job. She did well and liked the other girls in the office who were friendly and kind. Soon after being promoted to secretary to the Managing Director everything began to go wrong again. The strange feelings were back and people at work seemed to be plotting against her. Janet knew she needed help but was not sure who she could trust. Since moving south she had missed the social worker who had been very supportive and was apprehensive about contacting the social service office near her new home. Janet saw a doctor instead who promised referral to a psychiatrist. She waited a few days and then noticed a man was watching her flat. What was happening? Were the police going to stop her seeing the doctor? She booked into a cheap hotel, took some capsules and drank a bottle of cough medicine with a warning on the label not to exceed the stated dose. She was admitted to hospital and later transferred to a psychiatric unit. Her communication was, 'I am confused, nothing seems real any more. I feel I am being taken over and need help but I can't rely on anyone'.

It is important to be on the alert for those who are starting a serious depressive illness where the apparent suicide attempt may well be a failed suicide, the person intended to die and only failed by accident. Whilst it is helpful in clinical treatment to use psychiatric labelling such as schizophrenia, manic-depressive, endogenous depression, it is essential to recognize that the patient is a person, an individual. Generally, those who are mentally ill are only partly out of touch with reality and most of their needs are the same as the average person. Someone in a deep clinical depression and almost emotionally dead can still benefit from Samaritan befriending especially when combined with professional psychiatric treatment.

FOURTH COMMUNICATION: REACTION TO LOSS

In the fourth communication, we look at reactions to the loss of a lover, friend, spouse, gay partner, job or self-esteem. This is very much a bereavement situation but there are certain aspects which are different from reactions to loss by death, because the present separation is likely to trigger off the memory of other past losses which have not been resolved. The person who has invested all in their love relationship, job, intellectual activity or social status is truly bereft.

Raymond, forty, a successful solicitor, has always felt the need to give and wanted very much to be loved. His father was a regular naval officer who lived for the Navy. His mother had been killed in a road accident when Ray was twelve and at boarding school. Over the years he had had several gay relationships. For the last six months he had shared his flat with a young man of twenty-two. Ray was not only sexually attracted to Ben, he also felt he was needed by him and helped him in many ways. Ray knew that Ben might want a younger partner for sex, but was devastated when Ben did not need him any more as a friend or elder brother. It seemed to Ray that he was as isolated and grief stricken as when the Headmaster had told him of his mother's death. He drank some brandy and swallowed a large number of sleeping pills. A friend found him and he survived. Ray's communication was, 'I am so alone. I have lost everything that matters to me. I want to be loved. I do not want to die'.

Ray's communication is about the need to be cuddled rather than the wish to be dead. (For the psychoanalytically inclined, it may be worth considering the possible link with warm cuddling and wanting to get back into the womb, and even the mystical idea of salvation in death). People like him have to be dependent upon someone, they desperately need a mother figure, they are like a frightened child crying to be comforted. For anyone in this situation, overdosing is a deliverance. We need to remind ourselves again not to underestimate the underlying pains and anxiety which are associated with loss.

*Loss of social status*
James, aged thirty and unmarried, lived with his mother, a very demanding woman. His father died in an industrial accident when the boy was fourteen. James was always rather shy at school and had few friends. He had several O levels and an A level in Economics. He was a bank clerk, worked hard and was well liked at the branch in a small respectable West-Country town. He had had one or two girl-friends but was not confident enough to develop a long-term relationship. Although not really interested in politics, he got involved with the local liberals through a male colleague at the bank. To his surprise, several of the older members greatly admired him seeing him as a good example of the younger generation. As he was interested in figures, he became treasurer of the local committee. Everything seemed to be going well, except that he felt the need to expose himself. This trouble first started on a visit to Plymouth when he was nineteen. Since then he had tried hard to stop and was terrified of being caught by the police. At the same time, he had to admit that he felt the urge to take the risk. Then the worst happened. He was coming home from a meeting one evening at about eleven feeling fed up because the secretary, an attractive girl in her mid-twenties, had ignored his shy advances. He saw two teenage girls coming across the park and rushed out in front of them and exposed himself. James was unaware of a courting couple nearby. The man, thinking from the girls' screams that there was likely to be a rape overpowered James. He was duly charged, put on bail and referred for a psychiatric report. James was shattered. His case made headline news in the local press

and his so-called friends shunned him. He resigned from the Liberal Committee, although the Chairperson had tried to persuade him not to do so. He felt he could not face investigations by the local probation officer and another appearance in court. He took all his mother's sleeping tablets with whisky. He was found by his mother, whose early return from visiting her sister saved him from death. His communication was the same as Ann's.

She was forty, married with three children; two boys of ten and thirteen and a girl of seventeen. Ann worked as an accountant in a small business firm, had a good work record and had always been very honest. Her husband, aged forty-eight, with whom she got on well, was a clerk with the local council. Although both managed their finances well, they were often short of money. Ann discovered that it was possible to fiddle the books. After six months, when the auditors were due, she was horrified to find a deficit of almost £1,000. She was not the type of person to ask for help as she had always been taught to cope alone. She was panic stricken. Her husband, a Baptist, would be so shocked and her daughter was soon to go away to college. Ann went to London and booked into an hotel for one night. She took a large dose of paracetamol with gin. She did not die because she was found by an irate hotel manager who wanted the room cleared.

Both James and Ann were deeply shocked and hurt by the loss of social status that their offences were bound to create. They are both saying, 'I am ashamed, I can never hold my head up again. I shall be cast out by those who point the finger'. The overdosing of people in these circumstances may be well thought out, failing only by accident. Often it is a desperate plea for help and, not surprisingly, a physical need for sleep.

Those who are in trouble with the police, especially concerning sexual offences, experience a mixture of inner isolation and panic. It is not unusual for them to have kept the crisis to themselves and not told anyone. Overdosing may well be seen as an answer, or at least a respite from the tension. We should not interpret this as taking the easy way out. Those of us who have had the opportunity of receiving their confidences (certainly not uncommon for Samaritans and many professional workers) recognize that most have made great efforts to be responsible.

FIFTH COMMUNICATION: FEELING OF INADEQUACY

We encounter many who just never seem able to manage their lives. They have problems with relationships, cannot keep jobs, get into trouble with the police and often are addicted to alcohol or drugs. Some may have very aggressive personalities whilst others may be over-dependent on family or friends.

Linda, twenty-one, youngest of three, unmarried, had moved into the city from a small town and lived with her boy-friend. She was glad to leave home for when her father had had too much to drink he used to become very angry when Linda would not allow him to fondle her. Linda's mother suffered from depression and her two brothers were in prison for robbery. After three years her boy-friend left her and their two-year-old son Danny, for a girl who used to baby-sit for them. Linda's feelings for the little boy were mixed and more often than not sentimental rather than loving. Sometimes she felt threatened by him and would lose her temper if he cried when she got tired of playing with him. Her health visitor was patient but Linda did not trust anyone, especially social workers. She felt very lonely and started going to a pub in the evenings. When Danny was taken into care because of her inability to cope with him, Linda overdosed, taking all the tablets in the house with neat gin. She was found by the health visitor and soon recovered. It was her second overdose, the first being when she was only fifteen. This young woman was saying, 'I cannot cope, I feel helpless, I am angry because nobody really cares about me or wants to bother with me'. Unfortunately this last comment was true since most of her helpers had found her attitude too demanding.

Most of the people in the fifth pattern will have a history of disrupted family life and may come from areas recognized as deprived, places with high unemployment, or the subject of social concern. The overdose rate in prisons, both for those on remand and those serving a sentence, is well above average. Support from probation officers and others does often prove rewarding despite personality difficulties. Such support may save the person's life by reducing their suicidal behaviour, which is otherwise likely to increase the risk of actual suicide.

SIXTH COMMUNICATION: ATTENTION SEEKING

In our last pattern we look at those who could be said to give suicidal behaviour a really bad name. This is because they use it directly as emotional blackmail. In many ways, what they do is very simple. They take tablets in order to get attention and to change the emotional attitudes of their lover, relatives, friends or whoever does not comply with their wishes. They manage their lives by manipulating other people. There are some easily recognizable aspects of their behaviour – they will play hard to get and will present some wonderfully dramatic stories yet withhold essential information as it suits them. The difference between them and the other people we have considered is that they intend to control and manipulate the helpers. Whilst others are desperate for help and are taking very dangerous action as a way of coping, those of this last group never endanger their lives and make sure that they will be found. Their communication is, 'You have got to do things for me and if you do not, I will make you sorry'. People who can communicate only through this sort of emotional pressure, certainly have problems with relationships and can only be helped by not complying with their demands. They need to feel more secure and may respond to firm, consistent support.

These imaginary stories of typical suicidal behaviour show that we will encounter a variety of people on the second rung. There will be a great deal of overlap as clear-cut patterns are seldom found in practice. Nevertheless they are useful as a basic guide to understanding how varied the needs of desperate people can be. The question we must ask about those whom we meet on the second rung is, 'Do they want to kill themselves?' A great many acts of overdosing seem to be impulsive rather than not premeditated. However as Stengel pointed out

> Some warning of suicidal intention has invariably been given. Those who attempt suicide tend, in the suicidal act, to remain near or move towards other people. Suicidal attempts act as alarm signals and have the effect of an appeal for help, even though no such appeal may have been consciously intended[1].

It was Stengel who first examined the differences between those who attempt suicide, or engage in suicidal behaviour, and those who intend to kill themselves. Later in 1970 Kreitman used the term parasuicide to refer to any act deliberately undertaken which mimics the act of suicide but does not result in a fatal outcome. We will confuse the situation if we describe all overdosing as attempted suicide. As we have seen, it seems rather to be concerned with the communication of the desperation and loneliness associated with acute anxiety and dispiritment.

Overdosing is likely to bring about changes which can be for the better. Some people feel much happier when they discover they have survived. They feel that God, or perhaps fate, wants them to live. They may also experience a release of aggressive feelings and tension. However, there is always a small minority who are extremely upset to be alive. They intended to die and failed to do so, either by being found by accident or through miscalculating the strength of the tablets taken. Most of these will be suffering from clinical depression or have logical reasons for suicide.

Both Stengel and Kreitman warn us to be on the alert for misinterpreting the signs, noting only the strength of the overdose. For example, a man who took a few sleeping tablets and only became rather drowsy had intended to kill himself. He failed because he genuinely thought that such a dose would be fatal. A serious suicidal intention such as this must be picked up; he will not make the same mistake next time.

When a person has overdosed, it is essential to clarify why it happened at that particular time. Events leading up to the act need to be ascertained. With both Kate and Simon, there was an obvious build-up of emotional stress; their past social and psychological contributed to an apparently impulsive act. It is important to be aware of the personality of those concerned and how they relate to people and stress situations. Family background can be very relevant; with all the examples given, except Janet, early family history would have been particularly useful to point the helpers to a deeper understanding of the individual's emotional needs. Sally O'Brien, discussing reasons given for taking an overdose, writes,

> To ask why people commit or attempt suicide, is rather like asking why people encounter disaster or become ill. The act of self harm is a response to great unhappiness which can be promoted by an infinite number of factors. When people were asked why they had taken an overdose, their answers were invariably superficial, usually offering the most immediate reason they could think of and the problem or problems which were at the forefront of their minds at the time. For most of the people many aspects of their lives have been wrong for a long time. It was the most recent crisis which was given as the reason although often this was the 'last straw'. For example, the most common reason given was the break-up of a relationship. Yet after talking with the people for some time, it became clear that there were many other factors involved and that the broken relationship was the last support to go and acted as a trigger[2].

There are two reactions which the helper, whether professional or volunteer, should practice.
1.  To make every effort to accept the patient/caller as a fellow human being in a desperate state. How the helper feels will soon

become apparent to the distressed person, so he needs to empathize and show that he understands that suicidal behaviour is an expression of their inner emotional pains. It will be useful for the helper to have some insight into his or her vulnerability to sensitive areas of their own unresolved inner conflicts.

2. To make themselves available, with all possible skills and experience, to help the patient/caller to discover what is happening.

This implies that all overdosing should be taken very seriously and that the helpers have a responsibility to assess the possible risk of a repeat overdose, or actual suicide, in the near future. It is estimated that twenty per cent of those who overdose will engage in this suicidal behaviour again within the next twelve months. People like Tony, especially if their serious problems are not reduced, may become more dispirited and use overdosing as a way of coping.

In Sally O'Brien's study of people aged eighteen to thirty she,

was able to verify that 77 people (39%) had made a further attempt at self-injury during the following year . . . During the first 3 months following the initial overdose, 20% of the men, and 24% of the women, had repeated. After one year, however, the rate for men remained constant at 27% while the rate for women had risen to 41%[3].

It seems that those most likely to repeat have a history of psychiatric treatment or have been victims of considerable relationship problems. It is not easy for them to respond positively to help and often they do not seem motivated to improve their situation. A great deal will depend on the rapport which can be established with the helper. In many encounters there will be a lot of unexpressed anger. When this is turned inwards, the risk of a repeat overdose is increased. When directed outwards, there may be some positive results provided that, in spite of the conflict, the helper and patient/caller can maintain a good relationship. This may need to continue with the same helper over a year or more. Even when a person is able to respond positively to psychiatric treatment and psycho-therapy, a Significant Other needs to be available in a parental role. Social workers and Samaritans frequently fulfil this need very effectively. We shall be considering the repeating pattern further in Chapter three.

Some of the most tragic of our encounters will be with those who make great efforts to keep going without overdosing. Then the emotional pressures return often more urgent than before. Many will have a very poor self-image so they are still vulnerable to changing events, become caught up in another overdose. It is not easy to appreciate the sharpness of the pain they feel. A person with little experience of being wanted, accepted and approved of by parents has a built-in sense of worthlessness. Trouble and rejection are expected and quite often they help precipitate it as their destructive tendencies take over. In other words, the destructive re-action is used as an emotional defence against anticipated rejection.

Sheila, twenty, was the youngest of three, living in a large northern industrial city. All the children had spent most of their early life in care. Both parents were very inadequate and her father often battered her mother. In many ways Sheila had the worst time of all since her brother and sister had stayed with their grandmother when they were very young, whereas she had been taken into care twice, for six months when she was two, and again at the age of five. Her mother was very withdrawn, offering her little or no affection. Her father could be very rough but always made a lot of fuss of her and she maintained that he did love her. Sheila took her first overdose when she was thirteen. This followed a frightening row with her father when she was accused of stealing from the corner shop. Although Sheila was not very intelligent, she was shrewd and not afraid to take risks. There was never enough money at home as her father was unemployed and her mother unemployable. She hated school where most of her friends were continuously in trouble with the police. She had been shop-lifting in a small way since she was ten, stealing sweets or cigarettes, sometimes a packet of soup or an apple. She always shared these things with her mother, secretly hoping that these little presents would please her, but they did not seem to make much difference. The shop owner told her father that next time he caught her taking sweets he would go to the police.

The most distressing part for Sheila was that her father called her a slut and a dirty thief and threatened to throw her out and get her taken into care again. She knew that he also stole things – she and her sister used to keep watch while he tried to break into parked cars. The overdose was not too serious but it did get her admitted into hospital for a few days and a few more visits from a social worker. This had the effect of making the owner of the corner shop more friendly towards her although this had not been her intention. She was too naïve, and angry with her father, for such subtle games. The following year, Sheila was put into care after her father was sent to prison for eighteen months for robbery. When she was seventeen, she went to London where she worked as a live-in chambermaid at a second-rate hotel. She did quite well and met up with Tim, a twenty-five-year-old divorcee. She moved in with him sharing a large flat and he made her his secretary in the modelling agency he and a friend were starting.

Sheila could not believe her luck. Tim was so gentle and treated her like a lady. For a short time she was happy and then one evening he was late home. At midnight police came and took her to the station. They told her that Tim was pimping for prostitutes. The police did not believe Sheila's innocent re-actions to their questions which went on for hours. She felt trapped and, as in the past, very wronged. She realized that Tim was also involved in hard porn and that she would be arrested for assisting him. She panicked and took a large number of tablets. She was in hospital again and, as before, her actions initiated good social work support. Sheila's communication was a protest, as it had been with her father, 'I am being used. I have been let down again'. She did see overdosing, despite the risk, as a way of coping. Sheila had a built-in negative reaction to life's demands. This has the effect of making her, and others like her, natural victims of suicidal behaviour.

We need to recognize that all assessments must be seen as an on-going process, as people may improve or become more suicidal. We should be alert for signs of clinical depression, mood changes related to dispiritment and sadness, and for deterioration in the support systems. It is estimated that almost half of all suicides have a history of parasuicide, therefore it is important to check out the degree of possible risk. Some or all of the factors in the check list below, compiled by Kreitman and Dyer, may be present when assessing the actual possible risk of suicide following an overdose.

*Factors predictive of repetition of parasuicide (UK)*
1. Previous parasuicide
2. Previous psychiatric treatment, both in-patient and out-patient
3. Sociopathic personality disorder
4. Alcohol and drug abuse
5. Lower social class
6. Unemployment
7. Criminal record

*Risk factors for suicide following parasuicide*
General characteristics:-
1. Age (risk increases with age)
2. Sex (males – females)
3. Social isolation (especially with recent loss of job or partner)
4. Sociopathic personality disorder
5. History of multiple previous parasuicides

*Characteristics specific to current episode*
1. Depression – suicidal thoughts
    – persistent insomnia
    – feelings of hopelessness and worthlessness

– social withdrawal
– restlessness and agitation
2. Use of violent methods or medically serious drug overdoses
3. Circumstances of the act

*Circumstances of the act associated with suicidal intent*
1. Isolation (no one nearby)
2. Timing (so that intervention is unlikely)
3. Other precautionists avoid intervention or discovery (e.g. making excuses for not turning up when expected)
4. Not acting to get help after act
5. Final acts in anticipation of death (e.g. making a will, arranging insurance)
6. Active preparation for attempt (e.g. making special arrangements to obtain the means)
7. Suicide note.[4]


Jenny, sixteen, was an only child of older parents who seemed to resent her. Her father was a managing director of a successful business. Her mother's main concern had always been to look after her husband. Although her parents had never admitted it to Jenny, her birth had been a mistake. Her mother had never wanted a child and her father's main interest was work. She was well cared for, had plenty of toys and clothes as her father was very generous with money. Her parents often had to go abroad on business trips so Jenny went to boarding school from the age of seven. She soon realized that if she was to get any attention from her parents she must not cause them any trouble or make emotional demands. She was liked by her teachers as she was obedient and quick to learn. She did not mix well with girls of her own age-group and used to have 'crushes' on the older ones. She felt very lonely and saw the need to please all the powerful people around her. When she was thirteen her reactions began to change. One reason for this was that she became aware of her attraction to men. During the long summer holiday her parents arranged for her to stay with a family in France, to improve her

French and to leave them free to enjoy their own social life undisturbed. Living with the French family was quite unlike anything Jenny had experienced before. The parents were very caring and the three sons, aged thirteen, fifteen and seventeen, were impressed by how well she could speak their language. Her initial shyness began to disappear. As her visit was a success, she continued to stay with the family for most school holidays or they would come to her parents' house in London. On their third visit, they brought their nephew, Pierre aged twenty-four, who was soon to begin work in England. Jenny became his constant companion, showing him the sights and gradually falling in love. It was a glorious summer for her and, after her first sexual experience with Pierre, she felt really wanted and that all her romantic ideas about the 'marriage of true love' were coming true. Pierre had already had several girl-friends and had no intention of committing himself. When they met again at the beginning of the Christmas holiday, he told her that they would not meet anymore as he had found someone else. For Jenny, believing that love would solve everything, this was the end of the world. She took a large overdose of sleeping tablets. Her mother found her, called in a private doctor and she survived without going to hospital. Her parents dismissed the whole thing as adolescent foolishness. But Jenny could not face going back to school where she had boasted to her friends about her 'affair', and she felt unwanted at home. She took another overdose and her body was found in the park.

Things might have been very different if someone had taken the first communication seriously. Jenny was saying, 'I am miserable, I want to be loved but nobody cares'. She had a neurotic need for affection and approval. She had never had a feeling of well-being from her parents. Nevertheless, she was neither mentally ill nor clinically depressed. Jenny had expected far too much from the relationship with Pierre and had hoped to find, in marriage, an end to her feelings of inner loneliness. Her psychological difficulties could have been resolved with professional help and befriending. In her first overdose, Jenny was crying out for help. By the time of her second attempt she seems to have reached the point where she felt all the doors were closed. We recall how she never felt able to express her anger – now, in the last resort, she turns on herself.

It is not vital to discover whether a suicidal act was impulsive or premeditated. What is essential, when dealing with distressed persons, is to try to pick up what they are communicating. They will need help to verbalize their feelings because they will be confused by their inner emotional conflicts. All helpers, Samaritan befrienders or professionals involved in treatment and counselling, should enable them to express their negative feelings. Attention must be given to their apparent problems and any signs of depressive illness. These may not be identified until the caller feels it is safe to talk. Whilst it would be foolish to disregard the importance of the clinical expertise of doctors, I know from long experience, that positive feedback comes from the patients who thought their doctors understood them as individuals. Naturally, a good doctor/patient relationship is helpful in all cases, but in suicide-related problems it could make all the difference between accepting or rejecting on-going help.

The summary in Figure 3 may help to chart some possible routes through the complex suicidal channels strewn with partially submerged wrecks of emotional pain. Stengel helps us here when he writes,

> . . . uncertainty of outcome characterising premeditated attempts as well as impulsive suicidal acts. It is often believed that the latter need not be taken seriously because they are thought to be precipitated by the situation rather than by conscious suicidal intent. However, closer psychological examination of such attempts usually reveals previous suicidal thoughts[5].

Kreitman and Dyer, writing about intention in parasuicide point out,

The definition of parasuicide makes no reference to intention, which cannot be used as a criterion since the patient's motive may be too uncertain or too complex to be ascertained readily. When asked, 'why did you do it?', the majority will deny they wanted to kill themselves. Many will reply, 'I just don't know'. Since parasuicide is usually carried out at the height of an interpersonal crisis by an individual feeling desperate or confused, such obscurity of intent is not all surprising. Moreover, approximately two thirds of the men and nearly half the women who present as parasuicides have taken alcohol within a few hours of the act[6].

Kreitman and Dyer also stress the need for parasuicides to be assessed on a broad basis and this should include a psychiatric assessment.

Most help required by parasuicides is unrelated to their likelihood of suicide. Social crises require amelioration, the distressed require counselling support and very occasionally drug therapy, while the mentally ill require treatment appropriate to their condition[7].

As with all suicidal behaviour, we have to acknowledge that people have very mixed feelings about why they react to crisis situations by overdosing. This ambivalence for life or death is well illustrated in Jack L. Rubin's biography of the great psychoanalyst, Karen Horney.

She was a very loving and sensitive person and experienced times of deep dispiritment following her brother Berndt's death from a pulmonary infection at the age of 40. She was deeply upset and while on holiday with her family and friends went alone for a swim. When she failed to return after more than an hour, Oskar, her husband, found her clutching a piling in deep water, ruminating on whether to end her life or swim back to the beach. Much pleading was required by Oskar and his friends to convince Karen her life was worth living[8].

Many of those who overdose are very confused about what to do and find it extremely painful to cope with their conflicting feelings. This makes it difficult for them to be co-operative with would-be helpers. It could account for their apparent rejection of offers of help. Those who have a day or two's stay on a medical ward, sometimes arrange to discharge themselves before being seen by a psychiatrist or social worker. Many also ignore arrangements for an out-patient appointment with a psychiatrist. Commenting on the effect of overdosing in the 'Nursing Mirror', Bhagat and Shillitoe have some pertinent observations.

We may conclude that difficulties in relationship precedes the act until some interpersonal crisis precipitates the actual attempt. The attempt demonstrates to the partner that she is in distress. What clearer statement could she make than she no longer wishes to continue to exist in the present state of affairs? It generates powerful conflicting emotions in both partners. The husband or boyfriend may be filled with remorse and anxiety; he feels he is to blame; his failure is made public; he may decide to mend his ways and the act may bring them closer. On the other hand, it may drive them further apart, and a definite break in the relationship may follow. It may, for example, confirm his negative impression of her. In a sense, therefore, the act 'works'. After it, things are rarely the same again – they either improve or break down altogether. As for the 'patient', what of her chaotic feelings? She knows she is not ill yet she is occupying a hospital bed. She is unclear about her future, knows she did not really want to die, yet finds it difficult to admit this to the staff for fear of appearing a fraud. To admit to personal failure is to lose face, especially for the younger person, as the admitting doctor and many of the nurses may well be. Hostility breeds hostility and suspiciousness. Each person is playing a role which hides the true nature of the situation. They are caught up in a game which none of them really want to play . . . Naturally, self imposed illness is annoying, time-wasting and the sullen

'Leave me alone' attitude is provocative. A vicious circle of negative attitudes is formed. The patient can see that she is different from the others on the ward, and she is treated as being different. Fear also plays its part. The inexperienced nurse is afraid of saying something to upset the patient, perhaps being the cause of another suicidal attempt. The fear is nearly always groundless.

True, this type of patient *does* need to be treated differently from the usual medical patient – but in an open and accepting way that recognises their distress. They need to be able to understand the reasons behind their behaviour, to come to terms with it, and to realise that they are in acute distress, rather than just a passing nuisance. Hostility and lack of sympathy do not help, even though they are understandable reactions. With the exception of a very few highly manipulative and psychotic individuals, they are people like ourselves who find themselves in a situation they cannot tolerate. To react to this with a lack of tolerance is to increase the stress and conflict. How would you like to be treated? Put yourself in their shoes. To be sure, some of you, someday, will be wearing them![9].

In the medical ward of a city accident hospital, where all people who had overdosed were seen by the chaplains as a matter of routine, a number of patients were told about the Samaritans and offered the means to make contact. About twenty-five per cent accepted the offer and benefited from Samaritan support and befriending in hospital and in the follow-up outside. It was interesting to discover that about a further five per cent got in touch with the Samaritans six months to a year afterwards, saying they had been told when in hospital that they might get help if they did not want to overdose again.

At the Central London Branch of the Samaritans, on average twenty-six per cent of new callers per year have had a history of taking overdoses. About thirty-five per cent have quite marked suicidal feelings, thoughts and ideas, and of these fourteen per cent had some definite plans. It is almost impossible to estimate how many of those would have tried parasuicide or actual suicide without this special intervention i.e. Samaritan befriending, counselling and frequent arrangements for professional help.

In her study of young people who overdosed in Central London from 1975–1978[10], Sally O'Brien points out that the persistent need of those she interviewed was, 'I need to talk to someone'. She says,

> . . . with few exceptions, most of the services were unable to offer enough time for people to talk fully. Furthermore, many people required more than just being listened to[10].

The experience of the Central London Samaritans shows that where potentially suicidal callers were given support, and professional psychological help was activated, the situation greatly improved.

Now let us recall what we have discovered so far about the people we are likely to encounter of the second rung of the ladder. All have shown some kind of suicidal behaviour involving different degrees of risk to life according to the lethality of the act. The problems causing this behaviour are mainly concerned with breakdown in interpersonal relationships, long exposure to excessive emotional stress and basic personality difficulties. Very few are suffering from any diagnosable psychiatric disorder and where there is any, it is generally depressive illness.

We have observed that there has been a great increase in suicidal behaviour in the last thirty years in all Western countries, especially among young people between fifteen and twenty-five, with a markedly higher proportion of females. At the same time, we can also expect to meet a considerable number of older people. Overdosing and wrist cutting are both seen as a way of communicating a person's desperation, anger and distress and are a cry for help which should always be taken seriously.

A society which still finds it so difficult to understand actual suicides, accepts those who engage in parasuicide even less. This may be a major contributory cause of the increase of actual suicides, especially of those under twenty-five. Throughout history an intensity of emotions and acts of excessive enthusiasm are common among the young. Today, when we speak of 'youth culture', and 'teenagers', on the one hand we give them a more significant status in society than ever before, yet on the other, parents and older people so often do not want to listen and are not prepared to appreciate how much young people need them. Some of the trouble may be due to older peoples' jealousy of the greater freedom and opportunities of modern youth. These improved conditions create many additional demands with which the adolescent has to cope. For those who live in the depressed areas where there is little or no hope of a job, these demands are reversed. The problem then is not that there are so many opportunities for them, but so few. Therefore many are attracted to easy escape routes. These may include the quick uplift by stealing or the psychological high of glue-sniffing. There is a danger here that the 'negative scream' expressed by some in overdosing, will be shown in aggressive acts. Perhaps the other side of the overdosing coin is outward aggressive behaviour.

All this comes at a time when the need to find an identity is so important, as the young man or woman struggles to handle their emerging sexuality. Young people have to cope with a variety of choices, often charged with emotional dynamite. They constantly need to have the opportunity to talk out and take soundings of their emotional depths about how they can deal with the drama of their daily life.

Many children and teenagers become part of the tug-of-war created by marital breakdown, having to decide for themselves which parent to see, and having to cope with the trauma of a new mother or father. Many are over-exposed to emotional pains which no young person should be expected to bear. The premature break up of the family is likely to shake the foundations of a child's world. It is not surprising that they experience a lack of confidence when they are older and a bewilderment about the future. All of us, from time to time, need consolation and caring support from those who give a special meaning to our lives. When there are problems about drawing on parental resources, other forms of consolation, such as drugs, alcohol and violence may be sought. When the distress becomes unbearable, it may well result in suicidal behaviour to anaesthetize the emotional pains and to plead for help. We have to be aware of the danger that suicidal behaviour may be seen as a form of deliverance. Some young people may get caught up in the mystical idea of dying without really grasping the finality of death itself.

René Diekstra and Ben J. M. Moritz point out the enormity of the problem.

> The total rate of attempted suicides coming into contact with medical agencies in the EEC was estimated by Diekstra (1982) to be 215, with a range of 54 (Milan, Italy) to 440 (Edinburgh, GB) per 100,000 persons aged 15 years and over. According to results of 3 sample survey studies, 2 of which were carried out in the Netherlands and one in Gt Britain, this figure is less than one-third of the total attempted suicide rate (that is, attempted suicides that do and do not come into contact with medical agencies) 700 per 100,000 persons aged 15 years and over. Based on these figures, the total number of suicide attempts in the EEC in 1976 was estimated at 1,400,000 of which nearly 432,000 were seen by medical agencies[11].

It is recognized that adolescence is a time when young people are at the peak of their emotional vulnerability and therefore a period when emotional adjustments are needed. In the last thirty years, parasuicide seems to have become one of the major ways of communicating their conflicts. There are three key groups found in suicide prevention work;
1. Society: parents, teachers, neighbours, colleagues
2. Volunteers, as in the Samaritans
3. Professionals: social workers, therapists, general practitioners and psychiatrists

The future life of many adolescents will depend upon how tuned in the people in these three groups are to the warning signals of emotional vulnerability of troubled teenagers who have overdosed. We have an erudite reminder of our task from Professor Erwin Ringel, founder of IASP. When addressing the tenth anniversary of the German Society for Suicide Prevention in 1983, he spoke of the importance of follow up care;

The dispute between those attaching equal significance to both suicide committed and suicide attempted and others who are viewing suicide and suicide attempted as fundamentally different things, this in my appraisal, is a fictitious conflict. There are suicide attempts which specifically constitute something quite different from actual suicide, and again there are suicide attempts which as elements of a preliminary phase, directly lead up to a series of further suicide activities until the point is reached where the final event is death by suicide. As it is still difficult today to ensure a differentiation of the two groups, the priority initiative must be to take every suicide attempt as a matter of utter seriousness. Kurt Rohme has rightly pointed out that, according to present day standard of scientific knowledge, a suicide attempt is still the most intensive indication to the effect that a person is in danger of committing suicide. The consistent extension of follow-up care after suicide attempts then is, and remains, an essential part of modern suicide prophylaxis.

Research workers, who time and again proclaim that suicide attempts and actual suicide are different things are bearing responsibility for the fact that wide circles of the population are minimising the significance of suicide attempts, and frequently even ridicule a resolve in this direction. Indeed even the pioneer of modern suicidology, when introducing the term which he called an 'appeal function of the suicide attempt', was not spared misinterpretation. In Austria, it appears, the word appeal is mistaken as meaning extortion and, in any event, constituting something for which one must not 'fall'. Thus, scientists with the best of intentions have inadvertently provided people with pretexts for inhuman behaviour! For this very reason we must move all the more fast to put an end to the time in which everything was done somatically for people surviving a suicide act, only to leave them psychically, in a merciless way, to the vicissitudes of their fate[12].

We recall how, on the first rung of our ladder, we recognized that suicide prevention was the responsibility of everybody, not just of special helpers and professionals. Therefore, for those who overdose, the sensitivity and understanding of relatives, friends and workmates is essential. It would seem that as these kinds of problems are seldom associated with recognizable psychiatric illness, they do not respond well to the medical models of treatment and help. In fact in many cases, apart from the physical treatment needed for the effects of overdosing, the traditional psychiatric assessment could be done by a social worker or an experienced psychiatric nurse. There are plans in hand with the DHSS for this new approach. However, no matter how open and informal the psychiatric services may be, so much will depend on how people are able to accept, respect and care for each other. Carl Rogers writes,

> I believe that individuals are probably more aware of their inner loneliness than has ever been true before in history. I see this as a surfacing of loneliness – just as we are all probably more aware of inter-personal relationships than ever before[13].

He also points out that,

> in the West, the majority of us have time to experience our loneliness as we seek to find meaning to our lives. We then, of all people, must be aware of the deeper underlying changes by the human seeking after self realisation.

How do we cope with this need to find our personal identity? Today people are encouraged to talk more openly about their feelings than in the past. Modern education tends to include more student participation. In selection procedures for many business, professional and voluntary work good performance in a group is an essential requirement of acceptance. Press, television and radio give prominence to personal experience, so essential to uncover real feelings. We know many celebrities have a lot of stress and emotional problems which cause them to overdose and some die. Their suicidal behaviour naturally gets highlighted in the media and may be seen by some as a way of solving problems, or at least of communicating desperation. Many people, especially the young, are influenced by the behaviour of leading figures in the world of pop music, cinema and sport. The media offers very much what a society wants from them. It would be unfair to suggest that they encourage suicidal behaviour because they make available only that which is of interest to their public. It is ironic in this age of extensive technical communication, the age of 'public relations' that so many thousands of people, especially young ones, feel they can only communicate their inner emotional distress through taking an overdose.

The communications of those who overdose are about feelings and how to cope with them. Despite our more open society, talking about emotions and fears, is likely to cause anxiety. Added to this is the fact that we are passing through a transitional stage as so much has changed during the last fifty years. We are still in the process of trying to find ways of coping with the conflicts and uncertainties of our age. To a great extent, parasuicide is a reflection of the underlying desperation in our society and is being used as an expression of our struggle to survive. There is the temptation to go out and lose ourselves in the woods.

> The woods are lonely, dark and deep
> But I have promises to keep
> And miles to go before I sleep
> And miles to go before I sleep
> Robert Frost[14]

It will be obvious to any student of sociology that the prevention of suicidal behaviour, as a way of solving life's problems, cannot be achieved by the professional helpers alone, since it must reflect the unease and dispiritment inherent in Western society itself. In our scientific and technical age, there is a danger that we will think the experts must produce a cure – and anyway, it is all too complicated for the ordinary person. We have to acknowledge that, no matter how caring and understanding any society may be, it will not be able to provide positive answers to all life's problems. Although we try to relieve suffering and distress, at the same time we have to accept that conflict and suffering are part of the drama of day-to-day life. The search for wholeness has to emerge from society. This is demonstrated, only too clearly, by the emergence of AIDS and the awful truth that, as yet, there is no antidote to the virus.

It may be that the helping agencies have developed to try and cope with emotional conflicts, because we are now more aware, more anxious and desperate. The growth of the Samaritans, which now has 187 branches and over 21,000 volunteers, is a good example of how the community can be motivated to express care. So many of those who overdosed that I have encountered, find it very hard to care for themselves. This is not surprising because truly caring for yourself involves coping with the darker side, the destructive, negative and frightening aspects of one's self. If this was not bad enough, we also have to accept the necessity to be dependent upon others, even those we dislike. However, if we can give ourselves permission to care for ourselves, it will help us to become more mature, courageous and responsible for our actions. As we are all dependent, to a great extent, upon the values and political attitudes of society as a whole, we have to help the community life become less desperate. For some, this will mean active political involvement and for all of us a responsibility to sharpen our social consciousness. We need to work hard on overcoming our inner desperation because this is bound to result in an increase of dispiritment. Despite all our expertise, we get over-exposed. We have to grapple with knowing so much but we do not have the space to feel. We are so near each other, yet so far apart.

In the course of our encounters on the second rung, as with those on the first, we are constantly reminded of the importance of the role of the so-called ordinary man or woman.

REFERENCES

1. Stengel, Erwin, *Suicide and Attempted Suicide*, Penguin, 1964, p. 97
2. O'Brien, Sally, *The Negative Scream*, Routledge & Kegan Paul, 1985, p. 35
3. Ibid., p. 64
4. Kreitman, Norman, and Dyer, James A. T., 'Suicide in relation to parasuicide', *Medicine* 36, p. 1830, 1829, 1828
5. Stengel, Erwin, *Suicide and Attempted Suicide*, Penguin, 1964, p. 100
6. Kreitman, Norman and Dyer, James A. T., 'Suicide in relation to parasuicide', *Medicine* 36, p. 1827
7. Ibid., p. 1830
8. Rubins, Jack L. and Horney, Karen, *Gentle Rebel of Psychoanalysis*, Dial, 1978, p. 87
9. Bhagat, M. and Shillitoe, R. W., *Nursing Mirror*, 9 February 1978, pp. 26–7
10. O'Brien, Sally, *The Negative Scream*, Routledge & Kegan Paul, 1985, p. ix
11. Diekstra, René and Moritz, Ben J. M., 'Suicidal behaviour among adolescents: an overview' in *Suicide in Adolescence*, ed. Diekstra and Hawton, Martinus Nijhoff, 1987, p. 17
12. Ringel, Erwin, 'Suicide prevention, retrospective and outlook' in *Crisis, International Journal of Suicide and Crisis Studies*, Vol. 4, No. 1, p. 10
13. Rogers, Carl, *Encounter Groups*, Pelican, 1973, p. 110
14. Frost, Robert, 'Stopping by Woods on a Snowy Evening', *Robert Frost Selected Poems*, ed. Ian Hamilton, Penguin, 1973, p. 130

# – 3 –

# Failed suicides and repeaters

When you have wanted to die, and have made careful arrangements not to be found, imagine your confusion on waking up in
a strange room with all kinds of tubes and machines. You hear a
peculiar bleeping noise which seems to be getting louder, then
you drift off into some sort of sleep. A distant voice asks how
you are feeling. Soon the awful truth emerges – you are still
alive. Surely not, it must have worked. Yet it seems that you are
back in that terrible world of darkness and gloom. The girl's
voice is clearer now and vaguely you realize she is a nurse.
God, you must be in hospital – they will want to keep you
alive.

This will be the experience of many of those we will meet on
the third rung of our ladder. The majority will be very sorry to
have regained consciousness. They fully intended to kill themselves and only failed by accident. There will be others who will
deny that they really intended to kill themselves because of guilt
or to avoid being stopped the next time. As with all suicidal
behaviour there will be some ambivalence, assessing the degree
of intention in the suicidal is always a difficult task. However it
would seem to be useful to make this distinction between
parasuicide and failed suicide provided it is not an arbitrary
one. The exploration should assist the helpers in deciding upon
some future action and alert them to further risks of actual
suicide. Let us examine some of the encounters outlined in
Figure 4.

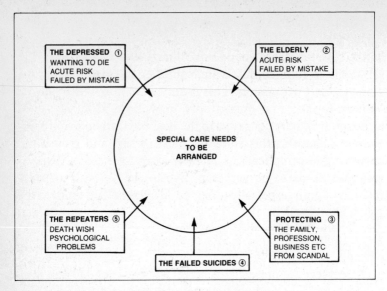

Figure 4: Management of failed suicides and repeaters

## 1. THE DEPRESSED

Those suffering from a depressive illness who may have tried to kill themselves when they were beginning to emerge out of the worst of their depression. This is quite common. They may be looking for the first opportunity to make a good job of it, although they may not say so to the hospital staff or any of their visitors. Those in this state are most at risk and may cause considerable complications in their assessment. The helper's response needs to be very sensitive to their possibly strong feelings of guilt, especially if that person has helped them in the past. There will be the feeling they have let you down and caused trouble. How the helper copes depends a lot upon their personal reactions and intuition at the time. It is generally helpful to let the patient express their feelings of guilt and their anxiety about letting people down. It is most important for the helper to let them see that you do care very much whether they live or die. Even when someone is so very depressed and intent on another bid for death, our loving, caring, just being there, gives some humane dimension to the bleakest of situations. The outcome is bound to be uncertain and likely to be very dependent upon how well the professionals, Significant Others and possible volunteers get to work. When patients are very depressed and there is a risk of suicide, they are most likely to be admitted to a psychiatric ward on a compulsory order. However it is often difficult for the doctor concerned, as the situation may not be straightforward. Relatives may be involved, saying they can or will take responsibility. Therefore frequently a number of risks are involved. Let us explore some of the likely problems and possible outcomes.

Liz was fifty years old, married with no children. She had suffered from depressive illness since she was in her twenties. She had had several admissions to psychiatric hospitals, having electroconvulsive therapy (ECT) and later drug therapy. For the past two years she had been doing very well and had taken a part-time job in a chemist for the last six months. Her husband, who worked at the local council offices, was very supportive but did not like her going into psychiatric hospitals. It had been a great joy to him that she had kept out of hospital for so long. Although he was very good to his wife he did feel rather ashamed of her illness. A few weeks ago Liz started waking up early in the morning feeling awful and very soon realized she was getting very depressed again. What could she do? Her GP, who was very understanding, would put her back on anti-depressants. He would not be pleased with her for stopping her medication. It very soon became too much for her and she swallowed a number of aspirin one evening when her husband was on night-duty. Although she took a very large dose she did not die but survived in intensive care. She did not mind being in a general hospital and co-operated well with the doctors. Rightly or wrongly she got the impression that if she co-operated and saw the psychiatrist she would go home. The ward sister then announced that she would have to go into a psychiatric hospital. Liz got her discharge from the hospital, went home to her flat on the tenth floor and jumped out of the window.

Like many people who suffer from recurring depressions, Liz reached a breaking point and could not face going back into a psychiatric ward. Unfortunately neither the doctors nor the nursing staff had been sensitive enough to realize how much at risk she was of another bid for suicide. Liz had not had a record of suicidal behaviour until she took the overdose. She was always a retiring person even when she was not depressed. It would seem that she certainly needed treatment, but there had been a failure to discover what was happening to her apart from a depressive illness.

One of the most dangerous pitfalls in situations such as that of Liz is to focus attention only on the depressive illness.

In 1949, Ringel examined 745 cases of suicide attemptors with the goal of determining their psychic state before, especially immediately prior to, their suicidal act. In the great majority of cases, he found a number of facts to occur with such regularity they they were summarized under the term 'Presuicidal Syndrome', consisting of

1. Constriction
2. Inhibited aggression, and
3. Suicidal fantasies.

These three factors reinforce each other. In the years since then experience has confirmed the diagnostic value of this syndrome[1].

Shneidman cautioned us against understanding suicide in terms of psychosis, neurosis or character disorder and recommended attention to the psychological constriction of feelings and intellect. Liz was suffering from depressive illness and had in the past reacted reasonably well to psychiatric treatment. It is likely that there had been resistance from her husband about her being admitted to psychiatric hospital, anyway it is reasonable to assume that for her, his attitudes did help to cause a constricting situation. The fact that it was quite unreasonable for her husband to react in this way does not alter the reality of the constriction or tunnelling effect on her. In his summary Sonneck makes these very relevant comments.

> People suffering from psychiatric disorders represent one group of high suicidal risk. The presuicidal syndrome is not part of any one psychiatric disease, but rather constitutes a common denominator of all psychic disorders. The factors of the syndrome vary specifically; similarly, the development, course and probability of recurrence of the syndrome are highly affected by the psychiatric disorder[2].

If, as part of the diagnosis, the reasons why she did not want to go into psychiatric hospital had been explored and if she had felt secure enough to explain, several possible courses of action could have followed, e.g. talking with the husband; exploring treatment at a Day Centre or the Out Patients Department; enlisting the help of the Samaritans, as a befriending support for both Liz and her husband. It is important to bear in mind how Shneidman recommends that frequent special support is essential for the Significant Other, as is well illustrated in this situation.

The attitudes of medical and nursing staff to the patient who unwittingly recovers from a serious overdose is going to have a tremendous effect on the outcome. As we discussed in the last chapter, hospital staff often find it extremely difficult to cope effectively with suicidal patients.

Suicidal patients are somehow special. They are surrounded by threat, worry, and often rejection. A special type of emotional climate is not only noticed by psychiatric consultants in the emergency ward, but also within the psychiatric unit and psychiatric staff itself. Many suicidal patients are known to be disappointed and to feel humiliated after receiving medical treatment and to say that they never would contact a doctor anymore because of a suicidal crisis. Several studies have been carried out in order to get more information concerning these special types of emotions and attitudes because it is thought that classifying those emotions which most harm the patient will lead to a better approach and contact to these patients. This will also have an influence on the prevention of further suicides[3].

It is not unusual for the carers to be inclined to believe that the patient/caller was not serious in their suicidal behaviour, this could be because the carers cannot cope with the inconclusiveness of these encounters. In my experience, this is not always recognized by the helpers who rationalize their impatience and frustration by assuming the caller is playing games or trying to gain sympathy, when actually it is carers who have the major problems as they fail to develop a rapport with their caller. People in crisis and those who are mentally upset may tend to be oversensitive to the attitudes of the helpers. It does not take long for the caller to discover whether you care or not and to discover how you really feel about them.

The Counsellors have come to realise that their personal intervention is so much more effective when it is carried out with spontaneous warmth and affection, than when they just go through the motions of interest and concern. The insincerity of professionally pretending cannot be concealed for long and even when the 'role-playing of love' is diligently sustained by experienced and well-practised counsellors, it is still insufficiently convincing[4].

This is not to suggest that the counsellor and caller disregard the dangers of over-emotional involvement and identifying too much with the caller's problems. Rather we are requiring the helper, whether volunteer or professional, to behave like a human being.

2. THE ELDERLY

It is unusual for there to be many failed suicide situations among those of sixty years and over. As we know the numbers of those who attempt suicide in the parasuicidal reaction or those who intended to die and only failed by mistake is much lower in those over sixty than in the younger age-groups. Lönnqvist and Achte make the following points.

According to Farberow and Shneidman (1961) in all suicidal attempts the age group 60 years up was only 6% in women and 8% in men in Los Angeles County in 1957. According to Ettlinger (1975) the corresponding figures were 7% in women and 12% in men in Stockholm in 1961–66. Distinctively higher percentages were presented by Parker and Stengel (1965) in Sheffield. They had come to the conclusion that in 1960–61 21% of women and 19% of men in all suicide attempters were over 60. In Finland the proportion of attempted suicides among the elderly (60-up) varies from 3% to 9% in different samples.

There are few follow-up studies of the attempted suicides among the elderly. Ettlinger (1975) had stated in Stockholm in 1961–64 that 7 out of 34 men and 4 out of 27 women (60-up) who had attempted suicide, had committed suicide during the follow up period of 5–6 years. In the corresponding sample in 1964–66 1 out of 43 men and 2 out of 29 women had committed suicide during similar follow-up period.

In this study the sample consisted of consultation records of 3267 attempted suicides during 1973–79 – the number of those over 65 years was 55 (36 women and 19 men). In the follow-up 1973–79 all those who had attempted suicide were traced and whether they had killed themselves determined by information on death certificate. During the follow-up period which had lasted 1 to 7 years, 20 persons of the 55 elderly suicide attempters (36.4%) had died. There were 5 suicides altogether (9.1%). Only one death was accidental and the rest were by natural causes. All suicides of the elderly were committed within a year after the key attempt.

The following cases were given in the appendix of the paper.

*Case 1.*
65-year-old former workman, married. He had severe alcohol problem for many years and before his suicide attempt he suffered also from paranoid fears and anxiety. In the course of few weeks he made several serious suicide attempts including an attempt to hang himself. On Christmas Eve he had taken an overdose of heart drug which caused serious intoxication. After the attempt he was in realities but depressed. He was advised for psychiatric care but he never went in. He hanged himself at his home at night six weeks after the key attempt.

*Case 2.*
75-year-old former truck driver whose wife had died two years earlier. He was physically fit but feeling depressed and lonely after the death of his wife. He was admitted to the psychiatric hospital after several suicide attempts. He was released from the hospital less than a year later. The following day after his release from the hospital he committed suicide by shooting himself in the head with the revolver, less

than a year after the key attempt. He had been treated for depression and was suicidal when he left the hospital.

*Case 3.*
68-year-old former mechanic who had suffered from rheumatoid arthritis for many years. Embittered because of his painful illness. His marriage had ended in divorce several years ago and he was depending on his lady-friend who, he thought, was getting tired of nursing him. He did not want to be dependent on anyone anymore. Several previous attempts of suicide, including an attempt to hang himself. Although the patient is very depressed he is not motivated for psychiatric care. Three months later he committed suicide at his home by hanging himself under the influence of drugs and alcohol. He had been continuously suicidal.

*Case 4.*
65-year-old packer, who had manic-depressive psychosis. She was depressed and had a strong wish to get to her dead husband. She made several suicide attempts and was referred for psychiatric hospital care. Seven months later she committed suicide by a lethal dose of lithium.

*Case 5.*
70-year-old widow, a physician. She had had depression for many years which had got worse since the sudden death of her husband a year ago. After that she went to psychiatric open care. She was continuously deeply depressed and wanted to die and get to her husband. After the suicide attempt she continued in psychiatric open care but committed suicide by morphin and sleeping pills three months later.

Both statistic analyses and case studies indicate that the actual factors relating to old age and ageing predispose the old people to risk of suicide. It is very often a question of depression and depressive crisis, often involving also elements of somatic illness and social isolation. In the small minority which consists of the most serious cases, the suicide follows rather soon after first attempt[5].

This study suggests that great importance should be given to any kind of suicidal behaviour of a person over sixty and that it would be wiser to regard all such situations as failed suicides. When making assessments of the suicide risk of the elderly it is important to recognize that they will have all the inconclusiveness and ambivalence common to younger people plus some peculiarities of their own. These will often include a feeling of not being wanted and of over-staying their time in society which will be accentuated if they are depressed. They may also deny that they need help and reject assistance from the medical profession or social services as it could mean going into a hospital or home. Many have a horror of going to an 'asylum', 'to the madhouse' or of being 'put away'. It is quite understandable that they dislike, and some react aggressively against, having their lives organized for them. Suicide could be seen as a way of gaining their freedom.

## 3. THE PROTECTIVE

Now let us consider those who try to protect their family, profession, or business from some scandal they have caused. A number of people in this situation see suicide as an answer to their problems. If they survive, it is generally by accident or by some unexpected intervention. It is important to appreciate how the situation may change for the better if those encountering the caller are able to arange some positive action. The following example illustrates how something very positive can emerge out of apparent ruin.

In my early days with the Central London Samaritans, a forty-year-old business man from Scotland misappropriated a large sum of money from his firm. He left home and booked a sleeper to London. On the train, he took a massive overdose of tablets and was rushed to hospital on arrival. He was very ill for about two weeks and was then transferred to the psychiatric ward. His psychiatrist created a very effective togetherness and gave excellent psychiatric treatment. With his patient's permission, he also asked for Samaritan support. The Samaritans provided befriending and contacted the patient's firm. However, they insisted on taking police action against our client and a warrant was issued for his arrest. The key figure here was the psychiatrist, as he would not consider his patient being taken into custody until he became less depressed. At this stage, the police did not know where the man was although they had reason to believe he was in London. The Samaritans were able to negotiate with the psychiatrist and the police about the caller. Of course, this was done with his full agreement and he was kept informed. When the psychiatrist decided his patient was well enough to face the music, he and the Samaritan befriender prepared him for the ordeal. By now he was much less depressed and no longer felt alone. As I was involved in the situation, I visited him in the cell on the evening following his arrest. We talked about how suicide was perhaps not the answer and about getting some Christian help – he was a lapsed Catholic. He was anxious about how the clergy would react. I arranged for him to make his confession to a very able Jesuit priest. He was befriended during his period in prison and helped to find a job on his release. It is obvious that things could have developed very differently, so much depended upon the mutual co-operation of everyone involved.

## 4. THE FAILED SUICIDES

There are those who fail to get it right simply because they made a mistake in the strength of the overdose required, so they are alive by accident. It is understandable that people are likely to assess the seriousness of a suicide risk by the amount of self-poisoning used. However, this is highly dangerous and disregards all the fundamental teaching in suicide prevention.

Jack, in his thirties, took a large overdose of distalgesic

tablets with a fair amount of alcohol. He lived in a flat on his own and there was no likelihood he would be found. Indeed no one did disturb him; to his shock and surprise he woke up two and a half days later. When he overdosed he was very committed to getting out and he saw suicide as the only solution.

Another danger is that often those who have failed by mismanagement or accident will deny they really intended to kill themselves. Therefore they are making sure that no one is going to be alerted and that next time they will be successful.

It is wise to be sensitive to unusual factors in car crashes where the driver, the only occupant, survives, or in sporting or climbing accidents. The injured party is, quite rightly, likely to receive care and treatment for physical injuries but the psychological factors may be overlooked. Those who had intended to kill themselves in one of these ways will be very cautious about communicating their intention to anyone. The helper needs to be someone who can be trusted to respect the patient's confidentiality from the authorities involved.

Lastly, we should recognize that people who have felt the need to die are obviously very upset, even if they appear not to be so. They may be seriously depressed, confused and just playing for time. Anyone in this position should be seen as at serious risk until the situation has clearly improved. Generally some time to feel into and assess their inner state will be needed.

*Two case histories illustrating how severity of poisoning does not invariably reflect severity of suicidal intention.*

1. A schoolboy of 15 was admitted to the Poisoning Treatment Centre following an overdose of about 30 tablets of diazepam. He was only drowsy, and required no skilled medical or nursing care. Inquiry revealed that for 5 years he had helped care for his mother who was in a wheelchair, and that she had died 5 months previously. He felt she still needed him and he heard her voice calling him. He wanted to

join her. He was very depressed with features of hopelessness, self-recrimination, social withdrawal, insomnia and
suicidal ideas. Since his mother died he had taken one other
drug overdose and had twice attempted to jump from a roof.
He was admitted for psychiatric treatment.

2. A schoolboy of 16, who was not apparently a regular drug
abuser, joined with some friends one night in taking drugs
stolen by one of them from a chemist's shop. He took the
drugs 'for kicks' with no conscious suicidal intention at all.
He took an unknown quantity of Tuinal (quinalbarbitone
plus amylobarbitone) and his friends called an ambulance
when he passed out. He was admitted to hospital deeply
unconscious and he developed a drug-induced pulmonary
oedema, requiring intensive medical care. Inquiry revealed
no significant psychiatric or social pathology and he was
discharged with no follow-up[6].

## 5. THE REPEATERS

A certain number of people who engage in suicidal behaviour do
repeat their suicide bids. Some of those who do so make sure
that their second overdose is successful, especially those aged
sixty or over. However, twenty per cent of younger people
repeat their suicidal action within a year. It is not easy to
decipher a pattern as there are so many different factors leading
up to the actual act.

Hawton gives some general pointers for increased risk of
repetition and suicide in young people.

The assessor should always try to estimate the risk of further
overdose, and of the adolescent committing suicide. Enquiry
must be made about whether the adolescent has a history of
psychiatric disorder or treatment, and of any previous overdoses or self-injuries even if these have not resulted in referral
to hospital. Knowledge of the consequences of a previous
overdose, or self-injury, may help in understanding the

current act. One important factor is the extent to which the adolescent's circumstances are likely to change as a result of the act. Various other factors, some of which reflect family pathology and others which reflect personality development, have been identified as suggesting risk of a repeat (Stanley and Barka, 1970; Headlam et al., 1979; Choquet et al., 1980; Hawton et al., 1982 b and c), and these are listed in Table 4. Those factors associated with greatest risk are probably a previous suicide attempt, personality disorder, chronic problems, behaviour disturbance, and alcohol or drug abuse.

*Table 4. Factors which may be associated with increased risk of a repeat overdose (or self injury)*
1. Being Male
2. Previous Overdose/Self-injury
3. Psychiatric/personality disorder/depression tendencies
4. Coming from a large family
5. Disturbed relationships with Family members
6. Alcoholism in family
7. Not living with parents
8. Chronic problems and behavioural disturbance
9. Alcohol/drug abuse
10. Social isolation
11. Poor School Record

The long-term risk of completed suicide, which is not insignificant according to the findings of Otto's (1972) Study of adolescent suicide attempts in Sweden, is higher in general among boys, those who make repeat suicide attempts, and those with psychiatric disorder[7].

In my experience of trying to care for and help those caught up in the repeating process, it is essential to explore what is going on inside the callers. It is very easy to label them as aggressive, manipulative, unhelpable and so on. I have found that when you give some special attention to detail, some of the following very simple patterns emerge, which may help to identify more clearly why they have a need to react with more overdosing.

Hopefully, the effect will make it possible for the helpers to empathize better with those who feel so desperate.

1. Many use overdosing as a response to stress or as a problem-solving device. In some ways it may be compared to those who get drunk as a way of coping when it all gets too much. From the experience of the Samaritans, some will also use overdosing as a way of bringing about changes in those around them for their own personal benefit. This may get them labelled as manipulative, yet it could be much more related to their feeling and indeed being inadequate personalities.

2. There are others who have suffered emotional deprivation in the past and when exposed to new criticism and further rejection, feel emotionally hurt. Their vulnerability is such that the pain is unbearable, although the incident that caused it may not have been so traumatic. What is significant is how their emotional wounds of the past are still raw and exposed. People who suffer in this way may overdose many times, often at risk of dying.

3. There are those who are very hurt and angry, but often unable to verbalize their need for attention or to express their anger. They feel helpless and alone so their aggression is turned on themselves by overdosing. They are rather like a clock which is overwound and the mainspring goes. As they are likely to experience many rough encounters, because of their own psychological problems and the hard attitudes of society, over-dosing – overwinding the main spring – is not so surprising. In this last pattern there is often a strong destructive tendency. The person may try very hard to be positive yet it seems some inner destructive force takes over causing them to break up a close relationship, lose a job and in the last resort, cut themselves or overdose.

All those in these groups have greater problems of one kind or another than the rest of the population and this is especially so of those in the repeating business. Farmer points out 'that in many respects individuals who poison themselves do not differ from the general population but that people who have more than one episode do'[8].

Let us consider how we can best help those who repeat to become more secure and so stop overdosing. At the outset we have to be realistic about the use of our limited resources, whether the help is from volunteers or from professionals. I have found this to be most important not only for overall management, but also because callers in this state need consistency and security. The majority of these callers have been let down, exploited and often badly treated by society. They are also likely to make the helpers angry, as some of their hostility overflows against the helpers who become antagonized.

Although each caller will have their own particular needs, some essential resources of help are required. Most will need someone who is able and willing to befriend and counsel them in a supportive way for many months or even years. At first this may seem impossible but it does happen through the care of social workers, the Samaritans, Christian groups, counsellors and therapists. It is essential for one of the helpers to be in charge and for the caller to know this and to have his/her confidence. Everything in this situation will depend upon the personal relationship which can be established between caller and helper. This is often reflected in the examples of seemingly strange partnerships:

1. The middle-aged social worker and the destructive young man who seems to be constantly fighting, either attacking himself or others, yet behaves in quite a different manner with his social worker.

2. The very inadequate young single parent generally mistrustful and unco-operative with all, except her Samaritan befriender, a seemingly very sophisticated lady.

3. The acutely dispirited caller who seems totally cut off, except from the apparently detached counsellor in whom she is able to invest some confidence.

All the above helpers have two things in common, they were prepared and able to empathize with these callers. It may be commented that this is surely a normal therapeutic requirement, but here we are trying to help those regarded as among the unhelpable. This does call for some special personal qualities, patience, even temper and generosity on the part of the helpers.

As most of the literature on those who repeat their suicidal behaviour points out, there is little presence of known psychiatric disturbances, therefore they are not likely to respond well to medical models of treatment. This does not mean that psychiatric supportive treatment need not be essential, but rather that overall care should be attempted through some befriending support and on-going counselling. We need to recognize that many of these callers are often very suspicious of doctors and social workers, seeing them as authoritarian figures. They are likely to respond more positively to the Samaritans or some other non-statutory group. They are also likely to be without any relatives or friends. Where there are relatives, it is likely relationships with them will be very strained.

Helpers working with those who have been so badly hurt emotionally will need to be prepared for slow progress and sadly, in some situations, none. I have known a number of people who have stopped repeating overdosing mainly due to the combined help of Samaritan befriending, on-going therapies, and medical treatment as required, with the provision of an overall management and back-up.

Jane, now in her thirties, started overdosing when she was twelve years of age and had five more serious overdoses, nearly dying in the last one. Her mother had serious emotional problems and was an alcoholic. She had a brother five years older than her with whom she had bad relations. Her father was not able to cope with his wife, but did give Jane some support. Her mother was very critical of her and from her earliest years she had felt unwanted. She felt very threatened by her peer group and so did not relate well at school. Not unnaturally she reacted by being very withdrawn and silent. This continued until she was sixteen years old. During that period she had several periods in a private psychiatric hospital (outside UK) where she had ECT and drug therapy. She found the staff were very kind and the hospital gave her protection from her peers and seemed to make it easier for her parents to take more interest in her.

From her earliest days her attitude to life and to herself was very negative indeed. She had all the classical symptoms of the depressive reaction, a poor opinion of herself, of her appearance, and the feeling of being unacceptable to others. At the same time, Jane had certain things in her favour, as she was intelligent and capable of gaining insight into her emotional reactions. There was also a lot of determination in her personality in spite of this deep sense of failure. Before she was sixteen she had taken two overdoses, at twelve and fourteen. She left school at fifteen and helped her father with the accounts in his firm. This was quite a successful time for her, as she had much better relations with her parents. However, she still found it impossible to have any friends and there were no social encounters. During this period, which lasted until she came to England aged twenty-four, she was very depressed and had two quite serious overdoses including one where she was out in open country and not found for three days. She did have some further psychiatric treatment, including ECT and anti-depressants. She did not have any counselling or psychotherapy and the reasons why she got into a suicidal state did not seem to be examined. She saw local Samaritans, who she says were not helpful telling her she needed a psychiatrist. She says that one of the reasons for coming to England was that she felt free to kill herself without the risk of being certified if it went wrong, as was threatened in her home town. It is significant that Jane saw suicide as a kind of insurance against having to face life when it got worse, which to her always seemed likely to happen. When in England her mother died and in spite of the many problems she had had with her, there was a great loss. She saw a therapist for a year, paid for by her father, but this did not seem to be helpful.

In 1981 she contacted the Central London Samaritans, after being in England for nearly two years. She was feeling very suicidal and desperate. She came to see me on a weekly basis, to help her talk about her feelings. I also arranged some on-going befriending outside our sessions plus the usual twenty-four-hour support from the centre as a matter of Samaritan routine. I formed the opinion, in consultation with a psychiatrist, that Jane was not in anyway psychotic and it was questionable if she suffered from clinical depression. She certainly had a lot of serious emotional problems and was very dispirited. She seemed to have taken on the role of being a mental case, an outcast, a negative person. She still had these feelings in spite of studying and passing two A level examinations since coming to England. I introduced her to a psychotherapist, who had been a Samaritan herself working closely with me for a number of years. Jane began therapy and soon made progress, however it was often hard going, as she had to work through a great deal of emotional pain. Jane also had the support of an excellent and caring GP. During this period she took two overdoses, and the last of which, in 1983, was very serious. Since then she has not overdosed in spite of the fact that her father died unexpectedly in 1986 and her psychotherapist had a severe heart attack and died suddenly in 1987. Jane was still seeing her therapist who had obviously become a very significant positive figure in her life.

Life is still not easy for Jane but she has become more outgoing and feels more able to relate to people. She has a dog which has been a great source of companionship to her. She still has to cope with the emergence of some negative feelings and has even wondered if her dog would have a better time living with someone else – when the dog is actually very well cared for and exercised more than average. Now Jane can face up to and examine her negative attitudes. She recognizes that it was sometimes necessary for me and her therapist to be quite tough and to encourage and help her get in touch with her inner positive resources. She sees now that overdosing had become a way of coping with severe traumas.

Jane's early pattern of behaviour is not uncommon. Her situation demonstrates that those who repeat overdosing as a way of problem-solving can be helped to change to a more positive reaction and stop the repeating. This can only be achieved with long-term care and commitment of several people, generally volunteers and professionals. As with Jane, there is always the danger that the caller will turn into a psychiatric case and use that as a possible defence against facing up more effectively to life's problems. Jane would be the first to acknowledge that her great psychological improvement was because of her therapist and the Samaritans.

REFERENCES

1. Sonneck, Gernot, 'On the phenomenology and nosology of the presuicidal syndrome', in *Crisis, International Journal of Sucide and Crisis Studies*, Vol. 17, No. 2, p. 111
2. Ibid., p. 115
3. Reimer, Christian and Arentewicz, Gerd, 'Physicians' attitudes toward suicide and their influence on suicide prevention' in *Crisis, International Journal of Suicide and Crisis Studies*, Vol. 7, No. 2, p. 86
4. Halmos, Paul, *The Faith of the Counsellors*, Constable, 1965, p. 157
5. Lönnqvist, Jouko and Achte, Kalle, 'Follow-up study on the attempted suicides among the elderly in Helsinki in 1973–9' in *Crisis, International Journal of Suicide and Crisis Studies*, Vol. 6, No. 1, p. 10, 11, 13, 17, 18
6. Kreitman, Norman and Dyer, James A. T., 'Suicide in Relation to Parasuicide', *Medicine* 36, p. 1829
7. Hawton, Keith, 'Assessment and aftercare of adolescents who take overdoses' in *Suicide in Adolescence*, ed. Diekstra and Hawton, Martinus Nijhoff, 1987, pp. 85–6
8. Farmer, R. D. T., 'The differences between those who repeat and those who do not' in *The Suicide Syndrome*, ed. Farmer and Hirsch, Croom Helm, 1980, pp. 192–3

# – 4 –

# Suicide

When we reach the top of our ladder we come to the finale of the drama of suicidal behaviour ending in actual death. Before, there were opportunities for debate, reducing the emotional tensions, befriending, and staying with them in their time of torment – even on the third rung when the risk of suicide was imminent, they were still alive. Now it is all over.

Those of us who have had experience of actual suicides among those who were especially significant to us as relatives, friends or callers, will realize how awful the emotional wounding of death by suicide is. On the fourth rung, we will need to make a brief survey of the ways and means of defining the greatest human power, that of killing oneself. Through the ages men and women have demonstrated their individual power to decide whether or not life is worth living by this final act. Chad Varah has always stressed that the object of the Samaritans is to help the suicidal feel that life is worth living. It is important to remember that suicide prevention, at its best, is not only about stopping a suicide but about helping the person believe that it is good to be alive.

Some of the following brief definitions of suicide give us some insight into the diverse interpretations of the feelings involved and an understanding of those encountering despair[1].

Suicide: the legal term for self-inflicted death
Sally Casper, counsellor, USA

I vengeful, killer, hate inspired – so I die;
I guilty, sinner, trapped – escaping death;
I hoping rebirth, forgiveness divine – live again.
Sarah Dastoor, psychiatrist, India

Fruit of illogical action resulting from 'funnel' thinking, which prevents a person from perceiving alternatives to self-destruction
Jozef PH.HES, psychiatrist, Israel

Suicide: Alienation's last word
Maria Gomezgil, sociologist, Mexico

Suicide is the most tragic decision of a man who found nobody to hold out a hand to him
Tadeusz Kielanowski MD, Professor of Psychiatry, Poland

Suicide is the chosen escape from pain, when there seems to be no other choice, nor hope of one
Monica Dickens, author, USA

Suicide is the act of self-ending precipitated when future existence appears unendurable
George Day, psychiatrist, United Kingdom

As can be seen from those few definitions, we will need to make some reflections into the realms of the individual, sociological, psychoanalytical theories, and look at some statistical data, current research and study of suicide prevention. Yet we must never lose sight of the primary goal of our task – to help the person struggling to cope with unbearable emotional pains. For the helper each caller, patient, client needs to be accepted and cared for as an individual. The special contribution of the Samaritans is their recognition that callers are people first and foremost and that their problems, even those related to suicide risk are of secondary importance. Although we will not live up to this ideal all of the time, because of our human failings and unresolved emotional conflicts, it is essential to keep trying.

Professional helpers in physical and psychological medicine would agree that there is a need to treat and care for the whole person. When Erwin Stengel was President of the Samaritans he frequently reminded us that he considered he both befriended and treated his patients. In simple terms, when a person decides to kill himself he is cutting himself off from society. He, or she, feels life is no longer worth living – for many suicide is seen as a blessed relief. Apart from a very few exceptions, suicide is the result of the build-up of unbearable emotional pain.

People who choose suicide have come to the conclusion they are on their own and experience a feeling of total isolation. They feel hemmed in on all sides. They feel trapped by excessive emotional stress and the horrendous demands of their particular predicament. The experience could be described as being caught in an emotional cul-de-sac of despair. There is an urgent need to escape, to get a release from the awful nightmare. What makes it worse is that the person will know this is not a terrifying dream from which they will awake. This experience is for real and has taken hold of the inner self. The pressure to escape is as much a physical urge as it is a psychological one. Some may feel rejected by those around them, though many will believe that no one can help. The overall darkness has enveloped the Significant Others and everyone else so they are as paralysed as the victim. Loneliness is the common denominator and, in the last resort, is a prerequisite to achieving death. The exception here is when a suicide pact is involved. There are always a variety of different causes for this 'suicidal loneliness' and 'suicidal vulnerability'. It is all too easy to over-simplify the presenting signs. The complexity of the situation is commonly found among those suffering from endogenous or severe depression.

Joe, fifty, had a good marriage with two grown-up sons. He enjoyed his position as a manager of a large store where he was well liked by the staff. He had always been quite fit until he had an attack of 'flu from which it took him several weeks to recover. He became severely depressed and was convinced everything about him was bad. He was very worried about the business although the store was doing well. His wife, family and friends were very supportive so Joe did not go into hospital even though his doctor had recommended it. He seemed to be getting better, but still sure that his family and the business would be ruined if he stayed with them, he killed himself in his car. While his wife was out shopping he closed the garage doors and the exhaust fumes were lethal.

Joe had a number of people to support him who would be seen, to the observer, as Significant Others. For him their very significance had been one of the reasons for his suicide – because they were so important to him he did not want to harm them any more. His state of loneliness was caused primarily by his endogenous depressive illness which made him feel he had to isolate himself from those who gave meaning to his life. The effects of the depressive condition had taken over and, for him, the only solution to this awful darkness was suicide.

Those of us who are concerned with the befriending, caring and treating of the suicidal do have to give special attention to the risk of suicide associated with depression. Stengel warns us,

Depressive illness or melancholia is the mental disorder with the highest suicidal risk. Its main symptom is a severe depression with profound pessimism, a feeling of futility and worthlessness and a tendency to excessive guilt feelings and self-reproach. Invariably depressed patients wish to die and many, though not all of them, commit or attempt suicide. The intensity of the suicidal urge depends not only on the severity of the depression, but also on the individual's past history. The likelihood of a suicidal act has been found to be greater among those depressive patients who had a history of a broken home in childhood than among those who grew up in a normal family setting. The etiology of this common mental disorder is still obscure. Only in a minority of cases can the onset of the illness be related to a precipitating event, such as bereavement. In all the rest the depression seems to occur without known cause. This is why it has been called endogenous depression. It usually subsides completely after several months but has a strong tendency to recur. It is an illness of adult life, it is not uncommon in middle age, and may occur also in old age. Its main danger is suicide. Some patients try to persuade their relatives to join them in suicide because they believe that they, too, would be better off dead. They only rarely succeed with adult relatives, but mercy killing of infants is not uncommon. This happens when a depressive illness following childbirth is not diagnosed in time. These cases of infanticide are particularly tragic if the mother, having killed the baby, survives.

These observations illustrate the vital importance of early diagnosis and treatment of a depressive illness. Its recognition is not always easy because depression is such a common condition and the differentiation of a depressive illness from an excessive depressive reaction to an upsetting event of everyday life, such as bereavement or disappointment, is often difficult, especially for the inexperienced. These so-called reactive depressions, which differ only in degree from normal depressive reactions, may also lead to suicide, but this danger is less than in endogenous depression[2].

One of the dangers is for us to underestimate the seriousness of a depressive state which can easily happen as the term 'depression' is used very freely. People talk about being depressed because of the weather when they are really fed up or sad. Depression, severe or less so, is not about being fed up or just feeling sad. The depression we are trying to define is the cause of hopelessness and despair.

As we know, the classification of depressive illness has been a great cause of debate among psychiatrists and is still going on. There are two basic questions; 1, Whether the depression is endogenous from within and a product of the personality and biological changes; 2, Whether the depression is reactive to external events.

Some support these two basic manifestations of depression, endogenous and reactive, others maintain there is only one type of depression which varies in intensity. These questions are relevant to suicide, as they affect how a patient will be treated and need to be examined in more detail in Chapter five. It is sufficient here to recognize that there is a proven strong link with depression and suicide and that all schools of psychiatry agree with this.

At all times helpers should remind themselves that people who are depressed or in a crisis of any kind, are most vulnerable to suggestion and persuasion. This is one of the reasons why the Samaritans will not accept as volunteers people who consider they have a mission in life to evangelize and promote their own religious or psychological therapeutic aids or political ideologies. The responsibility of all helpers is to do all they can to see the caller/patient has as many opportunities as possible to use all the available resources. Those in the 'front line', the sensitive neighbour or colleague, the Samaritans and emergency social workers, cannot afford the luxury of lengthy deliberation as decisions often have to be made quickly. This means that we all need to be able to react positively and have enough sensitivity and mental-health education to hold the suicidal person in a therapeutic embrace and try to reduce the emotional stress.

There are some people who are prone to inner loneliness and have little or no wish to feel close to others. All of us will have our particular neurotic reactions according to our upbringing and unresolved emotional conflicts. Those who experience a need to be cut off from others and feel alienated by society, are of particular interest. They are likely to react with a meaningless and futility to life which can produce a sense of hopelessness, the forerunner of suicide. It seems that these schizoid reactions are caused by the basic anxiety of being rejected because in childhood, there was little or no chance of developing an inner sense of well-being. The psychotherapists give special attention to the neurotic defences of their parents and define patterns of personality such as anxious, hysterical, depressive, obsessional and schizoid in order to promote individual healing. For us it is essential to recognize that our own apparent personal neurosis is reflected in society as a whole.

The schizoid reaction is also the forerunner of the depersonalizing of humanity, it is acknowledged that our scientific and technological age can diminish the personal value of the individual. Given the problems about identity and each person's role in society, it is not surprising that anxiety is very prevalent, both as an individual neurosis and as a common characteristic of the Western world. Indeed, this has been described by many as the age of anxiety because the validity of established political, religious and moral norms of the past is being questioned. Our modern means of communication make us more and more dependent upon each other. At the pragmatic level, one signal failure in a modern city can disrupt the lives of thousands of workers for several hours. Encounters with people, even superficial ones, become much more emotionally intense leading to heightened levels of stress.

During the last 200 years the rate of change in our Western environment has been faster and greater than at any other time in human history. It is worth recalling that our present-day isolation of men and women and our present age of anxiety can be traced back to the Renaissance, when we began to emerge from the feudal close-knit communities into stressing the values of individualism and rationalism. The faith in rationalism and science prepared the way for the industrial and capitalistic way of life. Many of our forebears were convinced that this kind of world would lead to a Utopia, but it would seem they underestimated their emotional and spiritual needs. We can surely only ignore our emotions at great cost to our integrity as people. We may recall how Freud came to remind us of our destructive instincts developing his theory of the death instinct in men and women. Few students of humanity could deny that we have a tremendous capacity for destroying ourselves not by natural courses, but in numerous power games of wars and revolutions. It is recognized that *homo sapiens* can be one of the most wantonly aggressive of all the animal kingdom.

So today we are very anxious and, very often, lonely. Kierkegaard seems to have some appropriate words for us.

I would say that learning to know anxiety is an adventure which every man has to affront if he would not go to perdition either by not having anxiety or by sinking under it. He who has learned rightly to be anxious has learned the most important thing[3].

It would seem that if we are to use anxiety positively, we need always to be tuned into our current cultural climate and how this will affect our emotional and rational reactions to the drama of daily life.

It was Jung who pointed out the human need to rebel, to protest in order to develop individuality. In literature we find writers like Herman Hesse commenting in 1927,

Now these are times when a whole generation is caught between two ages, two modes of life, with the consequence that it loses all power to understand itself and has no standards, no security, no simple acquiescence[4].

Albert Camus in his essay *The Myth of Sisyphus* begins by saying, 'there is but one serious philosophic problem and that is suicide'[5]. These comments are particularly appropriate to the 1980s because during the last seventy years in the West we have been exposed to ever-increasing diametrically opposed phenomena. On the one hand there is great success in prolonging life through medical science and on the other the developing of weapons capable of total annihilation.

Whilst it is most important to acknowledge that about fifty per cent or more of suicides are because of depressive illness or acute neurotic problems, it would be disastrous to ignore the social and political implications for suicide. This is well illustrated by the observations of Dr Robert Jay Lifton, a psychiatrist who studied the human psychological defence mechanism brought into being by survivors of Hiroshima and some Nazi concentration camps. He describes it as 'psychic numbing, if I feel nothing then death is not taking place'[6].

Today we are subjected to a great barrage of aggressive behaviour on television news bulletins where the deaths of literally thousands of men, women and children are common place. Alvarez writes,

In every age man faces a pervasive theme, which defies his engagement and yet must be engaged. In Freud's day it was sexuality and moralism. Now it is unlimited technological violence and death[7].

Yet we know that death is a taboo subject that is not freely discussed. Most funerals are arranged with the least possible overt expressions of grief and the crematorium, in spite of the many devout clergy and sensitive undertakers, tends to cushion the reality of physical death.

Many doctors in the past have sought to relieve terminal illness and prolonged suffering by ceasing to treat their patients. We now need to be alert to the dangers of planned or official death via euthanasia. It is not always appreciated that suicide can be infectious, so we need to be aware of any current danger signals indicating how prone we are to embrace suicide or the death-wish. Those involved in suicide prevention highlighted some of our present warning signals at the Twenty-fifth Congress of The International Association for Suicide Prevention in Vienna 1985, when special attention was drawn to the following.

1. The apparent marked increase in suicides among young people under twenty-five years of age, all over Europe and in America.
2. The increase in destructive behaviour patterns, i.e. massive suicide attempts, excessive increase in drug and alcohol dependency and undue risk taking.
3. Considerable increase in despair and a feeling of the meaningless of life related to unemployment and fear of nuclear war. Some American University students, it is alleged, always have the cyanide ready for when the holocaust arrives.
4. The conflicts and tensions created by the search of the young for an alternative dynamic meaning to life than that which they have inherited. Rejection of the goodies/badies mentality between East and West.

All these points highlight the gravity of the disturbances smouldering below the surface of our Western societies. The young especially are searching for a meaning to life and a change in the quality of life. Some of their efforts are short lived and lacking in responsible commitment. Others are very dedicated and have produced some amazing results in practical help given to the peoples of the Third World, the awakening of a sense of responsibility and urgency in promoting the needs of protecting and preserving our natural resources, and, perhaps most significant of all, their effective and compassionate commitment to caring for peoples of all ages through voluntary agencies. In spite of all these efforts of not only the young but also many of the older generation, we have to face up to the reality and consider the questions asked by Hans Kung,

But is it really impossible to change this firmly cemented society with its immovable structures and hierarchies? To be consistent, is not all that remains an exodus in order to live differently and better? Have the great programmes for changing Society of the last decades really made any decisive changes? Have the class-struggle concepts in the highly developed industrial society not been outdated, have they not each and all turned out to be ineffective? No, it is a question of the individual's subjectivity, identity, orientation to happiness, of personal experiences, positive plans for life, concrete everyday practice: this is the answer of the alternatives.

Today it must be a commonplace that a change in Society is possible only by a change of the individual and that conversely a change in the individual can succeed in the long run only with a change in society. The situation becomes precarious, however, when this bond between individual and society in the process of change threatens to dissolve. And this is the case not least when – to speak of the interpretation in religious terms, instead of psychological-sociological terms – the eschatological tension is removed between the 'already' and the 'not yet'. This tension that has to be endured can be of vital importance, for society and the individual[8].

This build-up of discontent and disillusionment is highly dangerous, as people become more frustrated and impatient for change. Some express their aggression outwardly making demands for immediate action.

It is not always appreciated that many who behave in this way are men and women of considerable integrity and intellectual abilities, who feel trapped in a meaningless and dehumanized world. It would be short sighted to underestimate their emotional vulnerability, as already for many the aggression is turned onto themselves in suicide, as they feel life is unbearable.

Thirteen thousand suicide attempts by young people, and recently also by children, in one year in the German Federal Republic represent a terrifying question to the adult world, which has no cause to be surprised when many young people adopt the slogan 'happiness now' and find themselves driven into a tragic conflict with reality. Here we come up against the same sociological symptoms to which the alternatives also react. 'Young people increasingly get the impression that the world of adults represents such a world of death', was the opinion expressed by Erwin Ringel, the Viennese expert on psychosomatics and one of the best known suicide re-searchers, 'and for that reason they refuse allegiance. They do not regard such a world as meaningful, they protest against it, they want a world that promotes life'. Ringel illustrates this with a poem by a school leaver.

I wanted milk
and got the bottle,
I wanted parents
and got a toy,
I wanted to talk
and got a book,
I wanted to learn
and got reports,
I wanted to think
and got knowledge,

I wanted a survey
and got a glance,
I wanted to be free
and got discipline,
I wanted love
and got morality,
I wanted a calling
and got a job,
I wanted happiness
and got money,
I wanted freedom
and got a car,
I wanted a meaning
and got a career,
I wanted hope
and got fear,
I wanted to change
and got sympathy,
I wanted to live . . .[9]

The writing on the wall plainly shows the urgent need for change and is a challenge to the hypocrisy and selfishness generated over the years by capitalism and the dogmatism of communism. It is not surprising that the young seek desperately for some alternative which will give happiness now and a deeper meaning to life. They feel let down and to some extent abandoned by the older generation who have not been able to give them a sense of purpose and meaning to life. In many ways this is not surprising, as many of their older generation were disillusioned with the quality and meaning of life in their day. Therefore the emergence of this crisis among young people is a timely warning that our time is running out in the West and that maybe the old and the young have much more in common than is realized. This can and does result in desperate reactions such as addiction of the religious or political fanatic, drug-taking and ultimately suicide.

The basic motive underlying the majority of the thousands of young people who engage in suicidal behaviour is a cry for help, a begging to be delivered from the anger and emotional frustrations caused by the breakdown of communication with their parents, teachers and other significant figures.

When writing about suicidal behaviour among adolescents, the overview by René Diekstra and Ben J. M. Moritz is most relevant.

Early in 1984 four young Germans ranging in age from 15 to 18 put an end to their lives in a remarkable way. Two of them jumped off an apartment-building together. The other two killed themselves, also together, using the exhaust fumes of a car. Public interest in the deaths, however, was mainly aroused by the publication of the suicide notes, in which the situation of adolescents in present society was expressed dramatically. Naturally, the gutter press were having a field day with the story and they threateningly predicted an epidemic of suicides among adolescents, if this was not already going on. Similar opinions were aired in more serious publications, repeatedly pointing towards the fact that for some time now, suicide among adolescents had been an ever growing problem that should mainly be imputed to a number of inauspicious social developments.

To which extent are these cries of alarm based on the truth? First of all, suicides like those of the four young West Germans, with social factors seemingly playing an important, though definitely not the only role, are by no means exceptional in history, including recent history. The mass suicide by the young girls of the Greek town of Miletus, related by Plutarch, could be seen as a case in point, and what happened in France about 14 years ago is certainly an example of it. In the course of the month of January 1970, reports appeared in a large number of the daily newspapers which caused a wave of horror. At a secondary school in the French town of Lille at least 7 pupils had attempted suicide within a short period of time. Two of them, Regis and Robert, aged 16 and 19 respectively, died in their attempts. In a suicide note one of them wrote that he could no longer live in a world which is in itself to blame and yet stands idly by and allows countless human beings, adults and children, to die brutally from starvation every day.

The tenor of the letter, and the suicide, almost certainly expressed the feelings of many of those who were young at that time, in an extremely painful but also recognizably moving way.

Adults were touched by it, which is evident from the speculations and commentaries that appeared after the incident. These mainly showed how difficult it apparently is for adults to understand how certain social problems can make such a devastating impression on adolescents. Relevant in this context is a study of the Task Force on the Psychosocial Impact of Nuclear Advances of the American Psychiatric Association, which proved that adolescents in general are far more deeply touched by the nuclear threat and what it involves, than was previously assumed. Suicide notes by adolescents also frequently refer to this.

To adults, however, sensing and understanding that these things can make such an impact amounts to nothing less than pleading guilty: to no less than admitting co-responsibility for a world that is so imperfect, so discouraging, that the next generation, growing to awareness, hesitates to accept the inheritance. Faced with the choice of having to say yes or not, since a return to being a child, to ignorance, is no longer possible, some adolescents pull out, banish themselves to death as the only hope for a better world, this being no world at all[10].

Carl Rogers writing on loneliness says,

I wish to speak more of the loneliness when the person feels that he has no real contact with other persons. Many factors may contribute – the general impersonality of our culture, its transient quality, its anomie – all elements of loneliness which grow more marked the more we are crowded together. Then there is the fear, which resides in a great many people, of any close personal relationship. These are a few of the factors which may cause an individual to feel he is closed off from others[11].

We are always involved in struggles for self-realization and each generation has to discover ways of coping with the demands of their times. The coming of Marxism and the development of various brands of socialism have once again brought new challenges to our society. Also the awakening of the peoples of the Third World and their search for better social conditions and the opportunity to develop their own societies.

Under the influence of modern technology the world has become a much smaller place and we have to recognize our need for each other. It may be argued that the first essential of suicide prevention is the promotion of positive togetherness between the United States and the Soviet Union and the commitment to actively working for racial harmony. The time is running out – we could lose the ability to understand ourselves and become victims of the psychic numbing. Therefore with Albert Camus we must acknowledge that there is one serious problem, that is suicide. Do we want to live or die?

We may only begin to find some answers when we reflect beyond the limitations of the study of suicidal behaviour, since so much of the evidence about suicidal statistics is very questionable and much depends upon the model used. The overall causes of suicide are recognized as numerous and very difficult to define. At the same time, we need to be aware of the crisis caused by the clearly documented radical changes of the twentieth century.

After Hiroshima we can envisage no war-linked chivalry, certainly no glory. Indeed, we can see no relationship – not even a distinction – between victimizer and victim – only the sharing in species annihilation.

More simply, just as the decay of religious authority in the 19th century made life seem absurd by depriving it of any ultimate coherence, so the growth of modern technology has made death itself absurd by reducing it to a random happening totally unconnected with the inner rhythms and logic of the lives destroyed[12].

Whilst it is important not to exaggerate the gravity of the situation nevertheless those who claim a commitment to suicide prevention and a concern for those in despair, cannot ignore the gathering storm clouds of total destruction. At the same time, it is most important to recognize that each generation produces its own special positive and negative contributions to its age. These may or may not have any significant effect on suicidal behaviour. At present, as with any age, we cannot predict accurately the sociological and psychological effects of our particular environment as there are always contradictions in the reactions of men and women. Some very neurotic and dispirited people may not feel in the least threatened by the possibility of impending annihilation. The idea of global suicide in nuclear war may be seen as a way of escape. Conversely, those who are more stable and caring may be moved to despair and suicide by the thought of the destruction of world civilization. Yet it is most likely that the majority of people, of all ages, are affected by the conflicts of their generation.

The inner loneliness contributing to suicidal behaviour may come from unresolved personal problems or it may be caused by reactions to what is happening at the particular time. For example, war, political or moral revolutions, famine or economic collapse are all likely to create a kind of collective despair. Conversely, the result may be harmony, depending upon how well people are able to cope at the time. In addition, some individuals and groups, not least adolescents, are bound to be affected by these social upheavals and become more aware of their inner loneliness. When this is added to the greater loneliness of, or a meaninglessness felt by, society, suicide is a probable outcome. These kind of reactions could be better described as causing a state of dispiritment, rather than depression, which clearly can lead to despair and suicide.

As we have noted earlier, all of us have our personal neurotic reactions and some of the most sensitive and intelligent among us have to be more aware than the rest. In every age there are the prophets who feel a responsibility to speak out about what is of fundamentally importance to humanity. In this age of anxiety it would seem that it is the existential philosophers who surely have a special significance for us.

Existentialism is concerned with a trend or way of approach in philosophy rather than the formation of a particular system. It is a rejection of the traditional rationalism and dogma of the past. Great importance is given to the individual as a person participating in the drama of daily living. We understand our existence in terms of our experience so that sensitivity and awareness are essential. Men and women have to take responsibility and make choices, which will mean living in a state of anxiety. We need to give as much attention to feelings as to reason and so reduce the separation between mind and body. This also opens the way for a more dynamic approach to life and can encourage greater attention to the quality of life. We could say 'to live fully is to be passionate', as living demands total giving and commitment to life. Being for the existentialist concerns what is happening to individuals here and now. The existentialist is, in the main, associated with Kierkegaard and became well known by the writings of Heidegger, Jaspers, Marcel, Camus and Sartre. It is significant that these leading existential philosophers of our century gave so much attention to suicide and the meaninglessness of life. Some may argue that they had their own inner personal unsolved problems and these are reflected in their philosophy. The test of their validity is surely whether what they say has special relevance to their time. Camus, writing in the introduction to *The Myth of Sisyphus* begins,

For me, *The Myth of Sisyphus* marks the beginning of an idea which I was to pursue in *The Rebel*. It attempts to resolve the problem of suicide, as *The Rebel* attempts to resolve that of murder, in both cases without the aid of external values which, temporarily perhaps, are absent or distorted in contemporary Europe. The fundamental subject of *The Myth of*

*Sisyphus* is this: it is legitimate and necessary to wonder whether life has a meaning; therefore it is legitimate to meet the problem of suicide face to face. The answer, underlying and appearing through the paradoxes which cover it, is this: even if one does not believe in God, suicide is not legitimate. Written fifteen years ago in 1940, amidst the French and European disaster, this book declares that even with the limits of nihilism it is possible to find the means to proceed beyond nihilism. In all the books I have written since, I have attempted to pursue this direction. Although *The Myth of Sisyphus* poses mortal problems, it sums itself up for me as a lucid invitation to life and death, in the very midst of the desert[13].

Camus is surely speaking to late-twentieth-century man who has, to a large extent, abandoned all the traditional ways of support. He is left to face psychological conflicts and emotional traumas without the shield of built-in sociological defences and the protection of religious ritual. What is so frightening, and terrifying psychologically, is that the over exposure to the nihilistic attack comes both individually and collectively. Camus invites us to live positively in the void, assuming it is our only chance of survival.

Those of us who have experience of psychotherapy will recognize only too well some of the signs, as our neurotic defences against the emotional demands of life are broken down or crumble as we begin to grow up and become more mature. We have to try to discover the meaning of life in spite of our anxieties within and around us. It is not surprising that death becomes very significant and the major question is, 'Do I carry on?' This is the reality for us. Kierkegaard in his existentialistic approach would distinguish between 'neurotic anxiety' and 'healthy anxiety'. With the former there is the anxiety caused by fear, a withdrawal from the conflict and so an inability to give oneself freedom to go forward. Whereas in the latter there are inner conflicts, but the anxiety increases a person's determination and awareness to fulfil the task. At the same time,

Kierkegaard does not in any way underestimate how hard it is to cope with anxiety. He recognizes that freedom is essential to the positive psychological development of the personality. It would seem for him that human beings have a great potential for creation.

> If there were not some possibility of opening up, some potentiality crying to be 'born', we would not experience anxiety. This is why anxiety is so profoundly connected with the problem of freedom. If the individual did not have some freedom, no matter how minute, to fulfil some potentiality, he would not experience anxiety. Kierkegaard described anxiety as 'the dizziness of freedom', and added more explicitly, if not more clearly, 'Anxiety is the reality of freedom as a potentiality before the freedom has materialised'. Goldstein illustrates this by pointing out how people individually and collectively surrender freedom in the hope of getting rid of unbearable anxiety, citing the individual's retreating behind the rigid stockade of dogma or whole groups collectively turning to facism in the inter-war years in Europe. In whatever way one chooses to illustrate it, the discussion points to the positive aspect of Angst. For the experience of anxiety itself demonstrates that some potentiality is present, some new possibility of being, threatened by nonbeing[14].

The existential approach recognizes that anxiety is an essential part of living and creativity. Today people are confronted by uncertainties on all sides; the Western need to be competitive, often to the point of physical and emotional exhaustion; the search for a meaning to life and finally death. Heidegger was very much concerned with death and for him, facing up to it was part of being. He saw humanity in a continual state of incompleteness, death itself giving meaning to life. He is trying to help men and women not so much to come to terms with the inevitability of death, but to take possession of it. With Jean-Paul Sartre, he considers that insufficient attention is given to death by the philosophers and recognizes the modern tendency to refrain from discussing death. For Sartre, death is a fact, something that cannot be understood and deprives life of meaning. He saw human beings as essentially lonely and isolated.

Karl Jaspers, like all existentialists, was concerned for people to be free to make choices, yet he also was aware of their constant exposure to the crises in daily life. People are surrounded by despair and total breakdown – the search for truth involves trying to transcend the nihilistic state. In a strange way, he suggests that death does become a fulfilment to life as there is a total embracing of the struggles of our suffering and disordered world. Hans Kung points out,

> With the rise of atheism, established in German philosophy particularly by Feuerbach, the problems of death acquired an oppressive weight of their own. What is obvious particularly with recent thinkers – Heidegger, Sartre and Jaspers – is the enormous seriousness and unusual effort not to remain mute in regard to death, but to bring it into discussion as part of human existence[15].

Paul Tillich, whose theology and philosophy are greatly influenced by the existentialist approach, warns us of the need to beware of how anxiety can lead to despair and a state of non-being. Hopefully, it will be apparent to all readers of this book that we urgently need to discover new ways of responding to the challenges of the modern world. It is not a question of debating humanistic, religious or political solutions, because, if we dare to be honest, we have passed beyond those.

As we have recognized earlier, there are always tensions between internal and external causes of suicide, but any study of suicidal behaviour must concern individuals and how they interact with their environment. In the existentialist approach the focus of attention is being – existence is the basic problem. Each person has fears, desires, hopes, needs and is involved in taking responsibility for himself. Tillich, a student of philosophy and theology, also actively participated in depth psychology and was well aware of the anxiety caused by the existential way of thinking. He saw men and women as the most vital of all beings, and able to transcend any given situation. Yet this vitality was dependent upon human intentionality. He was very sensitive to the contributions of sociology and psychology to both Christianity and philosophy. He also studied poetry and art, which were, for him, an expression of man's spiritual aspirations and insights. As we move from the philosophical considerations to those of literature, we shall have the opportunity to encounter the very personal feelings of the artists and grasp their reflections of the moods of society.

In literature, with the rise of the Romantics, suicide became a major preoccupation. It was during the Renaissance and the Reformation that the attitudes to suicide began to change, and the taboo on suicide, and the all-embracing power of the Church, decreased. It is significant that there are four suicides in the Old Testament, Samson, Saul, Abimelech and Ahithophel, and one in the New Testament, Judas. There seems to be little condemnation of these suicides but it should be remembered that, at the time, the Bible was not commenting on the ethical or sociological position of suicide. Later, the Church was moved to condemn suicide, to a large extent out of respect for life. The Christian theological argument is that life is a gift from God to man and only God is in control of life and death. During the Middle Ages suicide was unquestionably regarded as a sin. It was John Donne, Dean of St Pauls, who in 1608 wrote the first defence of suicide in English, *Biathanatos*. It was published, posthumously, in 1644. He suggested that suicide was not necessarily sinful and implied that man had a right to kill himself. Donne was known to be prone to suicidal depressive moods.

David Hume, in his essay 'On Suicide', published in 1777, was one of the first leading Western philosophers to introduce the concept that suicide is not a sin – resulting in a change of attitude towards those who killed themselves. Alvarez reminds us that

the traditional combination of genius and melancholy which had so preoccupied the Renaissance, was transformed by the Romantics into the Siamese twins of genius and premature death . . . Youth and poetry and death became synonymous; Keats died in 1821 at the age of 25, Shelley the next year at 29, and when Byron died two years later at 36 his brain and heart, according to the postmortem, already showed symptoms of old age[16].

(Thomas Chatterton killed himself in 1770, at the age of seventeen. He became the symbol of the Romantic poets.)

Goethe's novel *The Sorrows of Young Werther* depicting a despairing lover, set the scene for vindicating and encouraging suicidal behaviour. For the Romantics, suicide was a way of life, an expression of getting in touch with feeling alive. This attitude was very dramatic but it was fashionable and there was an epidemic of suicide in France in the 1830s. According to Alvarez,

> As the Nineteenth Century wore on and Romanticism degenerated, the ideal of death degenerated also . . . As the social, religious and legal taboos against suicide lost their power, the sexual taboos intensified[17].

Suicide was accepted as part of the daily affairs of society, however unfortunate to some people, and so it took its place in art. There was great concern for despair and death, and some writers, including Dostoevsky, were very preoccupied with the problem of suicide. Alvarez writes,

> On and off throughout 1876 Dostoevsky worried at the question of suicide like a terrier, and would not let it be. He ransacked the newspapers, official reports and the gossip of friends. He came up with suicides because of pride, 'swinishness', even faith . . . and continually he returned to the one idea that suicide is inextricably entwined with belief in immortality[18].

Dostoevsky had great inner spiritual struggles with his ambivalence to traditional Christianity and suicide which are reflected in *The Possessed* and *The Diary of a Writer*. He seems to be accepting a new kind of responsibility in the closing period of the nineteenth century, as he begins to act more as a prophet. The serious artist begins to become more passionately involved in the drama of despair, the meaning of life and in the twentieth century the possibility of global suicide.

Wilfred Owen, killed in France in 1918, was one of the British forerunners of modernism. In a letter to his mother, on New Year's Eve 1917, he writes,

> It was not despair, or terror, it was more terrible than terror, for it was a blindfold look, and without expression, like a dead rabbit's. It will never be painted, and no actor will ever seize it. And to describe it, I think I must go back (to Etaples) and be with them[19].

Some of the poets, whose works are most relevant to our discussion, are the Extremists, including Robert Lowell, John Berryman, Ted Hughes and Sylvia Plath. Alvarez points out,

> The operative word is 'control'. The Extremists are committed to psychic exploration out along that friable edge that divides the tolerable from the intolerable; but they are equally committed to lucidity, precision, and a certain vigilant directness of expression[20].

But it is with Sylvia Plath that the Extremist impulse becomes total and, literally, final[21].

> It is as though she had decided that for her poetry to be read, it must tackle head-on nothing less than her own death, bringing to it greater wealth of invention and sardonic energy than most poets manage in a lifetime of so-called affirmation. If the road had seemed impassable, she proved that it was not. It was however, one-way and she went too far along it to be able, in the end, to turn back. Yet her actual suicide, like Berryman's or like Lowell's breakdowns, is incidental; it adds nothing to her work and proves nothing about it. It was simply a risk she took in handling such volatile material[22].

It would seem the artist is offering a passionately human response to the dehumanizing events of our century culminating in Hiroshima – the passionate answer to Lifton's psychic numbing.

We began our discussions by recognizing that suicide is the result of a person's unbearable pain and stress. We quite rightly reminded ourselves of the need to look out for the effects of clinical depression. Now we have to be aware of the effects of dispiritment; despair caused, not by any psychotic disorder, but individual and social in origin. Alvarez writes of how the artists' feelings about suicide are very personal and not concerned with prevention and therapy,

> They view suicide not from the perspective of prevention but as a problem to be felt in the nerves and the senses, and powerfully expressed. What they offer, in short, is not solutions but understanding. And this seems to me at least as important as any more rigorously scientific approach to a desperately sensitive and confused subject[23]

THE SOCIOLOGICAL APPROACH

In the sociological approach to suicide, we can get some insight into how society, or the social group, affects suicidal behaviour. It was the French sociologist, Emile Durkheim, who opened up a systematic sociological examination of our subject. *Le Suicide*, written in 1897 but not translated into English until 1952, was one of the earliest studies of human behaviour. He stressed the need for social facts to be studied as realities external to the individual. For him, the suicide rate depended upon the level of outside controls created by society. The collective conscience of a group was the main source of control and social institutions, such as the family and religious groups, were extra sources of integration. Durkheim says,

> First of all it can be said that, as collective force is one of the obstacles best calculated to restrain suicide, its weakening

involves a development of suicide. When society is strongly integrated, it holds individuals under its control, considers them at its service and thus forbids them to dispose wilfully of themselves[24].

For Durkheim, each society had its now collective inclination to suicide and, unless there were changes, the suicide rate remained constant. This leads him away from any individual explanations and towards the study of social facts. Suicide rates are an instance of social facts and social facts are only explainable in terms of other social facts. They are recognized by their externality to the individual and the constraint which they exercise over him or her. This can be summed up in Durkheim's famous dictum, 'Consider social facts as things'. In rejecting subjective evidence, he did not accept analysis of case histories and suicide notes as relevant explanation of the suicide rate. He went so far as to claim that mental illness, alcoholism, racial or genetic factors did not have any effect on the data. He defined three types of suicide related to the disturbance between the individual and society.

*Egoistic suicide* occurs when the individual is very cut off from the influence and control of society – there is a marked lack of meaningful social integration. He used a comparison between the predominately Protestant and Catholic areas of Germany, and established a cause and effect relationship between religion and the suicide rate. The Protestant areas had high suicide rates, which Durkheim attributed to their emphasis on individualism, while the Catholic areas had low suicide rates which he attributed to the individual being given far more support and where a great deal of the weight was taken off the individual's conscience through sacramental confession. Stengel regarded this as the most unsatisfactory of the three as it includes most suicides due to physical and mental illness, as well as the suicides of the depressed and bereaved.

*Altruistic suicide* is when people are driven by a sense of duty to kill themselves by the customs and expectations of the Community – *Hari Kiri* of the Japanese military is a good example.

*Anomic suicide* takes place when there is a breakdown in the ways in which society controls and regulates behaviour; a breakdown of traditional patterns, religious faith and moral codes of behaviour. This is perhaps the clearest example of a social explanation of suicide for anomic does not refer to any single individual but to the whole society which is lacking in specifically defined norms of behaviour. Such a situation occurs, Durkheim argued, during periods of economic uncertainty such as slumps and booms, during which the suicide rate rose. On the other hand during periods of economic stability, people's standard expectations were fulfilled and the suicide rate went down. He also noted the high suicide rate among the divorced where the status quo of society had been disrupted. Therefore, for Durkheim, the suicide rate varied according to the external constraints on society and these were experienced as integration in egoism, regulation and morals in the anomic pattern.

Durkheim's method in *Suicide* was a pathfinder in methodology. His systematic study of the suicide statistics of European countries, which he presented in tabular form, was the first of its kind. His use of the comparison of suicide rates for various groups which, in accordance with his suggested rules of sociological method, was an improvement upon previous attempts at comparative sociology. A great deal of his findings still apply today, as O. A. Biller (1977) pointed out,

> in the week President Kennedy was assassinated there were no suicides in the 29 American cities Biller studied compared with an average rate of 4.35 for the same week 1956–1972. This would appear to confirm Durkheim's hypothesis that national emergencies can have the effect of lowering the suicide rate[25].

However, as Giddens (1965) points out, much of Durkheim's findings were already well documented, Giddens' argument was not questioning their findings but their methodology. Durkheim also directed his debate at Esquirol and others who viewed the suicide rate in terms of the distribution of mental disorder. Durkheim seems to be more aware of the limitations of his suggested methodology once he tries to apply it. He recognized that suicide statistics relied on subjective interpretations of the officials and this made him search harder for objective criteria which could be correlated with regular patterns of suicide rates, which would strengthen their validity. We owe a great debt to Durkheim for his pioneer work in beginning a systematic approach to the sociological study of suicide. Whilst it is true that the fundamental changes in the structure of society effect the individual, it is now recognized that the one cannot be understood without the other.

As Durkheim introduced the concepts of social integration, so Weber introduced the ideas of motivation, intention, bureaucracy, power, authority values and rationality. He distinguished between observational understanding of social behaviour and the motivations or subjective understanding. Social behaviour is dependent upon interaction between individuals, and it was the sociologist, G. H. Mead, who realized the emergence of the self was dependent upon social experience.

> The individual gets outside himself by seeing himself as others do (what C. H. Cooley called 'the looking-glass self') and by taking the attitudes of other individuals toward him. Often we literally do not know whether we are intelligent or beautiful until a set of individuals pass judgement upon us. Nevertheless the Self has two aspects which Mead calls 'I' and the 'Me'. The 'Me' is the organised set on internalised attitudes of others toward me. The 'I' is the individual's response to this set: it is, thus, the source of novelty, creativity, and uncertainty[26].

The approach of Weber and G. H. Mead is developed by Douglas in his examination of the social meanings of suicide. He believes that

> Durkheim's explanation of the suicide rate is neither operationally defined, nor based on date with a common social

meaning. Three points are at issue: First, suicide has many meanings; second, suicide cannot be explained until we ascertain what it is we are trying to explain; and third, the way one arrives at the meanings of 'suicide' is by observing the statements and behaviours of individuals who engage in suicidal behaviour[27].

Douglas claims that 'the meanings of suicidal actions are problematic'. Indeed there are cognitive, moral, and effective meanings of suicide. The usual procedure in sociologiy is to assume that the definitions of suicide are non-problematic and to analyse the official statistics, for example, death certificates or coroners' and medical examiners' records, as did Durkheim, Gibbs and Martin. Unfortunately, contends Douglas, there are about as many official statistics as there are officials and thus the official statistics are inadequate data for the study of suicide. According to Douglas the best way to proceed is by

> Trying to determine the meanings (of suicide) to the people actually involved, i.e. the meanings to the labelled rather than the labeller, rather than taking as the definitions the unknown but assumed definitions of unseen officials[28].

Douglas does give us a timely warning about the danger of relying on the validity of statistics of suicide and making all kinds of significant assumptions from the data.

Social psychology is of importance for sociologists and does incorporate some of Durkheim's theories. The social psychologist is concerned with individuals in relation to others. It is also about the psychological effects of social environment upon individuals and groups. The suicide rate is known to be highest among those working in professional and managerial jobs, medical and dental professions being most prone.

The suicide rate among university students is higher than in the corresponding age-groups in the general population. There is a big increase in adolescent suicides in Europe and America many of these are directly related to family problems and social change.

The right to die with dignity and the right to suicide are ideas which have become very prevalent in Western Europe and in America. During the last ten years, there has been a marked increase in the growth of organizations promoting euthanasia; in Great Britain, Exit – the Society for the Right to Die with Dignity (1935); in USA, Concern for Dying (1967), and the American Euthanasia Foundation (1972). Similar associations have been set up in Holland, West Germany, France, Italy, Denmark and in Canada. There is considerable support from all over the world for presenting their case for the right to die, including writers, sociologists and philosophers. The issues emerging from these discussions about the right to die and euthanasia have far reaching effects well beyond the importance and special integrity of those who, through advocating euthanasia, do so to relieve human suffering in terminal illness. Those of us who are familiar with Karl Menninger's three psychodynamics of hostility in suicidal behaviour, i.e. the wish to kill, the wish to be killed, and the wish to die, will do well to consider the possible long-term consequence of the promotion of suicide.

The sociologists Claude Guillon and Yves le Bonniec have produced a suicide instruction manual and claim anyone who finds their life unbearable should have the right to die. They are not by any means concerned only with terminal illness, but also with the distress and anguish caused by a person's environment. The philosopher Walter Kamlah defends the right to die as being morally permissible after careful deliberation. The writer Jean Améry seems to see suicide as the answer to unbearable failure caused so often by the state of society. He sees it as the special privilege of being a human being. Both Kamlah and Améry see suicide as a liberation from the confines of a self-imposed existence by the controllers of society, thus introducing a wider concept than advocated by those who want to terminate the seriously ill, who are exposed to physical pain and total dependence upon others.

Annemarie Pieper, Professor of Philosophy in Basle, discusses some of the ethical arguments.

A person who takes his or her own life in such a sick condition is not really the agent of death, but is only functioning as the tool of a stronger, dominating power. Campaigners for the freedom to take one's own life are not arguing that this group of pathological potential suicides, who doubtless need medical help, should be given this right. They are concerned with those who – like Améry, Kamlah and Roman – knowingly and willingly administer death to THEMSELVES and understand it as a free act.[29]

Pieper develops the argument that man, from an ethical point of view, does not have a right to suicide, but he is permitted to kill himself. Suicide is thus neither commanded nor forbidden in the universal sense. As the ultimate goal is freedom rather than life, Piper makes the point that,

> If the meaning of life does not consist in simply living, but in living as a human being and according to the standards of moral freedom, man does not exist primarily for the sake of life, but in order to exercise freedom[30].

She goes on to argue that

> Suicide does not open up any new freedom for the person concerned, yet if the person prefers death to a life that is not free then he is recognising the principle of inner freedom, even if it is only the freedom to end it all.

She concludes, 'there is no moral condemnation, as it is ethically permissible. Yet at the same time there is no right to suicide'. She makes the most important ethical and psychological point that you cannot regulate something which eludes and is bound to elude all regulations.

> For the category of the permissible cannot yield a bill of rights, nor a summons to commit suicide, nor propaganda for an act of this kind, which is only permitted as an exception

and hence must be left to the personal decision of the individual.

It is understandable that many people have become rightly concerned about the quality of the life of those who have their life prolonged by the expertise of modern medical techniques. It is by no means a new idea for those not influenced by any particularly religious belief relating to perserving life, to advocate euthanasia. What seems to be at stake today could cause not relief from pain, but the actual promotion of despair and suicide. Menno Boldt, a Canadian sociologist, writing about the notion of 'rational suicide' and 'the right to suicide' draws our attention to the danger of the effects of the promotion of 'the right to suicide' on the grounds that it enhances human dignity. He writes

> Advocates of the 'right to suicide' cite the 'right-to-life' provision, contained in various 'declarations of human rights', as meaning that society has an obligation to let its members choose their time to die. With this interpretation, they are reducing the ethic governing society's responsibility to the suicidal, to a gurantee of an individual's right to kill himself; I would argue that the 'right-to-life' doctrine contained in the classical manifestos does not imply that a caring society should allow and facilitate its distressed members to kill themselves. Rather, this doctrine speaks of the collectivity's responsibility to protect individual's right to a life with dignity[31].

We know that the meaning of suicide is being discussed not only by sociologists, philosophers and professional helpers but also by the general public. Boldt points out that we should take special note that the meaning we assign to suicide provides the young with clues to society's expectations. Young people may be beginning to see suicide as having a cultural sanction, as it is labelled 'rational' and advocated as 'a human right'. Boldt says 'Such cultural sanctioning of suicide has great potential to seduce young people into killing themselves when they come to grief'.


## THE PSYCHOLOGICAL AUTOPSY

The object of the psychological autopsy is to build up the picture of the recent life of the deceased. This is achieved by getting information about the deceased's life-style, relationships, habits and reactions from those who were significant to the deceased or worked closely with him. It would also be essential to talk with professional helpers, doctors and social workers. When the life-style of the deceased has been reconstructed it will be much easier to establish a more accurate cause of death.

> The professional personnel who constitute a death investigation team obviously should hold no brief for any particular mode of death, such as suicide, over any other. In essence, the members of the death investigation team interview persons who knew the deceased – the spouse, grown children, parents, friends, neighbors, co-workers, physicians, and so on – and attempt to reconstruct his life style. They focus particularly on the descendant's lifestyle just prior to his death. If the information they receive contains any clues pointing to suicide, their especially attuned ears will recognize them. They listen for any overt or covert communications that might illuminate the descendant's role (if any) in his own demise. They then make a reasoned extrapolation of the victim's intention and behavior over the days and minutes preceding his death, using all the information they have obtained[32].

This method does help to build up an overall picture, especially of the psychological behaviour of the suicidal immediately before their death. Also we gain a better understanding of their ambivalence and indirect seeking of help.

Suicide notes are often regarded by members of the general

public as being of special importance when considering the cause of a suicide or as an indication of the sincerity of the act. However, it would seem in actual fact that only a small proportion of those who kill themselves leave written notes or messages. The average seems to amount to between fifteen and twenty per cent. The common characteristics are not surprisingly emotionally expressed. They frequently include strongly aggressive feelings against those who were close to them or society in general. They often ask for forgiveness of loved ones. They have a considerable interest in what is going to happen after their death and often appear to expect to be still participating in events. There is considerable evidence to indicate that the writers of notes are interested in eliciting various emotional responses from those close to them. When considering the truthfulness and the significance of these notes, it is most important to remember that they are written under considerable emotional stress. They do not necessarily give a clear and precise picture of the situation of the deceased because, at the time of writing, he or she is most likely to be enveloped in tremendous emotional conflicts.

Eli Robins carried out a study of 134 suicides committed during a year period in the City of St Louis and in St Louis County, USA. This study has the benefit of providing both a medical and psychiatric clinical approach to the study of suicides. The study also included contacting family members, friends, neighbours, clergy and social workers so special attention was given to the social documentation. There have been only three such studies published in English in which 100 or more completed suicides were studied clinically by interviewing primary informants and additional ancillary informants.

B. Barraclough et al. *(West Sussex County, Gt Britain, 1966–68, 100 suicides)*

| | |
|---|---|
| Depressive illness | 70% |
| Alcoholism | 15% |
| Schizophrenia | 3% |
| Phobic-anxiety state | 3% |

Barbiturate dependence                          1%
Acute schizo-affective disorder                 1%
Not mentally ill                                7%
 Depressive illness + Alcoholism = 85%


**T. L. Dorpat and H. S. Ripley** (*Seattle, Washington, 1957–58, 108 suicides*)
 Depressive illness                        28%
 Alcoholism                                26%
 Schizophrenia                             11%
 Personality and sociopathic disorders      9%
 Organic brain syndrome                     4%
 Miscellaneous                              3%
 Unspecified psychiatric illness           15%
 No psychological information               5%
  Depressive illness + Alcoholism = 54%


**E. Robins et al.** (*St Louis, Missouri, 1956–57, 134 suicides*)
 Affective disorder, depressed phase       47%
 Alcoholism                                25%
 Organic brain syndrome                     4%
 Schizophrenia                              2%
 Drug dependence                            1%
 Undiagnosed psychiatric illness           15%
 Terminal medical illness                   4%
 Well                                       2%
Affective disorder, depressed phase + Alcoholism = 72%


Thus in three studies, completed over a ten-year period, we see that in combination, affective disorder, depressed phase, (or, as it is called by the other groups, depressive illness) and alcoholism were found to be the diagnoses predominantly associated with completed suicide with a mean of 70% of the 342 suicides studied. At the same time, schizophrenia, which has had the reputation of close association with suicide, was found to exist in a mean of only 5% of the overall samples[33].

The three studies show a high percentage of depressive illness and alcoholism as a major contributory cause of suicide. However it would be unwise to assume that the majority of suicides are related chiefly to psychotic disorder. We need to have more research into the role of the Significant Other and to discover what positive effect greater support can give, for example on those who are suffering from depression and alcoholism. Brian Barraclough and Marian Shea (1970) carried out a study entitled *Suicide and Samaritan Clients*. Those Samaritan clients who had killed themselves were identified by comparing the coroner's list of suicides with the Samaritan clients register in each of six towns in Southern England. Thirty-nine suicides were identified in this way, six more were found because, although they had died outside the coroner's area, the Samaritan branches knew of their deaths. Newspaper cuttings also provided proof of their suicides. The summary suggests that,

> Samaritan clients are most at risk of suicide in the year following self-referral when they have a high suicide rate of 357 per 100,000. Of the 45 suicides studied 71% (32) killed themselves within a year of self-referral, and 44% (14) of these 32 committed suicide within their first months as clients. About 4% of all suicides are former clients. Evidence suggests that Samaritan branches may differ in their ability to postpone suicide[34].

There were 929 suicides in the six coroner districts during the period of research, and thirty-nine (4.1%) of these had been Samaritan clients at some time before their death. Therefore the study suggests that those at risk will seek outside help if it is available.

Although we should always be aware of the limited usefulness and reliability of any statistics in the study of suicide rates it will be of interest to see some of the common presentations. First it is necessary to recognize that all these figures are bound to be an underestimation of actual suicides. Secondly, those statistics about parasuicide, or so called attempted suicide, are even more problematical, since it is impossible to obtain any detailed data. Most of the information comes from hospital admissions for self-poisoning and many who overdose do not go to hospital.

THE PSYCHOANALYTICAL APPROACH

This approach to suicide whilst certainly containing the common denominator of loneliness and effects of despair and

FIGURE 5: INTERNATIONAL SUICIDE RATES PER 100,000 POPULATION

| Country | Year | All | Male | Female |
|---|---|---|---|---|
| Hungary | 1977 | 40.3 | 56.0 | 25.5 |
| Germany (GDR) | 1974 | 36.2 | 46.0 | 27.7 |
| Finland | 1975 | 25.0 | 40.6 | 10.4 |
| Denmark | 1977 | 24.3 | 30.9 | 17.8 |
| Austria | 1977 | 24.3 | 34.8 | 14.9 |
| Switzerland | 1977 | 23.9 | 34.0 | 14.3 |
| Germany (FED) | 1977 | 22.7 | 30.2 | 15.8 |
| Czechoslovakia | 1975 | 21.9 | 32.5 | 11.8 |
| Sweden | 1977 | 19.7 | 28.3 | 11.2 |
| Japan | 1977 | 17.9 | 22.0 | 13.8 |
| Belgium | 1976 | 16.6 | 22.1 | 11.4 |
| France | 1976 | 15.8 | 22.9 | 9.0 |
| Bulgaria | 1977 | 14.4 | 20.7 | 8.1 |
| USA | 1976 | 12.5 | 18.7 | 6.7 |
| Canada | 1975 | 12.4 | 17.9 | 6.8 |
| Poland | 1976 | 12.1 | 20.6 | 4.0 |
| Norway | 1977 | 11.4 | 16.9 | 5.9 |
| Australia | 1977 | 11.1 | 16.0 | 6.2 |
| Iceland | 1977 | 10.4 | 17.0 | 3.6 |
| New Zealand | 1976 | 9.3 | 12.6 | 5.9 |
| Netherlands | 1977 | 9.2 | 11.5 | 6.9 |
| England and Wales | 1978 | 8.2 | 10.2 | 6.3 |
| Scotland | 1977 | 8.1 | 9.8 | 6.5 |
| Israel | 1977 | 6.5 | 8.2 | 4.8 |
| Northern Ireland | 1977 | 4.6 | 5.0 | 4.1 |
| Spain | 1975 | 3.9 | 5.9 | 2.0 |
| Greece | 1976 | 2.8 | 3.8 | 1.8 |

*Source*   WHO statistics

## FIGURE 6: SUICIDE METHODS IN ENGLAND AND WALES IN 1980

|  | % MEN | % WOMEN |
| --- | --- | --- |
| Poisoning by liquid and solid substances | 24.8 | 54.3 |
| Domestic gas | 0.4 | 0.0 |
| Other gas | 16.6 | 2.7 |
| Hanging, strangulation and suffocation | 29.3 | 17.2 |
| Drowning | 5.4 | 12.1 |
| Firearms | 8.1 | 0.4 |
| Cutting and piercing instruments | 2.7 | 1.8 |
| Jumping from high places | 4.3 | 4.9 |

Figures taken from *Suicides 1950–82*, published by the Office of Population Censuses and Surveys

depression, will introduce the dynamic effects of exploring the unconscious. This will result in greater sensitivity to aggressive reactions, guilt, hopelessness and the significance of unresolved emotional conflicts both in individuals and society.

The psychoanalytical approach reflects the discoveries of Freud who could be said to have caused a psychological revolution by his uncovering of the unconscious. He taught that human behaviour was not the product of our will power, but of instinctive drives and unconscious urges which moved us to act. This implies that we are dependent upon anxieties, fears, and feelings of love and hate coming up from the unconscious. Whether or not the reader agrees with Freud and others of the psychoanalytical school, their findings open up an entirely new reaction to human behaviour with the psychodynamic approach. For Freud and his followers suicide was seen as hostility directed against an introjected love object. This ambivalence, the possibility of being able to love and to hate at the same time, is one of Freud's great contributions to our understanding of our early development. In simple terms, the relationship between child and mother is of vital significance. The child is totally dependent upon the mother, or mother-substitute. He or she identifies with the mother and eventually the mother is drawn into the child emotionally. In this way a special form of identification or introjection is established. The

# FIGURE 7: DEATHS FROM SUICIDE IN ENGLAND AND WALES, 1973–1986

| | 1973 | 1974 | 1975 | 1976 | 1977 | 1978 | 1979 | 1980 | 1981 | 1982 | 1983 | 1984 | 1985 | 1986 |
|---|---|---|---|---|---|---|---|---|---|---|---|---|---|---|
| **MALES** | | | | | | | | | | | | | | |
| ALL AGES | 2250 | 2280 | 2184 | 2330 | 2363 | 2436 | 2564 | 2625 | 2765 | 2781 | 2812 | 2859 | 2949 | 2880 |
| 10–14 | 3 | 1 | 2 | 3 | 1 | 6 | 6 | 2 | 4 | 4 | 2 | 1 | 2 | 2 |
| 15–19 | 41 | 47 | 62 | 60 | 62 | 72 | 84 | 84 | 88 | 78 | 84 | 90 | 87 | 85 |
| 20–24 | 159 | 156 | 163 | 155 | 169 | 188 | 169 | 166 | 188 | 184 | 191 | 219 | 253 | 276 |
| 25–29 | 191 | 176 | 196 | 205 | 227 | 212 | 220 | 206 | 250 | 250 | 223 | 243 | 274 | 256 |
| 30–34 | 134 | 182 | 162 | 169 | 196 | 203 | 248 | 253 | 262 | 252 | 257 | 241 | 260 | 265 |
| 35–39 | 172 | 167 | 158 | 170 | 168 | 183 | 202 | 230 | 239 | 254 | 281 | 280 | 285 | 262 |
| 40–44 | 192 | 159 | 165 | 164 | 186 | 191 | 219 | 228 | 223 | 215 | 242 | 268 | 266 | 255 |
| 45–49 | 207 | 231 | 196 | 236 | 220 | 233 | 214 | 208 | 226 | 260 | 226 | 262 | 253 | 226 |
| 50–54 | 206 | 243 | 217 | 206 | 238 | 209 | 218 | 219 | 258 | 248 | 250 | 238 | 218 | 226 |
| 55–59 | 206 | 188 | 170 | 218 | 220 | 208 | 254 | 249 | 262 | 269 | 246 | 249 | 234 | 212 |
| 60–64 | 224 | 221 | 232 | 236 | 164 | 195 | 187 | 219 | 220 | 202 | 243 | 211 | 249 | 215 |
| 65–69 | 210 | 198 | 160 | 184 | 195 | 190 | 178 | 210 | 180 | 186 | 187 | 153 | 173 | 190 |
| 70–74 | 139 | 161 | 160 | 157 | 149 | 180 | 147 | 156 | 154 | 158 | 152 | 168 | 154 | 157 |
| 75–79 | 88 | 81 | 78 | 97 | 92 | 99 | 129 | 121 | 122 | 119 | 129 | 133 | 133 | 125 |
| 80–84 | 58 | 48 | 40 | 51 | 49 | 47 | 62 | 48 | 60 | 64 | 73 | 76 | 79 | 95 |
| 85+ | 20 | 21 | 23 | 19 | 27 | 20 | 27 | 26 | 29 | 38 | 26 | 27 | 29 | 33 |

| | 1973 | 1974 | 1975 | 1976 | 1977 | 1978 | 1979 | 1980 | 1981 | 1982 | 1983 | 1984 | 1985 | 1986 |
|---|---|---|---|---|---|---|---|---|---|---|---|---|---|---|
| **FEMALES** | | | | | | | | | | | | | | |
| **ALL AGES** | 1573 | 1619 | 1509 | 1486 | 1581 | 1586 | 1631 | 1689 | 1659 | 1498 | 1467 | 1456 | 1470 | 1246 |
| 10–14 | 4 | 1 | 2 | 4 | 5 | 1 | 3 | 1 | 1 | 3 | 6 | 1 | 1 | 1 |
| 15–19 | 35 | 28 | 36 | 30 | 32 | 29 | 35 | 38 | 27 | 23 | 24 | 20 | 21 | 23 |
| 20–24 | 67 | 69 | 60 | 69 | 98 | 67 | 61 | 72 | 52 | 55 | 65 | 44 | 52 | 55 |
| 25–29 | 77 | 89 | 82 | 77 | 68 | 82 | 78 | 63 | 72 | 74 | 55 | 68 | 61 | 78 |
| 30–34 | 72 | 80 | 82 | 82 | 94 | 94 | 94 | 83 | 92 | 83 | 61 | 60 | 90 | 58 |
| 35–39 | 87 | 94 | 85 | 91 | 76 | 103 | 97 | 110 | 84 | 96 | 110 | 110 | 89 | 96 |
| 40–44 | 130 | 108 | 104 | 105 | 107 | 111 | 106 | 125 | 124 | 100 | 93 | 101 | 93 | 65 |
| 45–49 | 146 | 143 | 136 | 107 | 139 | 114 | 159 | 140 | 133 | 121 | 116 | 120 | 117 | 87 |
| 50–54 | 181 | 205 | 166 | 161 | 169 | 153 | 168 | 164 | 161 | 143 | 134 | 150 | 135 | 120 |
| 55–59 | 162 | 152 | 135 | 141 | 180 | 162 | 183 | 193 | 184 | 151 | 152 | 144 | 144 | 104 |
| 60–64 | 150 | 168 | 171 | 159 | 144 | 150 | 170 | 146 | 154 | 154 | 159 | 170 | 155 | 128 |
| 65–69 | 166 | 174 | 156 | 156 | 136 | 183 | 172 | 170 | 193 | 153 | 136 | 124 | 145 | 113 |
| 70–74 | 122 | 149 | 130 | 136 | 156 | 149 | 139 | 174 | 174 | 145 | 151 | 133 | 148 | 115 |
| 75–79 | 88 | 87 | 96 | 93 | 119 | 117 | 98 | 133 | 105 | 103 | 101 | 101 | 110 | 118 |
| 80–84 | 55 | 49 | 47 | 49 | 39 | 52 | 43 | 58 | 68 | 64 | 60 | 78 | 76 | 55 |
| 85+ | 31 | 23 | 21 | 26 | 19 | 19 | 25 | 19 | 35 | 30 | 44 | 32 | 33 | 30 |
| **TOTAL ALL AGES M/FEMALE** | 3823 | 3899 | 3693 | 3816 | 3944 | 4022 | 4195 | 4314 | 4424 | 4279 | 4279 | 4315 | 4419 | 4126 |

Source: Office of Population Censuses and Surveys, October 1987

FIGURE 8: DEATHS FROM SUICIDE IN SCOTLAND, 1973–1986

| | 1973 | 1974 | 1975 | 1976 | 1977 | 1978 | 1979 | 1980 | 1981 | 1982 | 1983 | 1984 | 1985 | 1986 |
|---|---|---|---|---|---|---|---|---|---|---|---|---|---|---|
| **MALES** | | | | | | | | | | | | | | |
| ALL AGES | 253 | 260 | 226 | 249 | 246 | 274 | 292 | 319 | 340 | 366 | 344 | 361 | 387 | 410 |
| 5–9 | 0 | 0 | 0 | 0 | 0 | 0 | 0 | 0 | 0 | 0 | 0 | 0 | 0 | 0 |
| 10–14 | 2 | 1 | 2 | 2 | 1 | 1 | 3 | 0 | 0 | 0 | 0 | 2 | 1 | 0 |
| 15–24 | 31 | 31 | 27 | 30 | 33 | 37 | 37 | 42 | 51 | 47 | 43 | 45 | 53 | 69 |
| 25–34 | 30 | 48 | 33 | 44 | 46 | 55 | 45 | 55 | 60 | 66 | 53 | 75 | 68 | 76 |
| 35–44 | 46 | 40 | 37 | 53 | 43 | 47 | 49 | 56 | 69 | 59 | 67 | 62 | 75 | 81 |
| 45–54 | 50 | 50 | 47 | 36 | 42 | 47 | 55 | 66 | 55 | 75 | 78 | 59 | 81 | 64 |
| 55–64 | 49 | 38 | 42 | 45 | 49 | 46 | 48 | 45 | 53 | 61 | 52 | 61 | 53 | 58 |
| 65–74 | 38 | 40 | 26 | 28 | 19 | 28 | 38 | 36 | 32 | 39 | 39 | 35 | 35 | 43 |
| 75–84 | 7 | 12 | 10 | 10 | 11 | 11 | 14 | 18 | 17 | 19 | 9 | 18 | 20 | 17 |
| 85+ | 0 | 0 | 2 | 1 | 2 | 2 | 3 | 1 | 3 | 0 | 3 | 4 | 1 | 2 |

|  | 1973 | 1974 | 1975 | 1976 | 1977 | 1978 | 1979 | 1980 | 1981 | 1982 | 1983 | 1984 | 1985 | 1986 |
|---|---|---|---|---|---|---|---|---|---|---|---|---|---|---|
| **FEMALES** | | | | | | | | | | | | | | |
| ALL AGES | 183 | 177 | 201 | 181 | 176 | 165 | 202 | 196 | 177 | 197 | 161 | 158 | 182 | 158 |
| 5–9 | 0 | 0 | 0 | 0 | 0 | 0 | 0 | 0 | 1 | 0 | 0 | 0 | 0 | 0 |
| 10–14 | 1 | 0 | 1 | 0 | 0 | 1 | 0 | 0 | 1 | 1 | 0 | 1 | 1 | 0 |
| 15–24 | 9 | 13 | 19 | 22 | 22 | 9 | 20 | 13 | 12 | 11 | 9 | 7 | 13 | 12 |
| 25–34 | 22 | 17 | 24 | 26 | 15 | 21 | 27 | 25 | 13 | 28 | 23 | 16 | 22 | 21 |
| 35–44 | 22 | 28 | 29 | 28 | 19 | 32 | 27 | 29 | 19 | 33 | 26 | 29 | 23 | 22 |
| 45–54 | 41 | 39 | 43 | 39 | 42 | 32 | 50 | 43 | 44 | 35 | 27 | 28 | 32 | 22 |
| 55–64 | 45 | 34 | 42 | 30 | 34 | 34 | 42 | 42 | 44 | 46 | 34 | 35 | 45 | 28 |
| 65–74 | 29 | 32 | 29 | 27 | 38 | 25 | 31 | 29 | 29 | 23 | 28 | 27 | 29 | 36 |
| 75–84 | 13 | 14 | 11 | 9 | 6 | 10 | 5 | 13 | 11 | 18 | 13 | 14 | 14 | 16 |
| 85+ | 1 | 0 | 3 | 0 | 0 | 1 | 0 | 2 | 3 | 2 | 1 | 1 | 3 | 1 |
| **TOTAL ALL AGES M/FEMALE** | 436 | 437 | 427 | 430 | 422 | 439 | 494 | 515 | 517 | 563 | 505 | 519 | 569 | 568 |

Source: General Register Office for Scotland, October 1987

FIGURE 9: DEATHS FROM SUICIDE IN NORTHERN IRELAND, 1973–1986

| | 1973 | 1974 | 1975 | 1976 | 1977 | 1978 | 1979 | 1980 | 1981 | 1982 | 1983 | 1984 | 1985 | 1986 |
|---|---|---|---|---|---|---|---|---|---|---|---|---|---|---|
| **MALES** | | | | | | | | | | | | | | |
| ALL AGES | 32 | 39 | 36 | 42 | 38 | 38 | 54 | 54 | 68 | 57 | 87 | 72 | 85 | 101 |
| 10–14 | 1 | | | | | | | | 1 | 1 | 1 | | | |
| 15–19 | 3 | 1 | | 4 | 2 | 3 | 2 | 2 | | 5 | 7 | 1 | 7 | 11 |
| 20–24 | 3 | 2 | 9 | 7 | 4 | 4 | 12 | 8 | 8 | 6 | 10 | 9 | 11 | 8 |
| 25–29 | 1 | 2 | 4 | 7 | 5 | 3 | 3 | 7 | 9 | 3 | 8 | 5 | 10 | 6 |
| 30–34 | 1 | 1 | 3 | 2 | 3 | 2 | 6 | 2 | 7 | 5 | 8 | 5 | 8 | 13 |
| 35–39 | 3 | 3 | 3 | 4 | 1 | 3 | 4 | 9 | 5 | 5 | 5 | 8 | 12 | 10 |
| 40–44 | 5 | 4 | 3 | 4 | 2 | 2 | 3 | 6 | 4 | 6 | 7 | 8 | 6 | 8 |
| 45–49 | 4 | 9 | 4 | 2 | 2 | 4 | 2 | 1 | 8 | 4 | 7 | 7 | 3 | 8 |
| 50–54 | 4 | 4 | 3 | 2 | 2 | 1 | 4 | 4 | 4 | 3 | 5 | 8 | 9 | 12 |
| 55–59 | | 8 | 2 | 2 | 4 | 7 | 9 | 4 | 7 | 5 | 9 | 8 | 9 | 5 |
| 60–64 | 6 | 1 | 2 | 3 | 5 | 3 | 3 | 5 | 5 | 6 | 5 | 1 | 4 | 3 |
| 65–69 | 1 | 2 | 2 | 1 | 3 | 5 | 3 | 2 | 4 | 4 | 4 | 2 | 2 | 3 |
| 70–74 | | | 1 | 3 | 5 | | | 2 | 3 | 4 | 6 | 6 | 2 | 6 |
| 75–79 | | 1 | | 1 | | 1 | 3 | 2 | 3 | | 2 | 4 | 1 | 2 |
| 80–84 | | 1 | | | | | | | | | 3 | | 1 | 6 |
| 85+ | | | | | | | | | | | | | | |

**FEMALES**

| | 1973 | 1974 | 1975 | 1976 | 1977 | 1978 | 1979 | 1980 | 1981 | 1982 | 1983 | 1984 | 1985 | 1986 |
|---|---|---|---|---|---|---|---|---|---|---|---|---|---|---|
| ALL AGES | 38 | 23 | 20 | 26 | 32 | 32 | 22 | 27 | 22 | 36 | 55 | 37 | 32 | 44 |
| 10–14 | | | | | | | | | | | 1 | | | 2 |
| 15–19 | 2 | 1 | 1 | | 2 | 1 | 1 | 2 | | | 2 | 2 | | 3 |
| 20–24 | 1 | 2 | 2 | 1 | 1 | 4 | 2 | | 2 | 4 | 1 | 3 | 2 | 3 |
| 25–29 | 2 | 2 | 1 | | 2 | 3 | 2 | 4 | 3 | 2 | 2 | 6 | 1 | 2 |
| 30–34 | 1 | 2 | 1 | 4 | 1 | 3 | 2 | 5 | | 3 | 5 | 1 | 5 | 2 |
| 35–39 | 5 | 2 | 3 | 2 | 3 | 1 | 1 | 2 | 1 | 1 | 3 | 2 | 3 | 2 |
| 40–44 | 3 | 3 | 3 | 4 | 3 | 1 | 1 | 3 | 2 | 1 | 7 | 3 | 3 | 5 |
| 45–49 | 2 | 4 | 3 | 2 | 1 | 5 | 4 | 2 | 1 | 2 | 8 | 1 | 6 | 4 |
| 50–54 | 2 | 4 | 1 | 3 | 7 | 5 | 4 | 2 | 1 | 6 | 1 | 2 | 2 | 2 |
| 55–59 | 4 | | 3 | 3 | 5 | 2 | | 3 | 3 | 7 | 7 | 3 | 2 | 4 |
| 60–64 | 9 | 1 | | 4 | 1 | 1 | 2 | 2 | 3 | 7 | 8 | 8 | 4 | 4 |
| 65–69 | 4 | | 1 | 2 | 4 | 2 | 1 | | 5 | 2 | 2 | 1 | 5 | 5 |
| 70–74 | 2 | 2 | | | 1 | 2 | 2 | 1 | 1 | 1 | 4 | 3 | 1 | 3 |
| 75–79 | | | 1 | 1 | | 2 | | | | | 4 | 1 | 1 | 3 |
| 80–84 | | | | | 1 | | | 1 | | | 1 | | | |
| 85+ | 1 | | | | | | | | | | | | | |
| **TOTAL ALL AGES M/FEMALE** | 70 | 62 | 56 | 68 | 70 | 70 | 76 | 81 | 90 | 93 | 142 | 109 | 117 | 145 |

Source: General Register Office, Belfast, October 1987

emotional relations with the mother may be very good or very bad, generally a mixture of loving and hating.

There are two essential points here which are most helpful when caring for the suicidal. First, whether you use the psychoanalytical approach or not, there are always strong emotional and biological ties between mother and child. Secondly, the emotional effects of the relationship may help to produce a well-integrated personality or a very disturbed one. What is certain is that the original union will always have a major bearing on the psyche. You are stuck with it. As the child develops, what Freud called the Ego, or the Self, separates itself from the unconscious. The Ego is logical, moral, conscious and related to the outside world. The Ego is still linked to the unconscious and could be described as the manager of the relations between the unconscious and the conscious with all that implies in relating to the world outside. In addition to this there develops out of the Ego the Super-Ego, or internal morality. The Super-Ego contains the morals, rules and attitudes of the parents. Some therapists speak of the Good Mother and the Condemning Mother. Stengel writes,

In 1910 suicide was discussed at length in Freud's circle. Alfred Adler, who later dissociated himself from Freud, thought that the urge to inflict pain and sorrow on the relatives played a significant part in the motivation of suicide. A constitutional factor, i.e. the strength of the aggressive drive, was probably also important. Other speakers made some interesting comments, 'Only he who has given up hope to be loved gives up his life', 'Nobody kills himself unless he also wants to kill others or at least wishes some other person to die', 'Nobody kills himself whose death is not wished by another person'. All stressed the lack of love in the causation of suicide. Freud thought the study of 'melancholia', i.e. of depressive illness with strong suicidal tendencies, might provide the answer. Several years later he interpreted the urge to self-destruction as an attack against the loved person with whom the individual had identified himself. This theory implied that what appeared to be self-destruction was at least partly an act of homicide, i.e. directed against another person. Even the superficial observer sometimes notes how anger and aggression meant for others can be turned against the self. At the early stage of psychoanalytical theory aggression was still regarded as a perversion of the sexual drive and as a reaction to frustration[35].

Freud saw suicide as showing hostility; anger towards the introjected love object. In addition to this hostility there was a lot of anxiety and guilt. We remember that the Super-Ego has internalized the mores of the parents and so acts as a judge or controller of our behaviour. When things go wrong a person feels he has offended against the most precious parts of himself and so has great feelings of guilt, shame and helplessness. Many people seem to have a built-in condemning system as they seem programmed to put themselves down. The Significant Other, the internalized mother, is lost or withdraws, so they experience a severe state of loneliness. This can lead to anger against the internalized mother, against oneself.

Freud also developed the concept of the death instinct, first published in his essay 'Beyond the Pleasure Principle' in 1920. He came to this conclusion because the instinctive drive for preservation did not fit into aspects of human behaviour. He therefore postulates that from the beginning of life there is a destructive drive alongside the sexual one. This destructive drive is both passive and aggressive.

Although Freud's theory of the death instinct has not been generally accepted even among psychoanalysts, it did open up a much greater interest into the study of aggression in human behaviour. Karl Menninger in a very important book, *Man, Against Himself*, described a wide number of aggressive and destructive ways of human behaviour[36]. He included alcoholism, anti-social behaviour, self-mutilation, purposeful accidents, asceticism and martyrdom, with suicide as the most destructive. He also suggested that the drives in suicide are made up of the wish to kill, the wish to be killed, and the wish to die.

Some psychoanalysts rejecting the death instinct consider the human mind is incapable of conceiving death. Suicide is seen as a way of achieving a fantasized immorality. It is a way of defeating the fates and achieving some kind of emotional victory. It is worth remembering that this kind of reaction is not unknown in a number of young people who regard suicide as a kind of mystical death rather than actual death.

Summing up the psychoanalytical approach to suicide helps us to highlight the importance of our aggressive reactions and the need to assess the degree of guilt feelings in the suicidal person. Even if we do not accept these theories, it would be unwise to ignore the emotional psychological repercussions of the good mother or the bad mother and the reality of ambivalent reactions. The creation of an inner sense of well-being strengthening one to cope positively with all manner of stress is surely directly related to good mother care in all schools of thought.

If someone was to visit our world from outer space and carried out a survey on suicidal behaviour, they would surely draw attention to the apparent suicidal behaviours. Some people may well think of the death instinct as very relevant, as we accept that thousands are killed annually on the roads and in other forms of travel. In this century mass killings happened in two major European wars, the threat of global death by nuclear war is still a possibility and undue risk taking through drugs and alcohol is on the increase.

THE PSYCHOLOGICAL APPROACH

This sets the scene for observing the emotional and mental state of those who are suicidal. As we have discussed earlier, suicidal people experience intolerable emotional pain, feel trapped and need to escape. Their feelings of alienation, despair, the dispiritment are absolute. Shneidman, in 1976, noted four

general psychological features which seem necessary for a lethal suicidal event to occur,
1. Acute perturbation, that is increase in the general state of the individual's state of general upsetment

2. Heightened inimicality, an increase of self-abregation, self-hate, shame, guilt, self-blame and overtly in behaviours which are against one's own best interests

3. A sharp and almost sudden increase in constriction of intellectual focus, a tunnelling of thought processes, a narrowing of the mind's content, a truncating of the capacity to see viable options which would ordinarily occur to mind

4. The idea of cessation, the insight that it is possible to put an end to suffering by stopping the unbearable flow of consciousness.

This last is the igniting element that explodes the mixture of the previous three components. In this context, suicide is understood not as a movement toward death (or cessation) but rather as a flight from intolerable emotion[37].

If these four are considered in relation to the psychodynamic approach we will see how some unconscious unresolved emotional conflicts could be either a cause of, or add fuel to, the igniting process. For example, how easily acute perturbation would be increased by dormant rage against the internalized mother; how self-abnegation would be fed by the condemning mother and through the tunnelling of thought processes, plus the idea of cessation, vulnerability would be greatly increased in the absence of the loving mother. Here, we need to bear in mind that the loving mother would create a sense of inner well-being and a capacity for flexibility. We also need to recognize the effects of possible clinical depression, physical illness and the destructive aspects of the environmental climate of the time. When we try to sum up suicide, we have to say it is all this and more, yet at the same time each suicide is that of an individual person – who feels the need to leave all the rest, to abandon society. We recall Shneidman's statement 'There are many pointless deaths but there can never be a needless suicide'. He is saying that in suicide we have to appreciate that the person is trying to fulfil some urgently felt psychological needs. Those around the person may not understand and if they fail to recognize the essential, they are missing the whole point of the action and are failing to care for the person as another human being in distress. The helpers may not succeed in changing the person's state, but they should be able to identify his needs. Shneidman points out

> The focus should not be on 'Why' suicide has been chosen as the method of solving life's problems, but rather on solving the problems, so that suicide – chosen for whatever reason – becomes unnecessary (in that the problems are addressed and that the person sees some hope of at least partially satisfying, or redirecting, urgently felt needs which were essential to his suicidal scenario). In the past the treatment of suicide is the satisfaction of the unmet needs. One does this not only in the consultation room but also in the real world. This means that one talks to the Significant Other, contacts social agencies, and is concerned about practical items such as job, rent and food. The way to save a suicidal person is to cater to that individual's infantile and realistic idiosyncratic needs. The suicidal therapist should, in addition to other roles, act as an existential social worker, a practical person knowledgeable about realistic resources and aware of philosophic issues – a speciality which should be encouraged[38].

In this very basic approach of Shneidman we could say he is writing about good befriending, caring and trying to behave like a human being. Regarded as the father of American Suicidology, he gives us a stimulating new approach to our studies in his *Definition of Suicide* (1985). He draws valuable insights from the cosmological or world-view approach with special reference to Stephen Peppee's *World Hypotheses*. The personalogy, or understanding of the person approach, refers to Henry A. Murray's *Explorations into Personality*. He draws on valuable insights from the Systems Theory, expanded by James G. Miller in *Living Systems* and illustrates his presentation from the classical literature of Melville. His 'Ten Commonalities of Suicide' from the book mentioned above, *Definition of Suicide*, provides a unique portrait of the suicidal person's emotions, thoughts, needs and inner stresses.

In the past, suicide has been regarded as sin, mental disturbance or insanity; sociologically determined (Durkheim); psychodynamically determined by the unconscious (Freud); the result of physical illness, especially clinical depression, or alcoholism. In the more modern sociological theories, it is the result of urbanization and the breakdown of the traditional patterns of society, and the nuclear threat. What seems to be emerging is a multi-disciplinary approach to the subject. As always, we need to remember that we are encountering individual people who are unique, and everything will depend upon the rapport we can develop together. Because each person is so important, we must focus our attention on his or her needs. The person is now recognized as choosing suicidal action. There may well be many underlying causes, but our concern is with how the person, the individual, feels. We need also to perceive the person as being part of a greater environment. To quote John Donne, 'No man is an island entire of itself; every man is a piece of the continent'.

The Systems Theory of Miller reminds us to see the individual as interrelated to the immediate society and affected by it. Therefore, it is good befriending and good treatment to enable the suicidal person to have access to all the available sources of healing. These would include the Significant Others or befrienders, insights from the sociological, philosophical and spiritual fields, and the skills of psychiatry and psychology. We can study suicide from many angles, and we need to do so, yet we have to bear in mind always that suicide is about how we behave in response to living – in suicide we choose the ultimate negation, death.

Every age in history has its times of crisis and it is doubtful if situations were better or worse in the past. What is relevant is how we react to the reality of the here-and-now. The most subtle way to avoid facing up to the present is to bask in the glories of the past or to be terrified of the future. The crisis, the time of decision and reality, is now. We have a choice. Albert

Camus, answering the question, What can the artist do in the world today?, says,

> We must simultaneously serve suffering and beauty. The long patience, the strength, the secret cunning such service calls for are the virtues that establish the very renaissance we need[39].

REFERENCES

1. *Answers to Suicide*, ed. the Samaritans, Constable, 1978, p. 3, 7, 59, 89, 125, 179, 180
2. Stengel, Erwin, *Suicide and Attempted Suicide*, Penguin, 1964, p. 51
3. Kierkegaard, Soren, *The Concept of Dread*, translated by Walter Lowrie, Princeton University Press, 1944
4. Hesse, Herman, *Steppenwolf*, translated by Basil Creighton, Henry Holt & Co., 1947
5. Camus, Albert, *The Myth of Sisyphus*, Penguin, 1975, p. 11
6. Alvarez, A., 'Literature in the nineteenth and twentieth centuries' in *A Handbook for the Study of Suicide*, ed. Seymour, Perlin, Oxford University Press, 1975, pp. 46–7
7. Ibid., p. 47
8. Kung, Hans, *Eternal Life*, Collins, 1984, pp. 239–43
9. Ibid.
10. Diekstra, René and Moritz, Ben J. M., 'Suicidal behaviour among adolescents: an overview' in *Suicide in Adolescence*, ed. Diekstra and Hawton, Martinus Nijhoff, 1987, pp. 7–8
11. Rogers, Carl, *Encounter Groups*, Pelican, 1973, p. 111
12. Alvarez, A., 'Literature in the nineteenth and twentieth centuries', in *A Handbook for the Study of Suicide*, ed. Seymour, Perlin, Oxford University Press, 1975, p. 47
13. Camus, Albert, *The Myth of Sisyphus*, Penguin, 1975, p. 7
14. May, Rollo, *The Discovery of Being*, W. W. Norton & Co., 1983, p. 112
15. Kung, Hans, *Eternal Life*, Collins, 1984, p. 58
16. Alvarez, A., 'Literature in the nineteenth and twentieth centuries', in *A Handbook for the Study of Suicide*, ed. Seymour, Perlin, Oxford University Press, 1975, p. 33

17. Ibid., p. 40
18. Alvarez A., *The Savage God*, Random House, 1970, p. 218
19. Ibid., p. 242
20. Alvarez, A., 'Literature in the nineteenth and twentieth centuries', in *A Handbook for the Study of Suicide*, ed. Seymour, Perlin, Oxford University Press, 1975, p. 55
21. Ibid., p. 56
22. Ibid., p. 57
23. Ibid., p. 49
24. Durkheim, Emile, *Suicide*, Routledge & Kegan Paul, 1952, p. 209
25. Biller, O. A., 'Durkheim Lives', *New Society*, 1977
26. Giddens, 'Suicide problem in French society', *British Journal of Sociology*, 1965
27. Maris, Ronald, 'Sociology' in *A Handbook for the Study of Suicide*, ed. Seymour, Perlin, Oxford University Press, 1975, p. 99
28. Ibid.
29. Pieper, Annemarie, 'Suicide and the Right to Die', *Consilium* 3/1985, p. 179
30. Ibid.
31. Boldt, Menno, 'Defining suicide: implications for suicide behaviour and for suicide prevention' in *Crisis, International Journal of Suicide and Crisis Studies*, Vol. 8, No. 1, p. 3
32. Shneidman, Edwin S., *Deaths of Man*, Quadrangle New York Times Book Co., 1973, pp. 159–60
33. Robins, Eli, *The Final Months*, Oxford University Press, 1981, pp. xi–xiv
34. Barraclough, Brian and Shea, Marian, 'Suicide and Samaritan clients', *Lancet*, 24 Oct 1970, pp. 868–70
35. Stengel, Erwin, *Suicide and Attempted Suicide*, Penguin, 1964, p. 43
36. Menninger, Karl A., *Man Against Himself*, Harcourt Brace & World, 1938
37. Shneidman, Edwin S., *Definition of Suicide*, John Wiley & Sons, 1985, pp. 35–6
38. Ibid., p. 227
39. Camus, Albert, *The Myth of Sisyphus*, Penguin, 1975, p. 191

# – 5 –

# The immediate care
# and support of the suicidal

'There are many pointless deaths, but there is never a needless suicide', Shneidman[1].

'How could I possibly help anyone who wants to kill themself?' 'I just could not stand the strain.' 'They need doctors, psychiatrists, they are nutters.' 'If they want to die let them get on with it – why should anyone interfere.' 'People have a right to do their own thing.' 'It is their life, who am I to tell them what to do?' These are common reactions of those who have not been involved in any kind of suicide prevention activity. They are also the reactions of some of those who do not care for other people.

Most of these reactions are due to anxiety and selfishness. Let us take a look at their anxieties. Many people imagine that suicidal behaviour is going to be very dramatic, e.g. someone will phone up and say, 'I am going to kill myself', or 'I have taken a lot of tablets', or they will be sitting on the ledge of some high building waiting to jump. Others will imagine, that because they are 'nutters' (assuming only mad people want to kill themselves) they could be dangerous.

The second reason is selfishness. Many people will not admit to this and will take the easy way out by rationalization, e.g. 'those people are sick and should be put away', 'their life is not worth living so suicide is a blessed relief'. Some people are honest enough to admit they feel it is nothing to do with them, 'I have to look after myself first and cannot get involved'.

Those of us who are concerned about suicide prevention and trying to make life worth living, may point out to the anxious that the great majority of serious suicide risk people are not dramatic or threatening in any way. Those who have had many encounters with suicidal people, both as voluntary helpers and as professionals will all agree that there is very little drama. The great majority of the most suicidal people do not want to burden or worry others. They are so often pathetically grateful for a little time given to them.

To those who are selfish it is worth reminding them that their insistence that suicidal people are 'nutters', or should be allowed to do their own thing, could be part of societies defence against their own suicidal fears. If we are honest with ourselves, we have to recognize so often what we deny or attack about others is a reflection of some of our own unresolved inner conflicts. It is generally accepted that suicidal behaviour is a possibility for anyone irrespective of age, sex or personality. We could say that to be really pragmatic, to be maturely selfish, it is essential to be concerned for those at risk of suicide.

Both the anxiety and the selfish reactions are very understandable and to some degree will always be present in our encounters with people in crisis. It has been said that the only major problem for the Samaritans is how the volunteers react to callers. The latter with all their desperate and possible suicidal risk are not the major problem. This is not a cynical reaction, but one based on the recognition that both the caller and volunteer have needs. What is so remarkable is that so many men and women in the Samaritans who are drawn from the community can cope so well.

Carl Rogers in his book on encounter groups, gives a very clear and precise account of what happens when people feel it is emotionally safe enough to express both negative and positive feelings to each other. He points out how surprised he was to realize how much help can be given to psychotics and very emotionally disturbed people by other members of a group, who did not have any professional psychological or medical training. The helpers' contribution can be seen as an extension of what happens between human beings who are concerned for each other, such as the good neighbour, caring relative or friend. These people are not afraid to express some of their inadequacies and risk looking foolish. It is a normal reaction to be anxious when you have to face up to some new activity, e.g. being prepared for surgery, taking examinations, getting married, going for a job interview or being with a suicidal person.

How then does one cope with the first encounter? First and foremost you need to empathize with the callers and try to help them feel it is safe to speak of their needs. You then listen with patience and attention to what they have to say. It is helpful to feed back to the caller some of the actual distress they have communicated. If the caller says, 'it is all getting on top of me, I cannot sleep, making mistakes at work, feel so tired and now my boss wants me to move – how can I tell my wife?', after he has poured out some of these troubles, feed them back to show you understand. 'I expect you feel exhausted, on edge, a bit trapped, it must all be getting on top of you.' It is so important to give the caller space to be upset. Whilst we cannot expect to meet all the needs of the distressed, we can help them to unburden themselves. We should never underestimate the healing effects of listening and empathizing with someone in distress. This is especially true when people are suicidal, because many of the suicide risk periods are short-lived, that is why the twenty-four-hour availability with absolute confidentiality of the Samaritans, throughout the UK and Republic of Ireland, is so valuable. Whilst it is impossible to evaluate how much the presence of the Samaritans reduces the overall suicide rate, it is reasonable to recognize that they meet some of the essential needs of desperate people. Norman Keir sums this up very well when he writes,

It is astonishing how often merely talking about one's feelings can help. Many people go through life ignoring or suppressing their feelings. They find it difficult to speak about how they feel and they need help to do so. The act of talking about feelings allows the individual to develop a new perspective towards them. Often the attempt to articulate how he feels leads him to a new understanding of his predicament. Sharing suicidal feelings with another person may be the first step in breaking out of a closed pattern of thinking. Talking can soothe agitated feelings. Most importantly, talking is a way out of the sense of isolation that so many suicidal people have. The relationship between speaker and listener can provide the support that is needed for moments of crisis to be passed and survived[2].

It is estimated that over 381,000 annually contact the Samaritans for the first time and that twenty-two per cent of these indicate they had suicidal feelings and thoughts. On average twenty-five per cent of callers have on-going face-to-face encounters.

A highly suicidal state is characterised by its transient quality, its pervasive ambivalence, and its dyadic nature. Psychologists are well-advised to minimalise, if not totally to disregard, those probably well-intentioned but shrill writings in this field which naïvely speak of an individual's 'right to commit suicide – a right which cannot be denied'[3].

The immediate need then is to be available, to listen with sensitivity and patience. The second requirement is to stay with it, as we recall the risk time is transient, so there will be a few critical hours or days. During that critical period continuous support, befriending is required. It may be that it is necessary to have more than one helper involved. What is happening is that the helpers are becoming the Significant Other for the caller during the crisis period. We recall how the common denominator here is always loneliness, and so the effect of the helpers' presence is to reduce this and to begin to relieve some of the emotional pain. We need in the first instance to be with the person to try and lower the level of emotional distress. 'The immediate antidote for suicide lies in the reduction of perturbation.'[4] It is understandable that helpers encountering a suicidal person will be anxious to assess the degree of the suicide risk. We know that a number of schemes for measuring the lethality rating have been devised, but these should be used with caution. The intrinsic value of lethality checks for suicide risk factors can be helpful, as guidelines, if they are in continual use. How the person is feeling and the depths of their distress may not become apparent in the first encounter. Some people who are suicidal will deny it when asked and others may not realize themselves how much they could be at risk.

> Suicide is best understood not so much in terms of some acts of nosological boxes (e.g. depression or any of the often sterile labels in DSM-111) but rather in terms of two continua of general personality functioning; perturbation and lethality[5].

So the rule with people who are showing signs of being 'screwed-up', up-tight, very upset, lost, extremely negative, i.e. depressed or out of touch with reality, is to have regular checks on their emotional pain temperatures – which means keeping in touch with their feelings, i.e. at least twice in twenty-four-hour period or more if it seems appropriate, whether the encounters are with good neighbours, helpers, or professionals.

We have to recognize that it will not always work, as distressed people may decide to reject help. Therefore staying with the person, or at least keeping in touch, has to be arranged with patience and sensitivity to their needs.

When Shneidman speaks of 'many pointless deaths, but there is never a needless suicide', he is really giving us the key to understanding suicidal behaviour. Some of the difficulty in responding effectively is caused by the fact that suicide tends to be shrouded in mystery and fear. It is linked with murder, it is, after all, self-murder, therefore those who kill themselves are associated with sinister connotations. Society has tried to find ways of defending itself against this frightening kind of human behaviour. The victims are condemned, or declared insane – a common verdict of coroners is that 'the balance of the mind was disturbed' – or the defence is complete denial. On the other hand, Chad Varah, Shneidman and Ringel have all pioneered a more humane, caring and realistic approach to suicide. This is expressed by an attitude of acceptance, a policy of befriending and recognition of the needs of suicidal people and an under-standing of their underlying psychological conflicts. This results in volunteers and professionals becoming more aware and confident in their work of prevention.

If we examine Shneidman's ten common characteristics of suicide in Figure 10 in detail, we will begin to get the feel of their underlying emotions and grasp some of their needs. It could serve as a useful pattern, as a basic guide to all kinds of helpers. Although we consider each of the ten points separately, they are inter-related and are usually present in suicidal behaviour.

FIGURE 10:  TEN COMMON CHARACTERISTICS OF SUICIDE[6]

| Common Characteristic | Suicide (is) |
| --- | --- |
| 1. Stimulus | Unendurable psychological pain |
| 2. Stressor | Frustrated psychological needs |
| 3. Purpose | To seek a solution to an overbearing problem |
| 4. Goal | Cessation of consciousness |
| 5. Emotion | Hopelessness – helplessness |
| 6. Internal Attitude | Ambivalence |
| 7. Cognitive State | Constriction |
| 8. Interpersonal Act | Communication of intention |
| 9. Action | Egression |
| 10. Consistency | With lifelong adjustment patterns |

1. *The common stimulus* or *trigger* in suicide is unendurable psychological pain – 'I am feeling choked up inside, all screwed-up, cannot stand it any longer'.

There will be any number of significant external causes for

this situation. It is necessary to recognize the importance of the external aspects and essential to take account of how the person reacts internally to situations. Some will only experience a manageable amount of psychological anguish, for others it could be unbearable. This seems to have little to do with whether the person is a strong or weak character, but does seem to be related to the levels of psychological stress to which they have been exposed from the environment and from within their own emotional life in the past, e.g. serious losses in early childhood, little or no experience of parental support, depressive illness, etc. In fact, many people are thus exposed to levels of psychological pain which no one should have to bear.

*The helper's job* is to reduce the pain, the stress, to lower the emotional temperature, '. . . the main clinical rule is: reduce the level of suffering, often just a little bit, and the individual will choose to live'[7]. Keep in touch with their feelings.

2. *The common stressor* is frustration of psychological needs – 'I feel I want to scream, I'm very angry and can't get rid of it, I can't cope with people, I have had enough'.

Many situations cause a person's needs to be thwarted or unfulfilled. People seldom kill themselves because of their loss of material needs, rather it is the loss of status or place in society. There is an urge to be in charge, to be wanted and needed. We all have a need to find a meaning and purpose in life. How these are expressed is dependent upon each individual's situation. What is certain is that everyone will have needs to fulfil.

*The helper's job* here is to accept that the person's needs are real. This may seem to be obvious, yet it is not always easy for the helper to be able to recognize and accept the needs of the other, 'What is one man's flower is another man's weed'. The sensitive helper has also special needs within their role of helper, and that is to empathize with the person's needs and to be impartial. A person in crisis will quickly recognize any insincere reactions, not because they expect helpers to agree with them, but because they need understanding. When this is achieved, you are enabling them to have some space, for a while anyway, the heat is off. 'There are many pointless deaths but never a needless suicide'[8].

3. *The common purpose* of suicide is to seek a solution – 'I am in an emotional cul-de-sac, I must get out, suicide will solve everything'.

The message here is that suicide has a purpose in that it is solving a problem. It is the way out of an intolerable predicament and after careful consideration, is found to be the right solution. As there is always a lot of interest in whether a person really intended to kill himself or not, it will be useful to note the marked difference between suicidal and parasuicidal behaviour. The object of actual suicide is to solve a problem whereas the object of parasuicide is to reduce tension and to evoke a response.

It is important to remember that suicide is an omnipotent act; it proves to oneself and to others that you are able to take charge of finding the solution.

> The half dozen or more individuals whom I have talked to, who, in one way or another, have committed suicide and fortuitously survived have all said something like this. 'It was the *only* thing I could do. It was the best way out of a terrible situation. It was the answer to the problem I had to solve. I could not see any other way'[9].

*The helper's job* is to give the person the opportunity to talk about the terrible situation they feel the need to solve, by listening with patience, feeling and understanding. You need to recognize how very serious and urgent the problem is for the caller. In reality, the problem may or may not seem very serious to you. Great care should be exercised in getting into a discussion about the pros and cons of suicide as a solution. On the whole, people do not respond very well to those who try to argue them out of suicidal action, the indirect approach, care and alternative options are less threatening and seem more acceptable. You could ask them gently if they have considered this or that alternative, there is a need to help them explore the situation with you.

4. *The common goal* of suicide is cessation of consciousness – to sleep, to stop the racing thoughts, the pounding in the head, 'the closing in on me'. This means that the person is more interested in the long sleep, rather than death, and this can confuse the helpers. Quite naturally, they equate suicide with death and the end of physical life. Many people have found that when someone has finally made up their mind to choose suicide they seem quite relieved and positive. Some would see suicide as the trump card in the psychological pack.

*The helper's job* is to befriend, comfort, give human warmth and see in what way the unbearable stress can be reduced. Now is the time for some direct action to lessen the emotional suffering. It is important for the helper not to be deceived by the apparently more relaxed state of some of those they may see, as the goal, the act of suicide, is never born of joy, but only of black despair. You may not have another opportunity and you can begin by perhaps making an arrangement for the person to get some rest, or making sure that he or she will not be alone. 'What the suicidal person requires is only the efforts of a benign person, a decent citizen, a righteous champion, an effective ombudsman, a good Samaritan'[10].

5. *The common emotion* in suicide is helplessness; hopelessness – 'There is nothing I can do, no one can help me, it is too late. I am a failure. I feel so ashamed'.

As we have observed earlier, the common denominator of suicide is loneliness, at this point we encounter it with a vengeance. There seem to be two common causes of loneliness. The first is depression, whether designated endogenous or reactive. The second is the schizoid or cut off type of personality. When we speak of loneliness in these connections, we are going down to the depths of utter despair, isolation and nothingness. This kind of loneliness is nothing whatever to do with those who are experiencing a temporary loneliness through geographical or job changes, even bereavement. Here we are encountering the isolation and powerlessness so well described by Albert Camus and Franz Kafka. Rollo May and many other thinking people would speak not only of personal schizoid reactions, but would draw our attention to our schizoid society. The suicide risk seems to be greatest when a crisis emerges which creates a deeper sense of emptiness and a meaningless to living. In the same way, the helplessness and hopelessness caused by depression is quite different from that caused by great sadness or unhappiness. The depressed person seems impregnated by negative reactions to himself and, in severe depression, will be convinced of his own badness.

Shneidman, quoting from Professor Kenneth Colby's UCLA computerized course in *Programmed information for dealing with depression and suicide* (1984), states,

> In addition to hopelessness, people thinking of suicide often feel a terrible loneliness. That may shut one off from unfeeling others and one becomes numb, impervious to solace. Life, now grim as well as drab, loses its value and one determines to abandon it. Death seems the perfect release from troubles . . . Confusion will be ended and calm and control will finally be achieved[11].

*The helper's job* is first to recognize how awful the person feels, as there is no point in trying to persuade them that they are being too pessimistic. The very isolated and severely depressed are not likely to improve without professional help. What we have to react to initially is the suicide risk.

> What we fear is something worse than what we have. Often times persons literally on the ledge of committing suicide would be willing to live if things – life – were only a little bit better, a just noticeable difference, slightly more tolerable. The common fear is that the inferno is bottomless and we have to draw the line on internal suffering *somewhere*. Every

suicide makes this statement; this far and no further – even though he would have been willing to live on the brink[12].

The person can be said to be bleeding to death emotionally. If the helper is able to begin, as it were, to stem the flow of emotional desperation just a little, then some of the loneliness may be reduced. This may encourage the person to live as you have given a transfusion of hope, but there is still a need to be in close touch.

6. *The common internal attitude* to suicide is ambivalence – 'I want to live and I want to die, the battle goes on inside, I must kill myself but I could survive by accident.'

It is not easy for people to appreciate how the suicidal person can have such mixed feelings. 'It is the common internal attitude toward suicide: to feel that one has to do it and, simultaneously to yearn (and even to plan) for rescue and intervention'[13]. Yet, if we are honest, all of us have experienced ambivalent feelings and attitudes to people and events, therefore it is not surprising that when it is a question of living or dying, we have mixed feelings. As in most human activity, there are mixed motives and inner emotional conflicts which may well result in a person wanting to change from dying to living or vice versa.

*The helper's job* is to cash in on the ambivalence. We could say that all attempts at suicide prevention are doing just that – being realistic and recognizing that conflicting feelings and ideas are an essential part of the human make up. So it is here that the helper can begin to gently present some positive alternatives which later will need to be followed up and consolidated.

7. *The common cognitive or mental state* in suicide is constriction – 'I feel the barriers are up, all the avenues of escape are closed. There are only two answers – a miracle, or death – there will be no miracle, nobody can do any more, I think I am in a tunnel and there is no light at the end of it'.

The logical aspect of suicidal behaviour will depend to a great extent, upon the individual's particular style of reasoning. It is not possible to identify any specific rational approach to suicide. There is no doubt that, to the great majority of suicides, their action seemed to be quite rational.

> I am not one who believes that suicide is best understood as a psychosis, a neurosis, or a character disorder. I believe that it is much more accurately seen as a more or less transient psychological construction of effect and intellect[14].

This would seem to imply that we may have a person in crisis. This upsets them emotionally, so they try to work out a logical on-the-spot way out of their dilemma. Whether they succeed or not is very much a matter for debate. Some may argue that anyone facing such a crisis is not in a fit state to make a rational decision about the future. What is most certain is that, because of the heightened emotional tensions and anxieties, the individual's rational judgement is likely to be upset. This will probably cause constriction or a narrowing of available options. The suicidal person, in the main, wants to stop his consciousness in order to escape the pains and anxieties.

> One of the most dangerous aspects of a suicidal state (high lethality/high perturbation) is the presence of constriction. Any attempt at rescue or remediation has to deal, almost from the first, with the pathological constriction[15].

It is really very questionable how free people are to choose suicide. In reality a person's rational response is, in effect, a desperate bid to find an answer to an intolerable situation which is already overwhelming a clear and free intellectual response.

*The helper's job* is to recognize the person's fenced-in position, the constriction, and try to open up other ways forward, to encourage the person to explore other options, to widen their vision. Quite often the very act of talking about the actual situations in great detail and looking at some options which are presented by the helper, may begin to give the person confidence to explore other ways out of their predicament.

8. *The common interpersonal act* in suicide is communication – 'It is all getting too much, they would be better off without me, sometimes I feel like ending it all, I have lost interest, feel very tired'.

We know from the psychological autopsies that eighty per cent of suicides had indirectly indicated their suicidal state. It is not necessarily a cry for help, rather it seems to be an expression of a person's inner state. They are so upset and disturbed inside that they begin to transmit messages, quite frequently in the form of a whisper rather than a threat. The careful observer who knows them well may be able to recognize that they are behaving in an unusual way, e.g. putting things in order, omitting to do things they habitually do, acting out of character.

*The helper's job* is to be sensitive to the signals of change and distress given out consciously or unconsciously. Unlike the parasuicidal person where the communication is a call for help and rescue, here the person feels a need to inform and not to call out or ask. This is probably why many of these indirect signs go unnoticed. Therefore it is safer for the helpers to assume there is a risk of suicide whether apparent or not. Once again, this confirms the helper's need to ask questions about suicide. Granting permission to talk about suicidal feelings and plans could act as the vital trigger giving the person a chance to survive.

9. *The common action* in suicide is escape – 'I want to get out for good, I have had more than enough, this is the end, I cannot stand any more, I am not going to put up with it'.

It is quite common for men and women to talk of getting away from it all, escaping for a few days holiday from the pressures of work and so on. This is a way of getting relief and of renewing oneself. Religious people talk of making a retreat and so giving themselves an escape from the noise and bustle of the material world. The object of escape in this context is for improving and saving life. Whereas with those who use suicide as a means of escape, it is for a permanent change and an end to life.

*The helper's job* is to listen and act. There may not be much time, as the person is now on the verge of taking action. So the pills, gun or other lethal objects need to be collected by the helpers. On-going support needs to be arranged.

10. *The common consistency* in suicide is with life-long coping patterns. We all tend to be set in our ways, the well-established patterns of behaviour are unlikely to change without psychological intervention. Our defences against stress and in crisis are generally consistent.

It seems that as all of us tend to follow our built-in style of behaviour, it will also apply in most suicide situations.

> In suicide we are initially thrown off the scent, because suicide is an act which, by definition, that individual has never done before – so there is no precedent. And yet there are deep consistencies with life long coping patterns. We must look to previous episodes of disturbance, to capacity to endure psychological pain, and to the penchant for constriction and dichotomous thinking, for earlier paradigms of egression[16].

Therefore, for the care of the suicidal, it is appropriate to give particular attention to their personality and previous reactions in crises.

*The helper's job* is to research the history of the person's background wherever possible and to seek ways of using such information for their benefit. It is most valuable and generally beneficial in working out how best to relieve their suffering but there are some snags. Even when the person is beginning to receive professional help, caution should be exercised in taking a case history using the rather formal medical model. People at risk are extra sensitive and may not respond well to a formal setting. Care also needs to be taken when using an analytical or psychotherapeutic approach as long silences or psychological interpretations may be premature. Where the initial encounter was with a volunteer helper, the suicidal person may feel it is easier to talk about themselves and their past. Special attention needs to be given here to the danger of being too non-directive and too unwilling to encourage or arrange professional help when this is required. It can also be helpful to recall previous positive patterns of successful ways of coping. There are many men and women who have shown great courage and given evidence of considerable psychological strength which has gone unnoticed.

We have considered how suicidal behaviour does have some identifiable ingredients. Shneidman has outlined for us some fairly simple signals which should help us to empathize more closely with those in crisis, both as human beings and as helpers. The following is a summary of Shneidman's ten points.

The common characteristics of suicide (described earlier) have direct implications for saving lives. Here are some practical measures for helping highly suicidal persons, following the previously presented outline:

1. Stimulus (unbearable pain): *reduce the pain.*
2. Stressor (frustrated needs): *fill the frustrated needs.*
3. Purpose (to seek a solution): *provide a viable answer.*
4. Goal (cessation of consciousness): *indicate alternatives.*
5. Emotion (hopelessness-helplessness): *give transfusions of hope.*
6. Internal attitude (ambivalence): *play for time.*
7. Cognitive state (constriction): *increase the options.*
8. Interpersonal act (communication of intention): *listen to the cry, involve others.*
9. Action (egression): *block the exit.*
10. Consistency (with life-long patterns): *invoke previous positive patterns of successful coping.*[17]

In the next section, we examine some of the mechanics of how we pick up and work with callers/patients. We look at an emerging pattern of help geared especially to meet some of the needs of the suicidal.

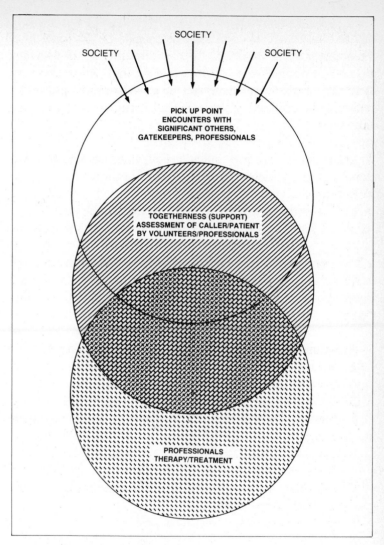

Figure 11: The mechanics of working with callers

## THE PICK-UP POINT

If we recognize, to quote Shneidman, that 'in the last analysis, the prevention of suicide is everybody's business', then how those concerned get on with each other will have a tremendous effect on the suicidal.

In Figure 11 you will see from the use of these circles that there are three significant areas which may be identified in providing help. You will notice the three circles interlock and this highlights the modern trend towards an inter-disciplinary approach.

In circle 1 are the sensitive and caring people of the community. This would include friends, Significant Others, gatekeepers, good neighbours and the Samaritans, as well as professionals, especially GPs and social workers. You will see those on the edge of this circle operate in the main on the frontier points of society and as we move into the circle they open the way for the creation of togetherness and support and professional help. This then is the pick-up point, those who are available should be likened to those who operate radar screens used so extensively in air and sea communications, for everything depends upon how well problems, new situations and changes are identified. We may have some excellent resources, very committed volunteers, deeply caring and expert professionals, but none of these will be used unless there is a successful pick-up or a meaningful response to a request for help. This applies to all our encounters and our difficulties are far more complex than those experienced in any radar operation, as we are trying to relate to people and not objects.

In very simple terms, we can expect to encounter at the pick-up point;
1. Those who want help and ask for it, sometimes they may be rather vague about what they need or want to receive, yet it is recognized beyond question that the most positive relationship and help can be given when the caller wants it.
2. Those who find it hard to co-operate, though they want and need help. This would include the very depressed, who do not

think they are entitled to help, some find it very hard to trust people, generally the result of bad experiences from early childhood, and those who get out of touch with reality and are likely to be labelled mentally ill or psychotic. Some will respond well to a sensitive encounter whilst others may consider co-operation is ridiculous or too dangerous.

3. Those who are very demanding and frequently make extensive use of voluntary and professional services. They often have a special capacity to 'wind up' the helpers with dramatic stories and sometimes threats of suicide.

4. Those who seem to be very inadequate, either presenting very dependent or aggressive reactions, often labelled chronic callers or patients. An early recognition is essential in order both to help the caller and to prevent the wasting of helping resources.

5. Some of the most suicidal people will be those who are referred to helpers by a third party or, as it were, dragged in for help. These kinds of encounters demonstrate again the need for the closest co-operation and mutual trust between the general public and the helpers, voluntary or professional. There are two fundamental distinctions to be borne in mind when seeking help. Voluntary bodies who insist on having a caller's permission and respect their confidence before taking any action, do not have any statutory authority or responsibility this is especially so of the Samaritans. The social services, GPs and psychiatrists have defined obligations to provide care, treatment and management. Most helpers, not least professionals, are uneasy about responding to third-party intervention. In some cases it will be necessary to section patients, detain them under the Mental Health Act, both for the care and protection of the patient and of the community. The modern approach in psychiatry is to section patients for the shortest possible period. This is in keeping with a more humane attitude. Unfortunately, at times it can heighten the suicide risk. It is the experience of most Samaritan branches, especially that of Central London, who average twenty per week, that, handled with sensitivity and understanding, the majority of people referred are able to accept help.

Those who provide counselling or psychotherapy, whether on National Health or privately, for individual or group work, insist that the person asks for such help. They would be required to enter into a contract based on mutual co-operation. The caller/patient must be free to stop the sessions or walk out of them. They must be free to make their own choices. This sometimes confuses relatives, friends and other helpers of those in therapy, because it may well involve the risk of suicide. However, these therapeutic units will have medical and psychiatric back up. DHSS referrals will have had a psychiatric assessment. It is not unusual for relatives and sometimes neighbours, to more or less force someone to see their doctor. Sometimes medical or psychiatric treatment is needed and can be arranged. What is unfair is to expect a busy GP to take over all kinds of social problems or be expected to treat and care for a patient who does not want help. The doctors and social workers tend to use compulsory powers of the Mental Health Act with great discretion, and quite often only as a last resort.

If you, as a relative or caring person, are concerned about someone who is very depressed, mentally ill, and a possible danger to themselves and others, and it is clear to you that they will refuse help, there is no point in involving Samaritans or voluntary bodies. They are likely to need a doctor and social worker with authority to take the appropriate action. Although they may certainly benefit later from some follow-up support.

Many people who are not involved in helping roles either as volunteers or professionals, will have had some experience of people in the five groups mentioned. In the course of our daily lives we often give support to many different people and for those of us with the care of children and the elderly the making of assessments as to their needs regarding medical help and crisis situations are quite common – therefore the average responsible caring man or woman can be invaluable for the suicidal at the pick-up point. Let us look at some examples.

The caring person who listens to the neighbour when they feel the need to talk about their worries. You may know about some recent illness in their family, a loss, trouble with police or the neighbour may just look down and seem upset. You begin to recognize their needs. It may be wiser to follow up a conversation with a visit or suggest he or she comes for a chat.

The milkman, shop assistant, hairdresser, policeman, lawyer, indeed any of those serving the community, the 'gatekeepers' as the Americans call them. Many of you will have regular encounters with your customers and clients, and although you may not have talked with many for any long period you are likely to be regarded by them as someone they can trust. As we have seen, to be trusted is a vital factor in the work of suicide prevention, so this should give you confidence to do a follow-up when it seems necessary. In a strange kind of way many people will already have regarded you as a sort of counsellor cum confidant. It would be sensitive and responsible for you to note any changes of behaviour; the man or woman who has a marked change in daily or weekly routine; those who stop gardening for no obvious reason; who are unwell, especially those living alone; hints of stress or anxiety, especially following a robbery or loss; an aura of detachment; a change in their appearance often for the worse; a withdrawal or just not being their usual friendly self. We must remember that suicidal people do communicate their need for help indirectly.

How you respond to any one of these people who are in distress and may be suicidal is up to you. Here are a few guidelines which are essential for all of us to follow.

1. Listen, give the other person a bit of time, you may not have another opportunity.
2. Try to be accepting, whether you agree or not – let them express their needs, hopelessness, frustrations.
3. After you have given them some space, do not be afraid to respond with, 'You are having quite a time of it', or 'Everything seems to come at once – it all gets on top of one', 'That sort of thing can hurt a lot'. If appropriate make some positive comments – you are coping well – have lots of patience, courage. You may consider it helpful to ask, 'Do you feel you can stand any more?', 'It's getting you down, isn't it?', 'Do you feel you have got to the end of your

tether?', 'I expect you feel you have had your lot?', 'Do you feel able to go on?' 'Can you see any way out?', 'Feel like snuffing it?'. You could certainly mention suicide, though some of the questions suggested may be a sufficient lead.

4. If the person has admitted they are suicidal, stay with the situation and make suggestions of help – go with the person to the place of help or make some definite arrangements. If the person is suicidal and will not seek help, you could try a third-party referral. The most valuable thing for you to offer is to see them later yourself, the 'keep in touch' idea may make all the difference.

There are some dramatic situations which are always likely to worry would-be helpers who are inexperienced or who are coping on their own. These are when the caller, as one of your relatives or friends, phones up in a great state, crying and saying they are going to kill themselves, they are taking the pills or it is all arranged, they cannot stand it any longer.

First, you must appreciate that it is a shock for you to get such a call, therefore it is natural for you to feel anxious, shaky and dry in the mouth, so try to calm down. Secondly, give your caller space. You could say 'I am so sorry, Bill, tell me what has been happening'. The caller may go on crying, saying, 'I am going to die', and not seem to be aware they have phoned you, so you need to keep on gently saying 'I am here Bill, I cannot help unless you talk to me about what is upsetting you'. It is quite likely the caller will calm down a little and begin to say what has happened. It can sometimes help to reduce the emotional tension, if you can ask some rather practical questions like, 'Have you been to work today?' 'Are you on your own?' It is also important for you to have some idea where the caller is, perhaps at home or at a friend's place. If he/she says they are at home and you have the address this could be most useful later on, especially if they are taking pills and perhaps drinking a lot. Thirdly, it is important to realize that ninety-nine per cent of the people who phone in this way want help, want to be saved from suicide. They may need to be persuaded gently and firmly and may not want any official involvement.

If things go reasonably well, you will probably end up in a face-to-face situation with them or will have arranged one through a third party. If it is you who see them and when you arrive they are conscious, do not try and rush them off to hospital or to a doctor. They may still need some space. Remember, as long as they are conscious they can still refuse to go anywhere. It is most essential to discover what worries them about a medical check-up at Casualty; they could be well known in the local community. If the person is conscious and has vomitted after a large intake of aspirin or paracetamol, remember it will have delayed effects, so if local help is unwise, it might be better to go to a casualty department some distance away. It is worth bearing in mind, without being cynical, that the dramatic caller is most likely to survive, the clinically depressed, quiet type is likely to die or kill themselves at the first opportunity. It is unlikely they will phone you for direct help, even if you are a good friend or loving relative. They will not want to bother you, will not feel entitled to your help. Although unlikely to make any direct reference to suicide, they may make a contact with you about something else. It could be just to ask advice about something quite ordinary, yet if you think about it, this is out of character, they are using it as a presenting problem, as a way of trying to communicate a more serious underlying worry. Perhaps they may just 'happen to be passing' and want to see you about a simple problem. They will go to their GP presenting some physical pains, say they cannot sleep, are out of sorts, have pains in the back, headaches and so on. If you manage to get below the surface, you may be surprised to discover how depressed and suicidal they are. If you provide them with the opportunity to talk about their deeper feelings, you may save a life. Of course more help will be needed and, in the case of depressive illness, medical-psychiatric help is essential. The effectiveness of the encounters in the pick-up area will depend not only upon your sensitivity but also on the caller's willingness to co-operate.

## TOGETHERNESS AND PROFESSIONAL TREATMENT

Those who have a successful pick-up encounter will be ready to promote togetherness and possibly seek professional help. We have to bear in mind that this is only the beginning. Now we have to help the caller/patient to feel secure enough to take the big step of trusting and co-operating with the helpers. Let us look at two examples.

Keith, a middle-aged accountant, became very upset following the break-up of his marriage. A colleague contacted the Samaritans and accompanied him to the local centre. He was seen by a female Samaritan who initially was concerned to help reduce the emotional pain. She achieved this largely by listening intensely, accepting his grief and some expressions of anger. Keith kept saying he had never got in this state before and it was the shock of discovering his wife was unfaithful and was going off with a neighbour. The Samaritan gave him permission, as it were, to be really upset. After nearly two hours he seemed calmer. By now the Samaritan has created a 'togetherness' with Keith, his problems were the same, the Samaritan had offered no solutions, but three essential things had happened.
1. His boss in a firm, but decisive way had told Keith that he must get help and had gone with him to a resource of help.
2. The Samaritan befriended him, gave of herself in rapt attention with acceptance and patience.
3. He was now no longer facing his crisis alone.

This was only the beginning. Keith was very dispirited and had been getting worse for the last two weeks, he could not eat or sleep, he was very agitated and felt a failure. Feeling more secure with Samaritan befriending, he was agreeable to seeing his GP, whom he hardly knew as he was never ill. So the togetherness moves into the professional circle and Keith is given some appropriate medical help, the Samaritans continue to befriend, and the circles overlap. He is becoming more able to assert himself positively, because those three helpers, the gatekeeper, the Samaritan and the doctor somehow restored his self-confidence, as they helped him to feel a person again.

Anna, thirty-five years old, a housewife with two children under five and a fifteen-year-old daughter from her first marriage, was becoming very depressed, which was not unusual for her. She had as bad a time with her second husband, as with her first. The only good spot in the situation was her GP whom she had known for three years. Although he had a very busy practice, Anna felt he always listened and he respected her wish to keep her children. She trusted his treatment with anti-depressants when she was going through a difficult period. He had established a togetherness, and because of this positive relationship, the bleakest of situations became bearable with dignity.

It is evident that so much of the future developments in all these encounters is dependent upon the quality of the relationship created between those involved. The great therapeutic value of a good doctor/patient relationship has always been recognized in medicine. However, putting it effectively into practice varies quite a lot and is often made more difficult by the scientific advances in modern medicine. So many people have come to expect quick solutions, there must be the right pill around or, for those preferring alternative medicine, the right homoeopathic treatment. Suicidal distress is about feelings of being upset, angry and afraid and people in this state need time to unwind. It is true that those suffering from depression will benefit from anti-depressants, but they improve faster with good human support.

> In the UK a general practitioner with a list of 2,500 patients could expect to encounter a suicide once every 3 or 4 years, accounting for about 1% of all deaths . . . The same general practitioner has 6 or 7 people on his list each year who became parasuicides[19].

These kind of statistics do not give a very real picture, as suicidal behaviour is not an illness like cancer or heart trouble, and this makes diagnosis so difficult.

Psychiatrists who consider these patients are at special risk may arrange for them to be admitted to hospital or make more frequent appointments. In all these encounters the doctor is dependent upon what the patient discloses to him; the patient may be too ashamed to speak about suicide or they may not realize how depressed they are. This is one of the main reasons why it can be very beneficial for there to be a group of GPs plus health visitor and community psychiatric nurse as part of the team. At the same time these would establish close links with the Samaritans and all other accredited helping agencies. Through the Central London Branch of the Samaritans and through many other centres, large numbers of people suffering from serious depression with suicidal ideas, have gained enough confidence and insight to see their GP or psychiatrist. The Samaritan emergency twenty-four-hour service is available at the pick-up point for direct telephone and face-to-face encounters.

## GROUPS AT SPECIAL RISK OF SUICIDE

*Young people*
'What we need is an older person to talk to' – serious statement of a fourteen-year-old girl in trouble with bullying at school with little or no contact with parents.

'I feel so lonely, all tied up inside, cannot explain' – girl of fifteen.

'She (mother) told me to get out, so I am not going back home' – fourteen-year-old girl.

'They (parents) nag me all the time about clothes, colour of my hair, etc' – boy of fifteen.

'My mates laugh at me because I have to be home at 10 pm' – girl of fifteen.

'Dad got a new wife and so they do not need me anymore at home' – girl of fifteen, whose mother died when she was thirteen and step-mother arrived two years later.

'I really loved him so much, it was not just sex – I'm sorry, but I cannot stand any more questioning' – girl of fifteen, in love with a man in his twenties, later she killed herself.

'I want to get away from home – no one speaks to me, I want to join the army' – boy of fifteen, pretending to be seventeen and at first only presenting an accommodation problem.

'I am going to bed early', she said. Parents accepted this explanation, in the morning they found her dead from an overdose of sleeping tablets. This situation, reported to the press was of a fifteen-year-old girl, who killed herself because of breaking with boy-friend. 'She loved him but she seemed OK.'

These are some typical examples of situations which upset adolescents, yet some of them do not seem at all important. All teenagers can expect to have some hassle with parents and figures of authority, so why all the fuss? There is a need to appreciate that what may appear very trivial to an older person can seem of tremendous importance to a fifteen-year-old. As we have observed, it is essential when helping the suicidal to discover the needs of the distressed person. As we explore the complex needs of the adolescent it will be helpful to refer to Figure 14. The pick-up point is of greater significance to the child or adolescent than to many older people, as the young tend to be more emotionally vulnerable and insecure, and wary of trusting adults. This is why so often the Significant Others for adolescents are from their own peer group. Although they may appear very mature and act in a sophisticated manner, they still have a long way to go in the process of their development. It will be useful if those in the pick-up group are aware of the most common warning signs of depression and suicidal risk in young people. Some of these are listed below.

1. Marked changes in mood, at home or school, long silences, expressions of unusual bad temper, inability to concentrate, lack of interest, withdrawal, getting out of touch with reality, sleeping late, appearing to become very lazy.
2. Expressions of a non-caring attitude, little or no reaction to

happy or unpleasant events. Sometimes talk of hopelessness and no point in living.
3. Rebellious reactions to parents or teachers, running away, getting into trouble with the police, etc.

Young people who come by way of third-party referrals, as with anyone coerced into help, will often be among the most serious and most difficult to help. Additional complications may arise with parents or guardians for those under age.

Mina, eighteen, was at university after doing very well at a select girls' school. She was the only child of doting, older parents who were over-protective. Student life came as a shock to her although, at first, she was very excited by the social life. Mina was attractive and popular with the male students in spite of her inexperience and shyness. She tried to adapt to the more critical and sometimes cynical ways of the academic approach to words. Towards the end of the second term, she became very anxious, missed lectures and seminars and stopped socializing. Fortunately for Mina, several of her year made her see the student counsellor. After counselling and then psychiatric help, she was able to return for the next term. Mina had become withdrawn, depressed and had really given up. She allowed herself to agree to arrangements made on her behalf. Without such intervention, she would have become worse and, in such a situation, suicide was a likely outcome.

Alan, nineteen, a science student, had a good record at school and was doing well at university at the end of his first year there. He was the eldest of three sons. There was very little expression of emotion in the family and any discussions were centred on intellectual subjects. His father was a lecturer in science, an able and erudite man. His mother was a Maths teacher and had suffered from attacks of depression. She had twice been in hospital for several weeks. Among Alan's friends was Sue, whom he had met at college. She was devoted to him but his emotional responses were very low key. When he became paranoid about her having an affair with her tutor, which was quite untrue, Sue did not break off the relationship. She realized that Aian needed help. He was very suspicious of his tutor and other members of staff and his behaviour became very unreasonable. Sue talked to Alan's tutor and both tried to help him but he would not talk with people he said were plotting to destroy him. He managed to cope until the end of term and even did quite well in several examination papers. During the summer, he became more disturbed, refusing to eat at home because he claimed that his father was trying to poison him. Eventually, he left home and went to a hotel and refused to leave the room the next day. He was aggressive with the manager, police were called and he was sectioned by psychiatrists under the Mental Health Act. Alan was not able to co-operate with any would-be helpers. In this sort of situation, the most effective helpers will be those who have the authority to detain a person under an order.

When trying to help children and adolescents, we have to recognize that, it is often very difficult at first for the helpers to be accepted and trusted. They are usually older, and to the young person sometimes much older. Achieving the togetherness in circle two is likely to be more difficult, and perhaps take longer, than with adults. It is useful to forget the age difference and concentrate upon what you have in common. We may illustrate this with two anecdotes. Graham Greene records a delightful story about communication between two human beings.

Pope John (XXIII) is caught by the camera talking to a little girl sick with leukemia – he speaks with extreme gravity and she listens with the same deep seriousness. It is impossible to say which of them is the elder, which will be the first dead. He speaks to her as an equal[20].

Some years ago, when my wife and I looked after a Samaritan hostel, a girl staying with us came into our bedroom early one morning as we were getting up. She sat on our bed and told us that she thought she had VD. It was her fifteenth birthday.

These are examples of profound human togetherness, which need no commentary.

For most teenagers, togetherness is very important, togetherness with parents, the gang, the group, togetherness in love and sex. We may be tempted to think that this is a modern phenomenon, but surely it is a very ancient youthful expression of grasping hold of life. Being alive means being in love, having sex, having special friends, special aspirations. Sometimes these may be experienced only in fantasy, but they are still very real to the boy or girl. Young people today have to adapt their search for living according to their changing environment. The basic vitality of seeking to be alive, of experiencing togetherness, is the same as in the past. Each generation has to discover its own special sense of human dignity, every individual needs to find how to be responsible for each other.

*What is going on behind the scenes?*
As helpers of the suicidal, we will meet many young people in their moments of crisis, despair, uncertainty, isolation, anger, frustration and disillusionment. Around them they see life and living, in their eyes filled with rejecting parents, demanding authorities, unreliable Significant Others, the joys and failures of togetherness, a lack of inspiration and the awful apparent meaninglessness of life. Many young people are very concerned about their identity, 'Who am I? How do I fit into society?' Twentieth-century youth has to manage with very few clearly defined reference points. There is little opportunity to find oneself. In the past, children and adolescents had little or no place in society and did not have the opportunity to make many choices. When Society is very structured and freedoms of choice are limited, many of our current identity crises do not arise. This has both advantages and disadvantages for all age-groups. We have seen that we are in an age of transition which also effects the behaviour of adults. Failure to recognize these changes will seriously hinder our mutual understanding, as both adolescents and adults have to face up to the realities of

life and discover ways of coping in a new age. Peter Giovacchini reminds us,

> The psychoanalytic philosophy contains some important lessons for those involved with troubled adolescents. It teaches us that an adolescent's attitudes and behaviour (as well as our own) are the results of forces within the mind that are beyond our conscious control. It also teaches us to try to understand why an adolescent is acting as he does rather than to pass judgement on him. The more open and receptive an adult is to this way of relating, the more an adolescent will be understood, which is the first step toward providing crucial support and help[21].

At the same time it is unrealistic to expect perfection in our relationships. What is most helpful is for the adult to be aware of their own weaknesses and mistakes. When adults feel the need to act in a superior way or feel bothered about waiting, as it were, on the responses of a fourteen-year-old, this is really an expression of their own anxieties. Children and adolescents are very quick to sense the degree of acceptance and sincerity in their helpers. As a general pattern, teenagers in distress tend to confide a great deal in each other. The sensitivity and ability to understand in their mutual befriending is a remarkable reflection of their inner capacity for togetherness. One of the other major attractions of the peer group is their mutual keeping of secrets. Young people put a great importance on confidentiality and regard this as a major part of trusting people. Some of this need is because they do not want to be laughed at and embarrassed. In addition, many are concerned about how parents, teachers, police and others will react, especially if they want to pass on information. So a very important part of our beginnings of togetherness will be for us to be able to offer absolute confidentiality. For some helpers, especially those of the statutory bodies, this may cause problems.

It is a great mistake to underestimate the ability of adolescents to be co-operative. If they feel their trust has not been abused then it is more likely that they will agree to a certain course of action. It is worth giving them time for discussion and helping them explore the various options.

I have talked with a number of runaways, thirteen- to fifteen-year-olds, and having reached togetherness following long talks, several have said, 'I am putting you in a difficult position, I know you will not tell the police, but I cannot stay with you indefinitely'. They will respond well to your commitment and maybe make a similar response themselves. They recognize that social workers and teachers are expected to report certain happenings or take appropriate action. It is far better, if there are certain statutory or school responsibilities, to explain the position quite clearly from the beginning. If there is a failure to be straightforward and, at a later stage, it seems necessary to break a confidence or take some action without prior consultation, any co-operation is most unlikely. Such action could precipitate suicide. Children and adolescents respect and appreciate honesty.

Disillusionment is another very common reaction. Young people have their illusions shattered when they see their ideas ridiculed and their ideals falling apart. The resulting emotional wounding is so deep because this is a time of experimentation when they are developing their self-confidence. Adults often remind teenagers how fortunate they are to have the time to do their own thing, therefore it is not surprising if they are upset and confused when their sincere efforts are criticized. Peter Giovacchini, when writing about us being understood explains,

Adult insensitivity – there is no one thing in and of itself that causes someone to end his life. A particular incident serves to be more like a straw that breaks the camel's back. With all the conflicts and pressures adolescents normally face in trying to create an independent adult identity, the camel's back metaphor is unusually apt.

Parents and teachers who make light of the distress an adolescent feels about a rejection, the loss of a friend, a poor grade report, or the sudden fascination with an ideology, may accomplish nothing more than making him feel totally cut off from the world. Such a response may serve to accentuate the terrible painful feelings of being odd or different. It may well dam up the turmoil, permitting the pressure to build and build within the child until he explodes in a destructive act[22].

Let us consider some typical situations presented to helpers. The fifteen-year-old who has run away, or left home because her step-mother told her to go – and meant it. The nine-year-old we will call Martin, who tried to impress his father with some special jokes he had picked up, he also desperately wanted his father's approval about his performance at school. He used to show him his exercise books, he could be quite a bright youngster, but father always put him down, made fun of his work and attempts at jokes. He soon became disillusioned, anxious and depressed. His mother, for different reasons, also found the father extremely difficult, she was aware how he put his son down.

The seeds of suicidal behaviour can be sown very early in life. Any child being brought up in an atmosphere such as Martin has been, may have little chance of developing positive reactions to life. We have not checked, but his mother probably had difficulties during his early rearing, as she had to cope with her husband's inconsiderate behaviour and possible jealousy of their young son.

Like all of us, young people want to be taken seriously and, as a girl of fourteen said, 'We need an older person to talk to'. What is needed is someone who will listen with empathy, giving their full attention, whether the young person is eight or sixteen. If they are given time, maybe a day or more, to unload their feelings and problems, they will feel able later to talk to their parents with greater insight and confidence. Rejection and mistrust will often make communication more complex; many will be confused about their worries and their attitude towards helpers. It is unlikely that they will have had much experience of someone who values them as a person, of someone who really wants them, loves them and cares for them. Deep feelings of rejection have become part of their personality which accounts for the inability to express their feelings and explain their problems to those who are willing to listen. Having a sympathetic listener is new and it is not surprising that they do not know how to handle this kind of experience, they are already trying to cope with the emotional traumas of growing up.

Maureen, aged thirteen with a brother of ten, goes to a comprehensive school in south east London. Her father, a publican, moved to a pub in north London to get a better job. Maureen stayed with her grandmother during the week. Her parents did not want her to move schools, or so they said. She was also parted from her dog. At weekends, she went home and tried to help her parents who were busy with the new pub, but they often just pushed her away. Before the move, she had begun to feel that they no longer wanted her and did not seem interested in her. She had a friend, Ruth, who had problems at home. Ruth had taken an overdose and been in hospital and thought it had helped to bring her parents closer again although this did not last. Maureen was more sensitive than Ruth and felt hurt and isolated living away from home. Her grandmother was kind and loving but over seventy and very deaf. Maureen did not feel that she should worry her, even if she could make her hear. She needed to be loved, she felt very frustrated, angry and helpless. She contacted the Samaritans, talked with several people and had on-going befriending with two volunteers. She wrote to them about her hopes and fears. For two years her situation did not improve and the doctor put her on anti-depressants. Maureen took a large overdose of the tablets and ended up in an intensive care unit. She survived and, for the first time, allowed the Samaritans to talk to her parents. The overdose and her near death acted as a catharsis for Maureen. She saw a psychiatrist but was not very co-operative. With the help of friends, her doctor and the Samaritans, she eventually became happier.

It is very important for us to remember that the great majority of teenagers cope with this period of their lives without undue emotional disturbance. If they are assured of emotional support in the form of a loving and caring mother-figure and the understanding and loving father, this promotes a sense of inner well-being and an ability to cope with some of the hard realities of life. If both parents are confident enough in themselves, they can accept the positive aggression and rebellious attitudes of the well-balanced teenager, as they strive towards healthy maturity.

If these two essential figures are missing or if the parents cannot accept or cope with the positive adolescent need to rebel and to seek independence, problems are to be expected. When the parental figures are absent, or emotionally inadequate, or too rigid, there will be considerable emotional confusion and anxiety generated in children and adolescents. The emotional needs to find a positive expression will grow out of proportion. The emotional traumas will manifest themselves in many different ways, such as running away from home or school, stealing, unusual sexual activity, heavy drinking and drug abuse, aggressive behaviour patterns, boredom and pronounced lack of interest and, in the last resort, suicidal behaviour, often with serious risk of death. Therefore it is most important to appreciate the seriousness of the risk of suicide, especially from the age of twelve upwards. Whilst it is very exceptional for children under twelve years of age to kill themselves, it can happen. We should recognize that the statistics of all suicides or parasuicides are always an underestimation of the actual figures. This is even more likely in the reporting of suicidal behaviour among children and adolescents. The overall death rate of the under twenty-fives in Western society is very low. If we look at the World Heath Organisation statistics of causes of death for that age-group, accidents will be top of the list, with illness second and suicide third. During the last thirty years there has been a marked increase in the suicide rate and suicidal behaviour of people under thirty years of age. Cynthia Pfeffer reminds us that,

In the United States in 1978, more than 3,000 families of adolescents who were 15–19 years old and about 150 families

| Dates | 10–25 yrs Males | 10–25 yrs Females |
|---|---|---|
| 1973 | 203 | 106 |
| 1974 | 204 | 98 |
| 1975 | 237 | 98 |
| 1976 | 218 | 103 |
| 1977 | 232 | 125 |
| 1978 | 266 | 97 |
| 1979 | 259 | 99 |
| 1980 | 252 | 111 |
| 1981 | 280 | 80 |
| 1982 | 276 | 81 |
| 1983 | 277 | 95 |
| 1984 | 310 | 65 |
| 1985 | 342 | 74 |
| 1986 | 363 | 79 |

(for more detailed age breakdown, see Chapter 4, Figures 6–9)
Source: Office of Population Censuses and Surveys

Figure 12: Deaths from suicide in England and Wales, 10–25 years old, 1973–1986

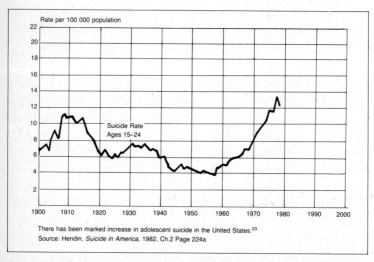

There has been marked increase in adolescent suicide in the United States.[23]
Source: Hendin, *Suicide in America*, 1982, Ch.2 Page 224a

Figure 13: Suicide rates in the United States of America, 15–24 years old, 1900–1978

of pre-adolescents (under 15 years) experienced the suicidal death of their child (Hart Vital statistics 1980). Furthermore, thousands of additional families have experienced suicidal threats and attempts of their youngsters. Recent data show that the numbers are still growing (see Ryerson, 1986)[24].

There has also been a massive increase in overdosing or attempted suicide between fifteen and twenty-five years all over Western Europe and in the United States with a much higher percentage of females over males. Health authorities have come to recognize suicidal behaviour expressed in overdosing as a major health care problem. It is estimated that in Great Britain there are over 100,000 hospital admissions annually for para-suicides, the total number for all European Common Market Countries is 1,400,000. Over sixty per cent of these are persons below thirty-five years of age. It is beyond doubt that many young people feel the only way they can solve their problems is by suicide or some kind of suicide attempt.

As we know, those who have had little or no experience of togetherness with parents or Significant Others will have some serious emotional wounds. At the same time we know that many young people who experience emotional deprivation do not use suicidal behaviour as a solution. We cannot expect to find any simple explanations, yet there are some situations and environmental influences which seem to increase the risk of suicide.

Firstly, adolescents are in the process of growing up and discovering about life, sex and death. They are concerned about their identity and developing attitudes to life. It is the age of intense feelings and risk taking, the primary cause of death of those under twenty-five is accidents. Their moods are subject to frequent changes with periods of happiness and dispiritment. For many it is the crucial period for developing their intellectual abilities and discovering new ideas. The majority in the West will be exposed to the demands of a competitive society. 'You have got to get your exams, go to college, earn money and have sexual experiences'.

Secondly, there is the effect of the nuclear threat. Diekstra says,

> Relevant in this context is a study of the Task Force on the Psychosocial Impact of Nuclear Advances of the American Psychiatric Assiocation, which proved that adolescents in general are far more deeply touched by the nuclear threat and what it involves, than was previously assumed. Suicide notes by adolescents also frequently refer to this[25].

Some adults may want to point out that in the past they have experienced threats of terrible impending catastrophies and not lost hope. Examples could be drawn from how young people coped with two world wars and persecutions on a vast scale. The difference surely is that in the past, even at its worst, there was the possibility of being able to take some effective action. Now, with the threat of nuclear war, there is nothing that can be done by pacifists or armed defenders, the outcome is annihilation. The acceptance of such an inheritance requires considerable courage and a determination for promoting fundamental changes. These may all be regarded as common demands made upon twentieth-century youth. Suicidal behaviour may seem an answer to unbearable emotional pains and an apparently hopeless life-style.

Thirdly, psychological wounding. Those who experience severe rejection are likely to develop negative and depressive reactions to life. Take for example the 'expendable child', a concept proposed by Sabbath and quoted by Pfeffer[26]. It seems the parent either consciously or unconsciously sees the child as a source of trouble and hindrance to their life-style. It is possible the mother did not want the child in the first place and so is jealous and angry with the child's natural demands for attention and affection. These feelings of hatred and deep-rooted rejection are picked up by the child and internalized as a state of inner worthlessness and hopelessness. So the way is prepared for suicide.

Other negative reactions may develop through a failure to

relate to one's peer group, to meet the standards expected by parents or school. Marital breakdown and divorce create tremendous anger and the sense of being let down. One of the most important aspects of the whole drama so frequently missed by even deeply caring parents is to assume that the ten-year-old, or even the sixteen-year-old, understands. Those of us who have had the great privilege of being the recipient of teenagers' deep feelings of hurt and let down will readily realize how emotionally battered they are in spite of their apparent image of indifference and sophistication. Some of them are fortunate enough to meet helpers who are able to get them to open up and to show them a positive way forward. Sadly, this does not often happen. The majority have to keep going at work, in social encounters and in the daily traumas of life, with little inner sense of well-being, except their own personal experience and their determination to survive. No one should be exposed to the severe loneliness and frustrations often experienced by these young people. The danger is that these psychological traumas will sometimes be manifested in anger or unacceptable social behaviour.

Fourthly, depression is often regarded as unusual in teenagers and is frequently not take seriously by adults. It is dismissed as moodiness or 'adolescent blues' yet it is well established by psychiatrists that children and teenagers do become clinically depressed. Diekstra points out that,

> All the symptoms of classic depression can occur in children and adolescents. The symptoms, however, are more often so misleading that they are misinterpreted, so that, unfortunately, depression is not recognised as such. For this reason depression in young people is sometimes referred to as 'masked' depression, where the real emotions are camouflaged[27].

Therefore, young people, especially children, do tend to express their feelings more in behaviour than words. They may become impatient, angry, regarded as troublesome by adults and teachers, run away, withdraw into themselves, steal, lie and play truant. Many of those involved in glue-sniffing, drugs and excessive alcohol are seeking some relief for their depression. Underneath these rather violent or destructive acts there is a lot of anxiety, confusion and hopelessness. One of the most hopeful things about working with children and adolescents is that the great majority do not want to kill themselves. This does not mean their suicidal behaviour is not serious, but given the chance of getting a better quality of life, they are more ready and able to give it a go than some older people. As the fourteen-year-old school-girl said, 'We need an older person to talk to'. She had a lot of insight, as what is needed is someone who can be trusted and will allow them to explore their feelings and accept them as a person. If we are realistic, even the best parents cannot always fulfil this role. The caring and listening parents will certainly help to create an inner sense of trust and well-being. Then the outside helper can encourage the adolescent to talk. Let us examine some of the more common situations relating to depression, using two imaginary young people.

Jill, nineteen, rather plain and slightly overweight, was at the beginning of the second year of a Social Science degree course at a polytechnic. She fell in love with her tutor, Nick, who was fourteen years older than her, and recently separated from his wife. The relationship lasted for six months before Jill's parents knew the identity of her man-friend. She did everything for Nick, was very loving and caring and amazed that such a presentable male could want her. She did not realize that Nick really wanted a 'mother'; he needed to be looked after which was why his wife had left him. When Jill became pregnant, she happily went off to tell Nick, but to her great shock, he was furious. He said she had trapped him and he would not see her again. She did not know what to do, she felt she had failed and let everyone down. Her parents, who were Christian and very anti-abortion, were shocked and not at all supportive. Jill felt so confused because in a way she was so pleased about being pregnant. How could Nick stop loving her just like that. She tried to talk to her mother but the latter seemed more worried about what the neighbours would say, and her father simply refused to discuss it. Jill left college and went to London. She was three months pregnant and managed to get an abortion paying for it out of her own savings. She became very depressed, attempted suicide and was admitted to a psychiatric hospital. In spite of the care and support of her doctors and the social worker, she killed herself with a large dose of paracetamol.

Tom, twenty, the eldest of three brothers, had completed his first year at university doing an honours degree in Science. He had got excellent results in his A levels and was well liked. His two younger brothers, aged sixteen and thirteen, were also doing well at school. Their parents were very ambitious for all their sons and wanted them to succeed and really fulfil all they themselves would have liked to achieve. They actually talked in this way to their sons and especially to Tom. Father was a manager of a chemist shop in a West Country town and Mother was a primary school teacher. Both were quite intelligent, but had come from a very deprived background in Aberdeen.

Tom always studied hard and really had little time for social life. He felt a desperate need to please his parents, they were so proud of him getting a place at university. Whilst his father always was supportive to Tom, he never seemed to be satisfied. When he got four of his O levels at grade A, his father only said, 'it will help you prepare the better for your A levels'. His mother, who was a very dour Scot, kept reminding him that he was the eldest and must be an example to his younger brothers. Sometimes Tom did wonder if they could ever be satisfied, but he needed to please them. Tom considered he had done quite well with work in his first year, he had managed to keep on top of his studies. He also had a bit of social life and had met Denise with whom he shared some project work. She was a very friendly and attractive girl, still it was all very platonic. Then the bombshell hit him, four weeks before the end of term, his tutor told him he did not think he would get a first class degree and so might not get on to any postgraduate work.

Tom was shattered, this was the first time in his life any teacher had even hinted he might not succeed. He had never failed an exam. He retreated to his room and avoided most of the end of term lectures. He felt a complete failure, he had let his parents down and the whole family. He soon became depressed, unable to sleep or eat and quite agitated. He could not tell his father – what could he do? He had so few friends and anyway what could they do? However he had reckoned without Denise's considerable attraction for him. When he did not turn up for the last meeting on their project with several other students, she went searching for him. He was most surprised when she turned up at his room, and more or less insisted on talking. At first, Denise could not believe he was serious about being a failure, then she realized he seemed to be in a kind of daze. She could not persuade him, after two hours talking, to see any college counsellors or doctors within the university. However, Denise was a determined girl and eventually she got Tom to agree to see her uncle who was a psychiatrist working ten miles away. The uncle recognized that Tom was depressed and suicidal. With only ten days left before he was due home, the doctor managed three sessions before the end of term. He helped Tom to begin to examine why he felt so upset, he helped him to see he was getting more ambitious than his parents. He gave Tom permission to consider not always having the need to be first. He asked Tom how many exams he had failed, and on hearing there were none, made him see that the reality of learning was not just about success or failure, it was about developing your inner resources and integrating knowledge. How could you give yourself freely to research and to experiment, if you were obsessed about success or failure? Before the last session the doctor asked Tom to phone his father and see how they reacted to his news. He did so, with help from Denise and was surprised when his father did not seem to grasp the great significance of not being able to get a first and the problems of postgraduate courses. He really only wanted his son to get a degree. With the help of the good doctor therapist and his generous girl-friend, Tom began to grow up. His thinking was so constricted. Tom had developed a kind of tunnel vision. This is not so unusual for young students.

The following comments from *The Study of the Suicidal Behaviour Among College Students* carried out by Peck and Schrut are relevant here.

What are some antecedents which might explain how the youngsters who committed suicide got to that point? Since the study revealed no major overt disturbances in the parents, how is it that parents are still seen as playing a major contributory role? Careful study of the individual students in the committed suicide group revealed a pattern among the parents of much overt striving for themselves and their children to be successful. While this is hardly abnormal in itself, in these parents it tends to compensate for their own feelings of failure, inadequacy, and insecurity. They must see their children as an extension of their fantasied successes, and therefore they are likely to block out other kinds of communication, especially those implying failure, from their children. These children learn early that only by being a perfect projection of their parents' fantasies will they win their approval. The parents of these students have great personal expectations from their children and place a greater onus of responsibility on them.

The failure of such a child to live up to parental expectation is often experienced as a great humiliation by the child whose super ego frequently continues to make demands of him far beyond those that the parents are actually making at this point in his life. These parental expectations of students who commit suicide are far more than the usual wishes for success that most parents have for their children. They represent a total lack of acceptance of their children as they are.

Children who commit suicide find that their efforts to express their feelings of unhappiness, frustration, or failure are totally unacceptable to their parents. Their feelings are ignored, denied, or met by defensive hostility: 'What have you got to be unhappy about; you have everything; we don't beat you; what do you want?' Such a response seems to occur often in these families, driving the children into further isolation with the feeling that 'something' is terribly wrong with them[28].

The following is a summary of their findings,

A study of all college students in Los Angeles County from 1960–68 revealed a suicide rate in this population that ranged from 5.1 to 7.2 per 100,000. This rate was somewhat lower than previous estimates and lower than the rate among a control group of non-college students. Despite the lower estimated suicide rate, suicide remains the second or third leading cause of death in this age group. When other suicidal behaviors, such as attempts and threats, are added, and the impact of all suicidal behaviors on significant others and the community are studied, the magnitude of the problem reaches great proportions.

According to data obtained on 65 college students, from 1967 to 1969, the typical student who committed suicide was withdrawn, isolated, and tended to not communicate well with his peers. Parents of these students, while not necessarily overtly disturbed, tended to cover their own feelings of inadequacy as parents by making their children into fantasied projections of themselves. They seemed to be uninvolved with the student himself, as he really was.

Those who committed suicide were mostly males, average-grade students, who had few social or sexual contacts, and who tended not to be involved with drug usage. There was little evidence that campus pressures contributed to their suicides.

The findings suggested that for students who commit suicide there is a common factor of social isolation and withdrawal and that lack of sexual experience or drug usage are symptomatic of this withdrawal.

The students who attempted suicide were mostly females, and they exhibited different characteristics from the committed suicide group.

Fifthly, we have to recognize that some adolescents will be suffering from psychiatric disorders which do cause serious behavioural problems. Diekstra estimates that about sixteen per cent of adolescents who are suicidal can be regarded as seriously ill in the psychiatric sense. This means they were suffering from psychosis; mostly from schizophrenia with a small number from manic-depressive psychosis. Unlike other adolescents they may not be so keen to talk to an older person. Like older people with these disorders, they are frequently out of touch with reality, become very paranoid and aggressive, wander from place to place and are not willing to co-operate with parents or helpers, even when they are most accepting and understanding. Although it is very difficult to help them it is worth persevering to try and achieve some degree of togetherness. Many who are the most mentally disturbed are very intelligent and well able to respond to a loving caring approach. Diekstra points out,

> Some studies suggest that suicide for certain psychiatric adolescents should be regarded as a reaction of the healthy part of their personality to the sick or psychotic part. Suicide would then take place in a lucid phase, when the adolescent is clearly aware of the degree of seriousness of the disorder. For this reason, the first few days or weeks after commitment to a psychiatric hospital are often dangerous. The fact of being committed and the situation the adolescent finds himself in – 'only lunatics around me' – are regarded at lucid moments as indications that people have given up on him, that he is a 'lost case', as one psychotic suicidal adolescent remarked. For the same reason, the risk of suicide immediately after being discharged from hospital is also relatively high. The adolescent is faced with the task of adjusting to normal life again and to 'normal' people[29].

One of the reasons why people in general find it difficult to understand those with psychotic illness, and this applies with all ages, is that a person with a mental illness is often out of touch with reality only in certain areas of life. In other respects he behaves in a normal way. Whilst the person who is very anxious and easily upset, the so-called neurotic, behaves in this manner more or less consistently. Some psychotic adolescents do kill themselves without any apparent warning using violent methods such as jumping in front of a train, hanging, leaping from a cliff or high building, or setting fire to themselves.

Now we have been able to explore some of the essential ingredients of creating togetherness and hopefully have identified some of the essentials for assessment of the needs, we come to the third circle, the professionals. It is most likely that adolescents who are suicidal are going to need counselling, perhaps psychotherapy, and for some even psychiatric treatment, given within the supportive setting of togetherness. On their own, that is with only befriending or only professional help, this will not be enough. Togetherness plus professional help could make their lives worth living.

### Elderly people

Elderly people, both male and female, are among the special risk groups for suicide; the average age is in the late fifties. People now live much longer in Western societies due to improved medical science, therefore the number of people with illnesses associated with old age are now greater. In addition to this, there are prominent sociological and psychological factors involved. People no longer live in close-knit family communities and it is the cry of both young and old to be free to do their own thing. These social changes mean that many elderly people become very isolated and this has an adverse psychological effect upon them, frequently leading to depressive reactions, feeling useless and suicidal. Living away from families also makes greater economic demands upon them which are still far from equitably distributed in spite of old age pensions and welfare benefits. Another growing problem is the emergence of some marked divisions between the attitude and life-styles of the young and the old. Social changes have happened so rapidly that it is not easy for many elderly people, especially those of less flexible personalities, to be open to change. This is very noticeable with immigrants who try to adjust to a world quite different from that of their earlier life. Although many elderly people will malign the young for their lack of moral standards and religious faith, it is noticeable upon further investigation that many of the elderly gave up their traditional religious affiliations many years ago. Therefore, in many ways, they do have a lot in common with the adolescent, as both have to cope with marked physical, social and psychological changes. Both will experience a good deal of alienation from those around them and frequently are not willing to co-operate with the helpers. It is most important for these two groups to make opportunities for relating more positively and being ready and able to develop a more dynamic approach to life and death.

> The death bed scenes of earlier days included family members crowding the dying chamber and standing in awesome silence awaiting the last solemn words of the departing elder. Such death bed scenes today are an anachronism and have been supplanted, in part, by the secret death of Suicide[30].

The helpers need to recognize that as with the young, the attitudes of society and the effects of the environment will play a very significant role in the future of the elderly. For example
– Loneliness and isolation are part of the cost of growing old in our modern Western society, yet alienation is not inevitable. It is not impossible for the different age-groups to integrate at some levels, but those concerned will need to work on it.
– Education for coping with growing old. It is surely a fundamental requirement to promote a better quality of life for the present-day elderly and make preparations for those who have not yet reached that stage in their lives. Whilst it is not surprising for many elderly people to be preoccupied with trying to keep going, we all have to die. It is tragic that although due to great strides in medical science we can expect to live longer, many people are not able to experience this as an enrichment of their lives because of their psychological problems

which are far from improved. Hopefully, more positive attitudes are developing as projects are put in operation through Age Concern and many elderly people are willing and able to become involved in voluntary work. One of the dangers with the greater interest in euthanasia and emphasis on physical fitness, is for the elderly, infirm or depressed to feel they should kill themselves. Like the young, they become disillusioned and many see no purpose in their lives. Therefore it is a matter of concern for all of us and we have to set about trying to grasp the reality of living and strive for passionate relationships.

As helpers, we will have to cope with the emergencies and crises which are the special problems of the elderly; the onset of serious physical illness; depressive illness often related to physical causes; psychological traumas, e.g. acute anxiety attacks; lack of self-confidence causing problems with relationships; a sense of total loss at the time of a bereavement; the onset of senility, psychotic or neurological illness; economic crisis, a sudden loss of income, anxiety over devaluation.

The warning signals for suicide risk will include all those we considered in Figure 2 (See page 30) plus extra attention when the person refuses to have medical help. Many will deny that anything is wrong even when it is clear to those around them that all is not well. The elderly person may be very fearful of going to hospital and needs to talk about this. Every effort should be made to give them opportunity to express their feelings. If the person is adamant about not accepting help, many elderly people are, then a choice has to be made about using the statutory powers for compulsory admission. This is always an extremely delicate decision to make and I personally feel the helper should try to assess how long the person is likely to live. There are some people for whom a move would achieve nothing but emotional pain; for others it could herald a better quality of emotional life for some months or years. This is especially so with those suffering from a depressive illness, acute anxiety or a readily treatable physical illness. This will cause problems for many voluntary helpers, especially the Samaritans, since it is paramount that they respect the wishes of their callers. However it is not always realized that social workers, health visitors and GPs are also very concerned to respect the wishes of their elderly people. Members of the general public are quick to condemn neighbours and the helping services when an elderly person is found after being dead for some considerable period. The elderly are very sensitive about their independence and there are many occasions when an aged person who is very much at risk both physically and mentally, can present a very rational reaction to visiting social workers or doctors. We have to remember that the cut-off type of personality of younger days is most likely to become more isolated and suspicious as they get older!

Each encounter will be different, but I think the helpers have to get straight in their own minds who they are going to serve. If they are responding to their own feelings of guilt and a need to control, then they will be serving themselves when they arrange for the elderly person to be put in a secure place. If they want to serve the deepest emotional and spiritual needs of the aged, then they have to accept the risks involved, as those concerned make their own decisions and by allowing this they may have provided the best possible help in our present state of society.

The proneness of the elderly to become severely depressed always increases the risk of suicide.

Depression is also common among the elderly. Its onset may be sudden or gradual and it may be mild or severe. In a survey carried out among elderly people who had recently been admitted to a general hospital, one third had experienced depression within the previous year. For many, of course, the reason for going into hospital – often loss of some sort – was associated with the depression. One in ten of those over 65 in the community suffer from depression, and one in three in residential homes. Some illnesses such as Parkinsonism, Arthritis if there is pain and loss of mobility, chronic heart and chest diseases and strokes limiting mobility may all lead to depression[31].

It is very important for helpers to realize that elderly peoples' depression and distress can often be relieved allowing their situation to be improved for a time. Helpers need to have short-term goals and to try and help the elderly person to co-operate with them on that basis. Many elderly people will seem confused and appear unco-operative. This is quite often because they are not accustomed to regarding depression as an illness and consider they should pull themselves together or die. As much as needing threatment they need to be understood and feel part of an extended family receiving its care and support. Many elderly people do have some remarkably successful operations and physical treatments without much attention to their emotional and psychological needs.

As with all callers, the elderly do respond well to being respected and valued as people and it is essential to try and discover what they consider is troubling them and what they need. It may not be possible to meet all their needs, they may be quite unrealistic, but to be listened to and taken seriously by the helper is most likely to be very therapeutic.

Elderly people are more exposed to loss than any other age-group; bereavement is very common and has some particular considerations which make their mourning harder to bear. There is for many a sense of total loss when their marital partner or special friend dies.

> The partner may be the only really close relationship that is left, the only remaining source of physical affection, and the only one who sees value and worth in the individual. The need for the partner may be very great even when there has been long term ambivalence. The likelihood of replacing him should he be lost is very small. (Cleveland and Giantureo, 1976, suggest that, of widows aged over sixty-five, fewer than 1 per cent will remarry)[32].

Those elderly people who have had little or no social contacts may have invested all their love and dependence upon a pet. When the dog, cat, bird or even goldfish dies, the loss could be just as severe as that of a human companion, therefore the helper must take it very seriously. Replacing a pet may be easy but care should be taken about doing this too soon. There may be a better response to a new pet if the dog or cat is a stray and needing special attention.

Although an economic crisis may come when an elderly person is coping well and is reasonably fit, it may trigger off serious suicidal ideas very quickly. Most feel protected if they are financially secure at an age when they are very vulnerable to dependence on charity or the Welfare state. In the last resort, as with young people, so much will depend upon the quality of togetherness that can exist between the elderly person and the helper.

*Doctors*
The suicide rate among male doctors is generally regarded as twice that of the male population, and among female doctors three to four times that of the female population.

Most papers on the subject of physician suicide report an incidence of two to three times greater than in the general population, with psychiatrists heading the list with twice that frequency. These rates are based on studies utilising death certificates and published obituaries. However, it is well known that suicide is generally underreported for a number of reasons. Therefore, the reliability of such data has been questioned, and any knowledge with regard to incidence must be considered incomplete. What seems to be more certain is that physician suicide rates vary from country to country[33].

Many people may be surprised to learn of such a high suicide rate among doctors, yet all health-care workers, including dentists and nurses are susceptible. Some suggest this may be related to the constant contact with death and disease. When looking at the problem from the voluntary sector, it would seem that the suicide rate among the Samaritans is higher than average; it must be pointed out that there has not been any carefully documented statistics carried out by the Samaritans to back this up, it is more a general impression. Some would suggest that all those who feel drawn into medicine and providing help and support for those who are sick or in distress, whether as professionals or volunteers, do so to meet their own psychological needs or to help combat their own depressive attacks.

There may well be some truth in these ideas, yet we do well to be realistic and appreciate that we all do things from mixed motives. Carl Rogers, when asked why people feel motivated to become counsellors, suggested we recognize the elements of power seeking, sexual curiosity, coping with our own sadness, worries, controlling others and trying to be helpful. One of the major factors among many doctors and helpers is a heightened sensitivity and awareness of the needs of others. This is likely to make many such personalities more prone to depression and suicide. According to Simon,

> A high risk period, for instance, occurs when a young physician leaves the protected environment of residency to face the responsibility of establishing a practice. Another high risk period exists when the physician nears retirement, when life may be viewed as not worth living without the gratification inherent in medical work. Other stressful events can be times when parents are dying, when children are leaving home, when chronic marital discord becomes more intense, or when competition with younger colleagues is becoming apparent[34].

Many doctors rely far too much on alcohol or drugs. 'It has been estimated that approximately 13% of all physicians develop a serious problem with alcohol or drug dependency at some point in their careers'[35].

Another very real problem for doctors is to whom they can confide. As one who has had the privilege of seeing a fair number of doctors in distress, I am well aware of how difficult it may be for a doctor to seek help for depression, anxieties, sexual problems and social attitudes about homosexuality. Personally, I think there are several reasons for these difficulties. The primary one concerns the personality of many doctors who tend towards perfectionism. The average medical student has had to produce good results in O and A levels, including several science subjects. This has meant a considerable amount of hard work, even for the brightest of pupils, and is generally associated with high-powered educational establishments. Usually one or both parents are physicians and even if the family is not medical parents will often have high expectations of their children.

When a person is brought up in this kind of environment they will have had little experience of failure or the second-rate. Of course, it is essential for any doctor of medicine to be meticulous, highly efficient, well educated and disciplined. At the same time there is a need to provide doctors with psychological education in sensitivity and self-awareness before and during their medical training. This is not only beneficial for the doctor's personality, but also for the better care of the patient. As soon as the newest doctor or intern is let loose on patients he/she will be exposed to life and death situations of the most terrible dimensions. Twenty-four hours in any busy hospital, especially where there is an accident unit, will expose doctors and nurses to horrors, tragedies, human misery and suffering well beyond the average person's comprehension. Added to these emotional strains they will have to cope with diagnosis and taking major responsibility for patient care. Even with improved modern awareness, doctors are expected to cope, and not to have emotional problems or worries. One of the reasons for higher suicide rate among women doctors may be because the medical world is very competitive.

Secondly, doctors are concerned about confidentiality and most use great caution. This can cause problems when they themselves need medical or psychiatric help.

Thirdly, for many doctors coping with death is extremely taxing, it has replaced sex as a taboo subject. Patients now have unreasonably high expectations as we all become accustomed to the remarkable healing powers of antibiotics, medications and surgical skills. When things do not improve we sometimes feel let down. For many doctors, death is seen as a failure.

Of central importance according to some authors is the medical ethic which requires a physician to do everything possible for everyone who needs his help. When one considers that physicians are on call 24 hours a day and are expected to perform at maximum efficiency at all times, this puts the physician under great physical and psychological stress, more so than members of other professions. This role strain begins in medical school and continues in medical practice with life-and-death responsibilities, described as clinical competence. Inability to cure many patients can promote intense anxiety. To keep abreast with rapidly expanding medical knowledge can add fears of vulnerability, especially whenever a patient is lost. Over-idealisation by some patients, public attacks to reduce one's self-image, loneliness and isolation in clinical practice, represent additional stresses to further increase role strain[36].

*What then can be done to help?*
A certain amount is, of course, being done by organized medicine in Britain and America to make it easier to identify and treat doctors who are emotionally ill or upset and possibly suicidal. We should be concerned with what kind of immediate help can be offered and I suggest that many of the problems of a doctor are related more to the stress caused by his or her personal life than that caused by the care of patients. I have been greatly impressed by the amount of care and responsibility shown by doctors for their patients when they have been under great personal stress. When there is undue strain in coping with relationships e.g. marital troubles, homosexuality, tensions with colleagues, added to the pressures of a busy doctor's day, there is a risk of emotional breakdown. Sometimes it can be embarrassing for a doctor to go to the local marriage guidance

or Samaritans, but there is always the centre in the next town.

The Samaritans have doctors as callers, both on the telephone and face-to-face. Doctors can be assured of absolute confidentiality and can remain anonymous if they wish, as with all callers. In the Central London Branch, the befriending would include making special assessments of needs and providing regular opportunities for talking through problems. I have a number of contacts with doctors, psychiatrists and therapeutic agencies for appropriate referrals. This can be of special benefit to doctors who have good reasons for keeping their problems confidential. Hopefully, those who feel the need for confidentiality because of guilt and anxiety, can be helped to get their worries in proportion.

For those of us who are concerned with suicide prevention, it is realistic to recognize that the medical and psychiatric services have a very significant direct and indirect role in this aim. The care and support of doctors is very much in the interest of overall health care and of improving the quality of life.

ALCOHOLICS AND DRUG DEPENDENTS

The rate of suicide among those who abuse alcohol and drugs is known to be high in Western countries. Recently, there has been a marked increase in the consumption of alcohol, especially among adolescents. Many people in all age-groups use hard drugs, heroin, cocaine and glue-sniffing, as a means of getting a high or as a way of coping with life's problems. People use the phrase 'drowning their sorrows in drink'. Diekstra tells us,

> The incidence of suicide among abusers of alcohol is high, 15% (Miles 1977). The same applies to the incidence of alcohol abuse among suicidal attempters (15–30%). Particularly with regard to adolescents, there is further evidence that

changes in their pattern of alcohol abuse might be causally linked to the incidence of suicide and attempted suicide, since it has been shown (Holding 1974) that the consumption of alcohol doubled between 1968 and 1974. Apparently, once individuals have taken to coping with the vicissitudes of life through the intake of mind-changing chemical substances like alcohol, the use of other chemical substances, like medical agents, for similar purpose becomes also more probable[37].

Helping a suicidal person who is an alcoholic or over-dependent on drugs is extremely difficult. Little can be done if the person is very high and suicide is a constant possibility for them. The risk may become greater when they have sobered up. What makes it so hard for the helper is that they may be out of touch with reality and so may not even remember talking to anyone when they are sober or have come down from a high. If the person is very inebriated, the helper may have to wait until they become calmer. Then they may feel suicidal and will need to talk. There is an opportunity now to try to create a togetherness with a view to helping to change the person's's attitude to life. Alcoholics Anonymous and Accept can be very helpful, but not everyone is able to work in groups or to agree with the ideas of AA. Generally, both alcoholics and drug abusers will need medical back-up. It is quite likely that a person drinking too much or taking drugs is suffering from serious depression and urgently needs psychiatric treatment. Conversely, they may be in a manic state because they suffer from manic-depression. The sad thing is that people will accept the manic state, or the life-and-soul-of-the-party type only for a while and there is not much sympathy for the depressed mood. Relatives and friends say things like, 'You drink too much, you are your own worst enemy, I am getting out' only making the situation worse. Strangers are less likely to trigger off violent reactions. Patient and understanding helpers may be able to initiate some positive help and treatment.

PRISONERS

The suicide rate is very high among prisoners and those in custody or on remand awaiting trial. It is estimated to be at least four times as high as those in the rest of the population. In the years 1969 to 1979, of 636 deaths in prison, 155 were suicides. Those on remand are especially at risk where the prison is very overcrowded. They often have to wait for six, or even nine, months before coming to trial. The average person becomes anxious and depressed seeing suicide as an attractive solution. Many of those accused of sexual offences have a very hard time and are shunned by the other prisoners. They are regarded as perverts even when very little has taken place between the prisoner and a child. Those awaiting trial for whatever cause have a lot of time on their hands and relatives and friends, if any, may live too far away for visiting. Those who have a prison record may feel that they cannot face another spell inside.

The suicide rate for unconvicted or unsentenced prisoners is three to four times that of the prison population as a whole. Furthermore, the proportion of suicides who are unconvicted or unsentenced has increased (37% in 1958–71, 45% in 1972–83, while in 1984 there were more unconvicted or unsentenced prisoners who committed suicide than sentenced prisoners). In recent years this increase has been greater than can be accounted for by the increase in proportion of prisoners who are uncommitted or unsentenced[38].

It would also seem that prisoners convicted or charged with offences of violence, especially homicide and arson, are significantly over-represented among suicides.

The situation with long-term prisoners is not good, as their suicide rate is four times higher than that of the prison population as a whole. It is agreed by all the studies that the weeks following reception, whether on remand or sentence, are the time of very high risk for suicide, and that forty-one per cent of suicides occurred in the first month.

*How can these suicides be prevented?*

Helping people in prison is bound to be extremely difficult by the very nature of their environment. It is neither the purpose of this book nor within the competence of the author to deliberate on prison reforms. As those concerned about the prevention of suicide, we need to recognize that so many people who are anti-society, or seem unable to cope with the just or sometimes restrictive laws of the community, are themselves seriously psychologically disturbed and frequently suffering from a psychotic disorder. This is not to suggest that those who expose their emotional disorders in murder, sexual attacks and unsocial behaviour should not be detained for the protection of the community, the obvious problem is how this is managed.

At this stage in our community development, this is very relevant as the large mental hospitals, the asylums, i.e. the places of refuge, are to be phased out. Maybe we need to ask if the heightened risk of suicide appearing among such diverse groups as young people, the elderly, doctors, helpers, prisoners, alcoholics and drug users is symptomatic of this age of acute anxiety. At present there is insufficient data to come up with any precise patterns of behaviour. At this stage we need to watch most carefully how consistent suicide increases are in these vulnerable groups, perhaps over a ten year period. Earlier, in Chapter four, we considered how we are living in an age of anxiety and transition. This is bound to be felt most strongly among those in these at-risk groups. Perhaps they could serve as useful monitors of the levels of stress in our society.

It is sometimes forgotten, or at least underestimated in assessing social change on the one hand how well those for whom the changes have been initiated adjust and co-operate with them; on the other, how much conscious and unconscious hostility such changes will trigger off in society as a whole. This is not to suggest that psychological and sociological conflicts are not necessary, and more often than not essential to progress, but we do need to help and support those caught in the midst of these struggles.

I am by no means a great supporter of the establishment (in case any reader rightly recognizes that this could be interpreted as a reflection of my own psychological problems, I would agree with them and be pleased to tell them I am still working on it, hence my empathetic remarks about Prison Officers). Those in the Prison Service have a tremendously demanding task and a difficult job at all times. It is most important to feel into their needs as well as those of the prisoners. The basic principle of effective suicide prevention is about needs and helplessness and about being human and caring for each other. We should be realistic and accept that for a long time to come, we shall have to accommodate within the prison system both those who offend society and those who look after the offenders whilst at the same time, protecting society.

One of the most important ways of helping prisoners at risk is to give them permission to talk about their suicidal feelings. This is emphasized in the Home Office Report of the *Working Group on Suicide Prevention.*

> We make no apology for dwelling on feelings; this is what suicidal behaviour is all about. And the view that the prison officer cannot afford to become involved in discussion of feelings – that his job is simply to keep an eye on prisoners and leave them to sort out their own personal problems – seems to us a betrayal of the professional ethic of the Service[39].

They go on to point out that special training is needed to help officers cope with the feelings of utter desperation and isolation, along the lines used by the Samaritans and Canadian prison service.

The need among those in prison, both officers and prisoners, to be more aware of feelings highlights a common human need. As suicidal behaviour is so desperate and disturbing it causes us to look more closely into how we respond to each other. What the Home Office Report says about feelings is equally applicable to school children, college students, doctors, drug abusers and alcoholics. Quite rightly, the Report writes of the need for training. We should also consider providing more education on how to understand the importance of feelings and emotions and how we respond to them. From this we could begin to create a more mature and caring society. Those of us who have experienced the care of prisoners and ex-prisoners will know that many have serious difficulties in coping with their emotions, especially aggression, either towards others or themselves.

As we conclude this chapter, we recap the essential points in some questions and answers.

*What do I do if I encounter a person in a crisis who feels suicidal?*
You do not **do** anything at first; to the caller, it is more important what you are going to **be**, any doing may come much later. You will,
1. Need to listen a lot
2. Encourage the person to go on talking
3. Help them to speak of their feelings
4. Give permission to use terms like 'suicidal'.
Hopefully, you will provide a sense of security and caring and begin to reduce the suicide risk. In your togetherness you will gradually find what you may need to do.

*How do I react to those who do not speak when at the end of a telephone?*
You will,
1. Need to be patient and gentle
2. Explain that there is no hurry
3. Give your name and suggest caller gives his or hers, but it's all right if they don't. Some people get a sort of stage fright and are lost for words.
4. Say 'I'm still here – tap your receiver, or cough to let me know you are still there and can hear me'. After ten minutes or so, the person may start talking, or become a silent caller but may speak after several calls.

*What can I do to be better prepared?*
1. Get in touch with your own feelings, e.g. about how you react to disappointment.

2. Try to recall some of the worst moments in your life, times when you made a fool of yourself or were ridiculed by others and how awful you felt.
3. Recall periods of loneliness and fear. If you have experience of serious depression, remember how isolated, hopeless and guilty you were at the time.
4. Check your behaviour patterns and note what others say about you, especially their criticisms.
5. Realistically love and care for yourself.

*How do I cope when I have talked to a person about emotional pains and suicidal feelings and he says he intends to kill himself?*
1. Use your togetherness to help him/her feel that you too are in touch with the desperate feelings.
2. Do not be afraid to ask how he/she intends to die – having got this far, you will not make it worse, you might sow some positive seeds
3. Stay with the person or arrange for someone else to stay with them or take them to Samaritans
4. Say you want to keep in touch – play for time.
Unless you have special statutory responsibilities, and these are limited, in the last resort you have to let the person make their own decisions.

*Is it helpful to comfort people and touch them when they are very upset?*
The immediate answer is yes. It is normal to reach out and comfort someone who is crying and distressed. If you are likely to see this person regularly, comfort by touching must be consistent and therefore limited. Sometimes it is helpful to allow and even encourage crying. People cry to express emotional pain and anger because they are hurt and frustrated. Behave towards the person you are helping in ways which can always be freely discussed with a colleague. Helpers, volunteers and professionals, need to be aware of and able to handle their sexual attractions. In the same way, we need to be wary of those who would like to become too emotionally involved with their helpers.

*How do you cope with people who need a lot of help and could become very dependent?*

Much depends on how suicidal the person is and what help is available. Most are not suicidal over long periods, the crisis comes and goes. It is important to get other people or agencies involved. Discuss the situation with the troubled person and ask how they can best be helped. Even some of the most demanding recognize the need for limits and these can make them feel more secure.

*How can you get help and support from others if you want to preserve confidentiality?*

It is essential to keep confidentiality and only to act outside it with permission. Talking with colleagues is allowed in volunteer and professional groups. In the Samaritans, volunteers would be expected to share their needs and anxieties about a caller with their director or deputy as a matter of routine. This is also common practice among professional helpers. People who are not part of a group can present the situation as a hypothetical case, not mentioning names, addresses or any identifiable details. Such a consultation can be a life-saver, both for the person needing help and the one giving it.

*How important is it to reduce emotional pain first?*

Very important as this may be your only opportunity. Do not allow the many current problems of the caller/patient to distract you from the primary task of this life-saving help.

REFERENCES

1. Shneidman, Edwin, S., *Definition of Suicide*, John Wiley & Sons, 1985, p. 126
2. Keir, Norman, *I Can't Face Tomorrow*, Thorsons Publishing Group, 1986, pp. 143–4
3. Shneidman, Edwin S., *Definition of Suicide*, John Wiley & Sons, 1985, p. 234
4. Ibid., p. 230

5. Ibid.
6. Ibid., p. 231
7. Ibid., p. 124
8. Ibid., p. 126
9. Ibid., p. 129
10. Ibid., p. 130
11. Ibid., p. 133
12. Ibid., p. 135
13. Ibid.
14. Ibid., p. 138
15. Ibid., p. 139
16. Ibid., p. 148
17. Ibid., pp. 231–2
18. Ibid., p. 238
19. Kreitman, Norman and Dyer, James A. T., 'Suicide in relation to parasuicide', *Medicine* 36, p. 1827
20. Greene, Graham, *Collected Essays*, The Bodley Head, 1969, pp. 400–1
21. Giovacchini, Peter, *The Urge to Die*, Penguin, 1985, p. 188–9
22. Ibid., p. 168
23. Diekstra, René and Moritz, Ben J. M., 'Suicidal behaviour among adolescents: an overview' in *Suicide in Adolescence*, ed. Diekstra and Hawton, Martinus Nijhoff, 1987, p. 8
24. Pfeffer, Cynthia, 'Families of suicidal children' in *Suicide in Adolescence*, ed. Diekstra and Hawton, Martinus Nijhoff, 1987, p. 127
25. Diekstra, René and Moritz, Ben J. M., 'Suicidal behaviour among adolescents: an overview' in *Suicide in Adolescence*, ed. Diekstra and Hawton, Martinus Nijhoff, 1987, p. 8
26. Sabbath, J. C., 'The suicidal adolescent – the expendable child', *Journal of the American Academy of Child Psychiatry* 8, pp. 272–285. Quoted by Pfeffer, Cynthia, 'Families of suicidal children' in *Suicide in Adolescence*, ed. Diekstra and Hawton, Martinus Nijhoff, 1987, p. 133
27. Diekstra, René, 'Renée or the complex psychodynamics of adolescent suicide' in *Suicide in Adolescence*, ed. Diekstra and Hawton, Martinus Nijhoff, 1987, p. 44
28. Peck, Michael L. and Schrut, Albert, 'Suicidal behaviour among college students', *HSMHA Health Reports*, Vol. 86, February 1971, pp. 149–56

29. Diekstra, René, 'Renée or the complex psychodynamics of adolescent suicide' in *Suicide in Adolescence*, ed. Diekstra and Hawton, Martinus Nijhoff, 1987, p. 67
30. Lesnoff-Carabagliag, 'Suicide in old age' in *Depression and Suicide*, ed. Soubrier, J. P. and Vedrinne, J., Pergamon Press, 1983, p. 581
31. Jeffreys, Peter, 'Care in the elderly' in *The Samaritans: befriending the suicidal*, Varah, Chad, Constable, 1983, p. 148
32. Raphael, Beverley, *Anatomy of Bereavement*, Hutchinson, 1984, p. 312
33. Werner, Simon, 'Suicide among physicians: prevention and postvention' in *Crisis, International Journal of Suicide and Crisis Studies*, Vol. 7., No. 1, p. 1
34. Ibid., p. 7
35. Ibid., p. 5
36. Ibid.
37. Diekstra, René and Moritz, Ben J. M., 'Suicidal behaviour among adolescents: an overview' in *Suicide in Adolescence*, ed. Diekstra and Hawton, Martinus Nijhoff, 1987, pp. 21–2
38. *Report of the Working Group on Suicide Prevention*, Home Office, HM Prison Service, 1986, p. 95
39. Ibid., p. 53

# – 6 –

# On-going support

'I am feeling a bit calmer, it helped a lot to talk during the last few days, now I have got to try and sort things out'
'It is good to be alive, someone somewhere did not want me to die'
'Things are a bit better, I do not feel so hopeless and I suppose the psychiatrist will want me to go into hospital again, more pills and living with a lot of crazy people, is it worth it?'
'I am not going to have any more pills, I am better without them, begin to feel alive, not all doped up'
'I wonder if it would help to get some hypnosis, I do not want to go back to the psychiatrist any more'
'What my son needs is someone to sort him out properly and not just encourage him to talk about his feelings'
'The National Health is hopeless, nobody cares, I will try some alternative medicine'.

Some typical comments of those who may no longer be feeling suicidal and are uncertain about the most suitable help available for them. The big question is, what happens now? It is obvious to most of the helpers and callers/patients that they will need a lot more care and support. For many the change of attitude is only temporary and they feel very insecure, but some will be in a more positive and hopeful situation. They have worked through the pick-up encounter and have had some experience of togetherness with volunteers and for some both volunteer and professional support. This is really only a gap in the clouds, and is likely to be very temporary, more dark clouds are on the horizon but now at least the suicidal part of the storm may be over. The helpers have to be very cautious about assuming it is safe to relax. They may feel now is the time to ask, 'What shall I do for the caller?'. 'What is the best way of helping?' It is true some will need to continue medical treatment already begun, or will be beginning treatment, but it is necessary to give as much attention to being, as to doing. The caller needs help to discover what he has been doing and how he has been coping, leading up to the present crisis, therefore the helper can be used as a facilitator and resource person. The wise GP or psychiatrist tries to keep their patients well informed about what is happening. It is not so easy if a patient is in extreme depression or out of touch with reality.

Among people who are suicidal, there are those who are clinically depressed and in urgent need of anti-depressants, before any other kind of therapy can be explored. There are those who are mentally ill and may need a period of hospitalization. Sixty per cent or more may suffer from a certain amount of reactive depression, be very anxious and psychologically upset in various ways. The help and support anyone of these may continue to have depends on the knowledge and competence of the helpers and co-operation of the callers. If a state of togetherness has been achieved by the relative, friend, Samaritans, GP or social worker, then a good start has been made. We need to know what is on offer. In Figure 14 we have a summary of what is available. Although there is a division in the circle between the volunteers and the professionals, this is only for the sake of clarity. It is essential to realize that as both are resource people their help is inter-related.

### WHAT IS ON OFFER

There is frequently a certain amount of misunderstanding and confusion about basic roles so let us briefly begin by describing what each has to offer.

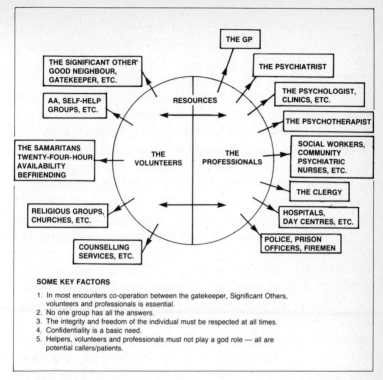

THE GP

THE PSYCHIATRIST

THE PSYCHOLOGIST, CLINICS, ETC.

THE SIGNIFICANT OTHER' GOOD NEIGHBOUR, GATEKEEPER, ETC.

THE PSYCHOTHERAPIST

AA, SELF-HELP GROUPS, ETC.

RESOURCES

SOCIAL WORKERS, COMMUNITY PSYCHIATRIC NURSES, ETC.

THE SAMARITANS TWENTY-FOUR-HOUR AVAILABILITY BEFRIENDING

THE VOLUNTEERS

THE PROFESSIONALS

THE CLERGY

RELIGIOUS GROUPS, CHURCHES, ETC.

HOSPITALS, DAY CENTRES, ETC.

COUNSELLING SERVICES, ETC.

POLICE, PRISON OFFICERS, FIREMEN

**SOME KEY FACTORS**

1. In most encounters co-operation between the gatekeeper, Significant Others, volunteers and professionals is essential.
2. No one group has all the answers.
3. The integrity and freedom of the individual must be respected at all times.
4. Confidentiality is a basic need.
5. Helpers, volunteers and professionals must not play a god role — all are potential callers/patients.

Figure 14: Sources of on-going help

## The Professionals

*The general practitioner (GP)* is, as you will realize, the key figure in all medical care and treatment in the UK. It is most important to understand the very special role of the GP in order to be better equipped to help the suicidal. All people in the United Kingdom are expected to register with a GP relevant to their geographical area. This means in theory, and works well in practice, that everyone is in the care of a GP. This is why if you are referred to a specialist consultant it is usually done through your GP. After the consultation, the specialist reports back to the GP, who is likely to monitor long-term medication and liaise as required with the specialist. Another very important factor is that the GP provides a twenty-four-hour emergency coverage. Many GPs work as part of a team of doctors and are supported by community nurses and psychiatrically trained community nurses and the health visitors.

The GP is the custodian of the patients' health care which includes physical and psychological aspects. The majority of people who suffer from clinical depression, schizophrenia and general psychological and neurological problems are treated by their GP with referrals and consultations as required with the appropriate specialist, psychiatrist or neurologist. Many GPs, even in this very mobile society, are still the family doctor, often for many years. Therefore, they are frequently in the unique position of knowing the whole family very well and having a good understanding of their physical and psychological needs.

*The psychiatrist* is first and foremost a doctor of medicine who has specialized in the care and treatment of disorders affecting thought, emotions and behaviour. Those doctors who want to make psychiatry or psychological medicine their speciality have to undergo four to five years of special training in mental and emotional disorders. They are of special significance in suicide prevention, as their experience and treatment of all forms of depression and schizophrenia is considerable. It is most important that psychiatrists should not be seen as unusual doctors you only go to when you are 'round the bend' or going to be 'put away'. For some years, modern psychiatry has greatly encouraged doctors to have a more therapeutic approach encouraging them to be more aware of their own emotional strengths and weaknesses. In general you can expect the psychiatrist to be very understanding and supportive.

*The neurologist* is a doctor of medicine specializing in the diseases of the brain, such as tumours, effects of nerve injuries, and epilepsy. In Great Britain neurology and psychiatry have developed as separate specialities, although there will be a considerable amount of overlap.

*The clinical psychologist* is taking an ever increasing role within the setting of psychiatric departments in hospitals. He is not qualified as a doctor of medicine, but has done a degree course in psychology, studying mental and emotional behaviour. They provide quite a lot of assessments in psychological testing for intelligence, memory and personality problems, helping in the process of a diagnosis or progress in treatment. A greater part of their work involves on-going therapy sessions, especially related to the behavioural approach. Whilst there are more clinical psychologists working with the National Health Service, a large number are in private practice.

*The psychotherapist.* As many of you will know, there are a number of types or models of exercising psychotherapy. Broadly speaking, the psychotherapist's function is to help the patient or client gain psychological insights into their emotional behaviour, therefore the therapist is most concerned with feelings and is using therapy as a means of helping clients work through some of their emotional problems and defences which cause anxiety, depressions, inner-isolation or obsessional reactions. Therapy is given individually and in groups. It may last from a period of months to two or three years. The approach is fundamentally non-directive and the co-operation of the client is essential. The psychotherapist's training varies according to the particular model of therapy, however it will generally take five or more years and will include a period of several years in personal therapy or analysis. All accredited therapists work under supervision. They are not medically trained, though some psychiatrists also become psychotherapists. Since they work a lot with acute emotional problems many of their clients are suicidal.

*Counsellors* have a lot in common with psychotherapists and could be described as providing a much less intense or less in-depth model of help. There are a number of counselling services, some run by paid workers and some by volunteers. Selection and training will vary according to the particular kind of service. The work of counsellors is of particular interest in suicide prevention; it is quite usual for universities and polytechnics to have a counselling service provided for students. In some schools there are counsellors allocated to each year's intake so that a pupil has the same person as a sort of tutor throughout their school life. The role of counsellors in places of education is to some extent vocational, but they also give invaluable therapy in helping reduce anxiety levels and emotional problems where there is sometimes a possibility of suicide.

*Social workers, probation officers, health visitors, prison officers, psychiatric nurses and police.* The roles of these are more generally understood except perhaps the community psychiatric nurse (CPN). All these workers are part of the government statutory services except those working with religious groups or charities. In all areas of the UK, there is a duty social worker available to cope with social or psychiatric emergencies. The CPN is a new development in psychiatric care and support, located more in the community rather than being hospital based. These nurses are responsible for supervision of medication for psychiatric patients living in the community and often give counselling and overall support.

*The clergy*. The role of the clergy will vary according to the particular way they exercise their ministries. Some will limit their work to their particular congregation of worshippers and to evangelization. This applies to many clergy, and also laity, of the major faiths – Christian, Jewish, Moslem and Buddist. There is, however, quite a large number of clergy who regard the pastoral care of the distressed and suicidal as an essential part of their ministry. It should be remembered that all British hospitals, prisons and HM Forces establishments have Anglican, Free Church and Roman Catholic chaplains, either full- or part-time, paid for by the State.

*Hospital services*. Although the function of hospitals is obvious to all, it is worth noting some of the excellent changes in their approach to psychiatric care. The large old-fashioned mental hospitals are closing down and the care and treatment of people with mental and emotional problems is becoming community based. This means psychiatric units will be much smaller and part of the overall hospital service. The emergence of Day Centres is of special importance where counselling and support is provided for psychiatric patients given by a multi-disciplinary team, psychiatrists, psychologists, social workers and nurses.

There are a number of special units provided by the National Health, such as Adolescent Units for young people of school age, alcoholics and drug dependents, and special Psycho-therapy Units such as the Cassell Hospital, Richmond; the Portman Clinic, London; and the Henderson Hospital, Surrey. Because of the changeover from the old psychiatric hospital approach, the walk-in clinic is developing. The world famous Maudsley Hospital in London has run a twenty-four-hour emergency psychiatric clinic for many years. All hospitals with a casualty unit will have access to a duty psychiatrist. The availability and service provided will depend a lot on the resources and demands of the local area.

## The Voluntary Services

For our purposes, we could divide voluntary services into those who offer a personal service from specially selected people such as The Samaritans, Relate (formerly Marriage Guidance Council), Cruse, etc., and those who provide a self-help service such as Alcoholics Anonymous.

Mind, the National Association for Mental Health, is the largest and most active voluntary organization in Britain concerned with matters of mental illness. Mind does a great deal to act as an advocate for the needs of psychiatric patients.

*Holistic living.* Many of you will have experience of what is sometimes called the 'holistic approach', 'alternative medicine', 'holistic medicine', as a different form of healing. These definitions can be very easily misunderstood and for the sake of good and effective health care it is most important that we are able to see the wood for the trees, as there are many unscrupulous people who take advantage of people's search for healing.

The word holistic means whole or complete, therefore the holistic approach to health care is concerned with the whole person, Body and Mind. Harmony could be described as one of the key words, as it involves harmonizing the emotional, mental and physical. Many of those involved in the holistic approach to medicine and health care are not advocating anything very new. They are reminding men and women that while the scientific and technical discoveries and their use are of tremendous importance for treatment and healing, it is essential to respect the needs of the whole man. Many generations of healers of religious persuasions or of humanistic philosophies have advocated tuning into nature by attending to the reduction of psychological stress, to better diet and to body care. This is sometimes expressed in meditations, yoga or giving special consideration to improving the person's environment. Scientific medicine has tended to specialize in particular ailments, often of necessity, but the holistic approach tells us that sickness is an expression of dis-ease. We are reminded that if there is a thorn in the foot, the whole body bends down to remove it.

The holistic approach is a timely reminder to twentieth-century men and women that we are often more concerned with treating and responding to symptoms rather than a cure. As there is bound to be a lot of stress and dis-ease behind suicidal behaviour, the holistic approach is very relevant. However, it is most essential for helpers to realize that sincere competent advocates of the holistic concept do not intend this as an alternative to more traditional medicine. The aim is surely to use all that is best and most effective in scientific medicine whilst recognizing that they should always be used within the framework of the whole person.

A DISCUSSION ON HOW BEST TO USE WHAT IS ON OFFER

The views I am putting forward are based on my thirty years' experience of encountering people who are in a crisis or feeling suicidal in Samaritan, accident hospital, and parish situations.

*If, according to your list, there is so much help around, why are so many people still in such a bad way?*
First, I would point out that although we have a variety of excellent professional and voluntary services, many have to cope with excessive demands upon their resources. This is especially so in the inner city areas. It is interesting to note that the World Health Organisation in their last report *North West Europe* attributed the very low suicide rate in the UK compared to other European countries, to the excellent health and welfare services. They did not mention the network of the Samaritan centres operating all over the country.

Secondly, so much depends upon what use people are able to make of these services and how effectively those who care for them initially manage the situation. Sadly, many distressed people are unaware of the options and some feel unable to use them.

It is most important for the helpers to realize that it is essential for us to forget our pet theories and to beware of our prejudices. We must concentrate on what the caller needs in their crisis situation. We are still in a transitional stage in the National Health Psychiatric Services, as the closing of large hospitals and the development of small units is taking place. This is further complicated by acute financial problems in many areas.

In recent years there has been a marked increase in the provision of what may be described in very general terms as the talking therapy. This is expressed in counselling, psychotherapy for individuals and groups, and sex and family therapy. All have become much more available both through the NHS and through charitable associations. It is therefore very beneficial if helpers, whether voluntary or professional, make themselves acquainted with the facilities available in their area. This presupposes a willingness to co-operate and to trust other sources of help.

Thirdly, although there is a lot of room for improving the existing professional services, it is unrealistic to imagine they can provide cures or answers to all our emotional needs of anxiety and dispiritment. Psychotherapy and drug therapy can be of great help where there are definite psychological problems and psychiatric disorders. There is a danger of overburdening the professional therapeutic services, even if they are greatly extended; whereas the greatest and most natural resource for healing, for therapy in the widest meaning of the term, is to be found within our society. It is for this reason that the idea of befriending, especially within the Samaritan context, is so encouraging and essential for the future well-being of our society. This has the effect of helping many people to be more responsible for themselves and encouraging them to live. At the same time, an atmosphere is created in which the expertise and resources of the professionals are more wisely and economically used for the benefit of those who most need it.

Lastly, there is the possibility that the community voluntary bodies, such as the Samaritans, may be turned into the specialist role, because modern Western society is so accustomed to expecting the specialist solution. It is still early days for the Samaritans, but there are some signs that members of the public and media would like to see them in this role, rather than as responsible caring representatives of the community.

The Samaritans are vulnerable as it is questionable if attitudes to suicide have really changed at depth. Elizabeth Salisbury, a very experienced Samaritan and Editor of the Samaritan Magazine, said,

> I doubt if the great majority of the population is that accepting of suicide. The Samaritans certainly are, but although they represent a variety of men and women they are still a small proportion of the whole. I think that perhaps this is not so strange, as the human instinct to preserve life is very strong indeed. Could this be why so many of us become Samaritans? Although we are understanding and accepting of suicidal behaviour, we are not supporting it. I feel that, on the whole, the general public are very anxious and uneasy about suicide and so quite often they are suspicious of those very much involved in helping people in suicidal situations.

She gave the example of a friend whose son had killed himself; she felt very little sense of support from the community at large and was made to feel in some way guilty. Another friend's son was killed in an accident and the attitude of neighbours was more supportive and accepting. Elizabeth went on to suggest that maybe society does need to reject the idea of suicide, as people kill themselves only when they are very dispirited or in a clinical depression. She considered this was a matter needing much more thought and discussion, because at present, quite apart from the Samaritans' views, there is a lot of discussion about whether or not people have a right to kill themselves.

We went on to discuss how people were ashamed to speak of their emotional problems and how this was especially true of men. During our conversation we touched on the question of emotional involvement in on-going befriending relationships. Elizabeth, who has experience in long-term befriending, freely admitted that for her it was essential to have some strong emotional rapport with her caller. This could be emotionally draining when the caller was feeling very low. I was intrigued to hear how Elizabeth described the encounter, 'You would begin chatting about unimportant things, then get down into the depths'. She would share her caller's sadness, not infrequently crying with her, and later they would come through the ordeal and might even be able to smile or laugh. She felt sometimes people imagined that, because you were encountering the other person in their darkest hours, you had to remain in the darkness. In her experience this was neither good for the volunteer nor for the benefit of the caller. Here we have, in my opinion, an excellent example of the development of a natural caring human relationship which arises out of the contrived setting provided by the Samaritan emergency service. Elizabeth also made the point that while you could certainly be of some help without feeling a rapport with the caller, more profound lasting help would only be possible when there was reciprocity between you. These points are particularly relevant to our question, as people needing help and those who try to give it, both have to begin to give of themselves openly and freely.

*What is most helpful for those who are suffering from depression?*
To try and answer this important question usefully, it divides into two parts. The first will be essentially practical and realistic, the second part will be longer and will open up discussions on ways of coping and some possible means of help. We know that depression is one of the most common factors leading up to a suicidal state and it is a most controversial disability for diagnosis and treatment.

Firstly, there are three ways of helping.
1. Those who present the classical symptoms of depression, (Fig. 15) commonly described as endogenous depression, or as part of the manic-depressive illness. Here medical/psychiatric treatment, generally with anti-depressants, is essential. In severe cases, admission to hospital will be necessary, for others treatment will be given by Out Patients or the GP.
2. Here the depression is less acute and may be reactive to external problems. Callers can be usefully helped by anti-depressants and talking therapy, or counselling.

3. Others who have complex psychological problems and lots of repressed anger which may manifest itself in some depressive reactions and anxiety. These generally need some long term psychotherapy or other psychological help.

*NB* All three groups will need support and befriending from their Significant Others who may be relatives, lovers, friends, Samaritans or professional workers.

Secondly, we consider some of the very complex problems presented by depression. For many years, there has been a debate as to whether depression is due to clinical, psychological or sociological causes or all three. The scientific research has not yet produced conclusive findings. Our priority has to be the needs of the patient/caller as they are presented to us. We should not get carried away by any of the popular theories of our period.

In my experience, when you have a person showing the extreme or classical symptoms of depression (Fig. 15) in some ways it is easier, as medical intervention is essential. At the same time, there are some serious risks involved. In some encounters, the caller may already be having treatment and there does not seem to be any improvement. I have found that people suffering from depression related to biochemical causes (as with endogenous depression) or related to other mental disorders, do respond well to anti-depressants. However, there are two essential requirements here.

(a) It is most important, according to the guidance of my most trusted psychiatric consultants, for the patient to be closely monitored by the GP or psychiatrist during the period of treatment, which could last for several weeks or months. If the patient has good relations with their doctor it is fine, but if there are problems then, with permission, it is generally helpful to talk with the doctor. During my encounters with many hundreds of GPs and psychiatrists positive co-operation was the norm. Most doctors feel relieved to know that their patient, who could be suicidal, has the support of one or more caring people. I think it is generally more beneficial for the person to be seen by a consultant psychiatrist, since they have more experience

| REACTIVE | ENDOGENOUS |
| --- | --- |
| SADNESS | ACUTE SADNESS — HOPELESSNESS |
| DIFFICULTY IN GETTING TO SLEEP | VERY EARLY WAKING |
| LACK OF CONCENTRATION | UNABLE TO CONCENTRATE |
| WORRY OVER DECISION MAKING | INABILITY TO MAKE DECISIONS |
| ANXIETY (SOMETIMES) | AGITATION |
| SERIOUS RISK OF SUICIDE (SOMETIMES) | CONSTANT SERIOUS RISK OF SUICIDE |
| FEELINGS OF GUILT (SOMETIMES) | PERSISTENT FEELINGS OF GUILT |
| ANGER | SOME ANGER |
| DEPRESSED MOOD CHANGES (SOMETIMES) | DEPRESSED MOOD CONSTANT |
| LOSS OF SEXUAL INTEREST | MARKED LOSS OF SEXUAL INTEREST |
| LACK OF EMOTIONAL RESPONSE (SOMETIMES) | EMOTIONAL DEADNESS |
| PARANOID REACTIONS (SOMETIMES) | FREQUENT PARANOID REACTIONS |
| FEELINGS OF ISOLATION (SOMETIMES) | GREAT SENSE OF ISOLATION, NOT WORTHY TO SEE PEOPLE |
| IN TOUCH WITH REALITY | OFTEN OUT OF TOUCH WITH REALITY |

Figure 15: Signs of depression

in treating depressives. We also have to be particularly sensitive to their psychological needs, as the clinically depressed are in severe emotional pain. In addition to expert psychiatric treatment they will need generous amounts of tender loving care.

It may be not too difficult to help to get the right treatment under way, but getting on-going loving support could be a major problem, yet the success of the treatment will often depend upon the quality of the support or befriending. This is well illustrated with those who give up the medication, because of lack of support from any Significant Other. It is not that the treatment programme is not likely to have positive results, it is a question of whether the patient takes the prescribed dose. I do not feel I am exaggerating when I say this is a most critical point in relation to whether the person kills himself or gets better. We know that it would be most unusual for anyone of us to leave a relative, friend or work colleague suffering from 'flu, or a severe chill with a high temperature, to sleep out on a winter's night, yet with our depressed friend or relative we may become disillusioned, angry or just feel it is all too much, when they find it so hard to make any positive emotional response. When you are suffering the deepest of depressions you are emotionally dead inside and find it almost impossible to express any emotional reactions to someone's befriending. I recall seeing a sixty-year-old female client, since dead, who was diagnosed as suffering from a manic-depressive illness. When supporting her befriender in the early stages of the depressive phase, it was necessary to reassure the befriender that although her caller hardly talked when she used to visit her and never seemed pleased to see her, her befriending visits were part of the overall life saving process. When she came out of her depression she used to say how much it had helped to have those encounters with her Samaritan befrienders and how sorry she was she could not express any positive response at the time.

Befriending and psychiatric treatment are the two essential ingredients in the presentation of suicide related to recovery from this kind of depression. It is true that sadly these kinds of depressive attacks do reoccur and so it is important for the caller to be in regular contact with their doctor and have good support from trusted friends.

Taking a look at the other expressions of depression where the symptoms, certainly to the inexperienced, are less apparent, we need to recognize that the effects can be just as severe as in a classical depression. Great care needs to be taken in distinguishing between deeply felt emotions of sadness and hopelessness resulting from negative and pessimistic thinking, and being just fed up or very unhappy. We are thinking about people who are really very depressed and possibly suicidal. Some people, especially adolescents, will mask their depressive reactions. Sometimes this is characterized by unusual behaviour, or as a denial, as in the smiling depressive. The big danger here is that the unusual symptoms are often misleading and so go unnoticed. René Diekstra reminds us that,

> In order to comprehend this well, one has to realise that, contrary to the current view in medical and psychological science, depression is in fact not so much a clearly defined syndrome or clinical picture, but rather an effect or state of mind resulting from psychic collapse and hopelessness or impotence. Viewed in this way, the symptoms of depression are nothing but the complex of actions, thoughts and fantasies needed to be able to withstand, avoid or cope with this effect. Naturally, this complex is determined to a great extent by the psychological development, social background and environment of the individual concerned and can therefore vary greatly in the various phases of the individual life. However, in spite of this wide variability, in three respects there are strong psychological similarities between the various forms of depression[1].

He then refers to Beck, who developed 'Cognitive Therapy', based on the idea that poor emotional experience and disturbed thinking, especially in early life, causes one to get into the three patterns of negative thinking regarding oneself, the future, and the environment that characterize the depressed person. All this could be very relevant to deciding the on-going help required, because there may be a greater need for counselling with or without anti-depressant drug therapy.

It will be obvious to the reader that if all these negative patterns of thinking are very active, the risk of suicide is highly likely to recur again. What can be most valuable here is for the caller to have some talking therapy through which some of the options for the future may be explored so that the depressed person begins to become less constricted in their attitudes. The caller's view that he/she 'is always at fault', 'is always a failure', or 'cannot help behaving the way they do', may need to be explored, questioned and challenged. The caller is going to need a great deal of support and it is important to create an opportunity for talking without delay. They will want to clarify their needs and it may be that if the caller has built up a rapport with a helper, who we must realize may have become a Significant Other, at least for the time being, the on-going talking should begin with that person. We must not underestimate the special importance of togetherness for this could be of more value than special counselling skills. So much will depend upon what is available and the readiness of the caller to accept the need for such help.

Writing about counselling and helping, Stephen Murgatroyd reminds us that,

> Many of those who seek the help of counsellors or voluntary workers in helping organizations utilise what is known as 'the medical model' of helping. They assume that, once they have described what is happening to them (described the symptoms), the helper will understand (diagnose) their problem (illness) and give advice (offer a cure) which will lead them to resolve their problem (get better) and function normally. They expect their helper to undertake most of the work, but the reality should be that it is the person in need who does most of the work. The medical model is not the predominant model being applied[2].

Interestingly enough many people react to the GP or psychiatrist in the same way, though sometimes with greater intensity, as they consider 'the doctors should have a solution, it is their job'.

I have found that many people who are depressed and over-anxious who are able to recognize that improvement, to a large extent rests with them and their willingness to co-operate, can be greatly helped. Although much will depend upon their particular problems, they will need time to recognize and work through their negative reactions. The essential is that they get the opportunity to share their feelings with a mature, sensitive and emotionally-adjusted person. This can be defined as counselling, listening, healing or befriending, as the person is helped to take more responsibility and also to release some of their untapped inner resources. Many good friends, Samaritans, teachers, GPs, social workers, and clergy fulfil this role. Some will need to have the much deeper and more precise emotional help given through psychotherapy, involving more detailed discussion and examination. At the same time I know that a number of callers who will benefit from some on-going counselling and listening may also need anti-depressants or other drug therapy in order to manage the intensity of their inner emotional turmoil. It is quite unreasonable to expect someone who cannot sleep, who feels all twisted up inside, unable to eat or to concentrate, to get by with only talking therapy. Similarly, it is most unwise to encourage people who are ready and able to work through their emotional and mental reactions to mask them with drugs.

As helpers, whether voluntary or professional, we have to recognize we have not yet worked through all our own psychological hang-ups. We must beware of the possibility that the caller might become a pawn in our own particular unresolved neurotic, therapeutic or psychological debates about treatment and care. I wish to stress this point very strongly, as I have some experience of the failure of a number of suicidal people suffering from being caught up in such conflicts. Our motto should surely be, 'Always mobilize all the resources available for the sake of the suicidal person'.

*You have mentioned talking therapy in your reply to the question on helping the depressed. Would you be more explicit about benefits of being listened to and is it not dangerous for anyone to play the amateur therapist?*

First of all I agree that it is most dangerous for anyone to take on any roles they are not competent to handle. So amateur psychiatry is out. This does not mean two human beings cannot come together to discuss their problems. We must always guard against the idea that we can only share our worries and problems or confess our misdeeds with some kind of designated voluntary or professional helper. I am not suggesting that the Samaritans, marriage guidance counsellors, clergy, doctors, social workers and lawyers are not some of the best confidants, but I want to stress that when you want to talk with another human being irrespective of their role, when you find a friend, feel free to do so.

For those unaccustomed to counselling experience it may help to explain briefly the fundamentals behind talking therapy. Stephen Murgatroyd suggests that help is differentiated not by the person helping, but rather through the nature of the help itself. He writes 'I cannot agree that only certain kinds of people (for example, professional counsellors with specified academic qualifications) should be allowed to provide particular forms of help'[3]. The talking or listening help, sometimes defined as counselling or befriending, involves listening to the other person, giving the other space to express their innermost feelings and thoughts without condemning or condoning and with complete confidentiality. This is very much borne out of the teaching of Carl Rogers, the great founder of the non-directive and client-centred therapy. This has been called by some the 'peaceful revolution' of this century. Carl Rogers put a great deal of focus on what he believed was in a person and their potential for healing, therefore the emphasis is on the person discovering their own solutions to problems. Through talking so seriously with the counsellor or other person, he or she is used as a mirror to reflect back to the caller their ways of behaving. Therefore, there is a reflecting back to the person not only of their negative reactions, but also their positive potential.

In some such relationships there may be some deep psychological interpretations, dependent upon the depth and type of encounter undertaken. You will see that this facilitating kind of approach oils or eases the rigidity of the emotional and intellectual activities. I have seen countless numbers of callers who started off emotionally defensive and intellectually constricted. After a few telephone encounters and several meetings with a Samaritan, their parish priest, or a good friend, they have experienced a great deal of relief of inner tensions with the beginnings of valuable psychological insights. This experience will often help a person needing some long-term deeper therapy, to have the motivation and courage to pursue it. There are however some necessary safeguards.

1. keep constant watch of the levels of depression,
2. those with long-standing deep-rooted anxiety, cut-off, schizoid, depressive, obsessional and hysterical reactions will need skilled psychological help over a longish period, sometimes befriending support is also needed,
3. those who are unable to maintain a reasonable degree of commitment and co-operation are not likely to benefit.

I would say the great asset of the good counsellor or befriender is a sensitivity to a caller's needs and a wise comprehension of what is possible. It seems to me that befriending and counselling have some common ingredients, so there is an overlap making it unnecessary to stereotype precisely our ways of helping.

The following is an excellent first-hand account from a caller who is now a Samaritan volunteer, of how positive the effects of a befriending encounter can be.

*Being There*
'I . . . I . . . I,. . . I'm going . . . to kill . . . going to kill myself . . .'

That was the faltering beginning of an interview that I had, in a small room on a wet and windy Spring night a few years ago. It had taken me ages to say that first word – it could have been one minute, or fifteen; the actual measurement of time was of no consequence to me. I didn't know what had made me visit the Samaritans that particular night, beyond the apparently insignificant reason of wanting to tell someone that I was going to die. I wasn't expecting 'help', and certainly the thought of somehow being 'saved' either from imminent death or from the continuation of a miserable and depressed existence had not even crossed my mind. What other third possibility could there be?

I had attempted suicide a year or so earlier and had been (or so I was informed) 'lucky to have survived'. But for what? In the hospital the day after having my stomach pumped, the duty psychiatrist came round and asked his prepared list of questions, hurrying me through my incoherent answers and showing only the barest interest in matters of 'how', let alone 'why'. I was referred for psychiatric assessment which, when it eventually took place (some two months later), similarly I felt that I was being used as an object in someone else's game; any wishes, needs, desires, that I might have had were subjugated to the professionals' structure and to their apparent need to see their own behavioural theories 'proved' in at least one person's reality. The group to which I was referred turned out to consist basically of some members displaying their hang-ups in a form of public masturbation, and others acting as voyeurs. Neither 'role' was any use to me, and I soon gave it up.

Life didn't get any better. The resources of my family, friends, and work colleagues all appeared exhausted. The feelings of uselessness, self-loathing, misery, and depression had all but enveloped me . . . so what could the Samaritans, what could one untrained, ordinary volunteer, do?

Well, he welcomed me warmly, he made me a cup of tea, and he sat down opposite me. Then what? Well, he didn't exclaim with horror when I eventually managed to mutter my opening sentence. And he kept saying 'Mmmm . . . ?' to encourage me to explore my feelings in greater depth. He allowed me to talk about suicide, death, questions of guilt and punishment, everything and anything that came up, subjects that I had thought I would never reveal to anyone. And he sat still, paid attention, kept eye contact, and he didn't become embarrassed when I cried and he didn't try, in subtle or unsubtle ways, to stop me from doing so. And he took all my testing-out, and the anger and hatred that I unfairly directed towards him. And when the downward spiral of investigation had finished, when we had reached rock-bottom and all my secrets had been revealed, and I just sat there, an empty shell on the brink of leaving and walking under the nearest bus, he didn't give the slightest indication that the interview had ended, or that it should end there. He too just sat there, and there was, I can quite clearly recall, a very long silence.

Something happened to me in the course of that silence that I had previously no knowledge or conception of. It is my belief that it was, in essence, a religious experience, that God used that volunteer, and the Samaritans, to save me. Life now is so different that it seems almost as if another person, not me, must have lived those awful days before that night. The first tentative steps back upward began in that holy silence – of a journey still being undertaken today.

Neither the volunteer nor I knew or sensed at the time what was happening. It was only over the coming months when I looked back in some wonder that I came to regard that evening as the turning-point. Immediately afterwards, while I did feel better, I still just expected the depression to return in time. And when, several years later, I saw the volunteer again, he could only say that he had felt no sense of being any help to me!

But he was, simply by being there, *really* being there, with me, demonstrating his patience and his concern – 'ordinary' human qualities that could not be trained into people. You can imagine my delight a few years ago when I was accepted as a Samaritan volunteer myself. Given that I am only alive today because of them, I now have at least the chance to begin to repay the debt that I owe. Of course, tomorrow, as yesterday, I may be a client again, but for today I have the great privilege of being in the other chair of that interview room, and can hope, and pray, that I may be used in the same way as that other volunteer was used on that wet night a few years ago.

*Do you think there are times when it is necessary to adopt the opposite of the non-directive Rogerian approach and be quite definite?*
There are times when the non-directive, very accepting approach will not be helpful to anyone. Chad Varah, who laid great stress on the Samaritans not giving advice or directing callers, was not prepared for Samaritans to be abused or exploited. He directed that some callers could not be helped by the Samaritan approach and firmly told them so. The more difficult situations arise when you have a very suicidal person not wanting to accept help. I personally think that if someone gets in touch with you or your agency for help, you should do all you can to prevent an actual suicide.

What do I do if someone asks me to stay with them on the telephone or sit with them whilst they die? I do not think it is caring or responsible to enter into a contract to assist in anyone's suicide in this setting. I realize that on the telephone you may not have much of a choice, but you can be explicit about your intention to try and keep them from dying. In the face-to-face encounter you can clearly indicate your position and not co-operate in any way. I do not consider this is being over-directive and disregarding the caller's feelings and needs. It is quite unrealistic to assume that because someone says they want to kill themselves in your presence or with your co-operation in the building of a known suicide prevention agency, this is really what they want rather than a conscious or unconscious plea for help. I have only known of one Samaritan caller who must have died within a fairly short time of ending her conversation on the telephone. I have never known of a caller wanting a Samaritan to enter into a contract to aid or support their suicide. All those callers I have known or supervised who have overdosed in the centre or in our hostel were very pleased to have been taken to hospital and helped to recover. Sadly, the many callers known to me who killed themselves never wanted to make demands on anyone.

The following is a very appropriate story in *The Therapist's Dilemmas* by Windy Dryden[4]. He recalls a joke about Carl Rogers who was working with a patient who said, 'Well, Dr Rogers, this is the last time I will see you because I am going to commit suicide'. Rogers reflects on the patient's feelings and the patient opens the window and says, 'OK Dr Rogers, I am leaving'. Rogers reflects further, whereupon the patient jumps out of the window. Rogers looks out and says 'plop', reflecting to the very end. In reality Rogers has talked about that and said, 'Look, in no way would I have allowed that person to jump, I would have stopped that person'. Asked why, he responded, 'because a strong feeling would have bubbled up and led me to take action'.

*What is the best way to help those who are in a suicidal crisis situation, because of possible action involving sexual or fraud offences?*

Here we are encountering people whose suicidal action is dependent upon how their particular crisis can be resolved. This means they will need the crisis intervention type of help. Although the caller is likely to see suicide as the only solution to their predicament, the depressive factor is often very transitory, e.g. if the situation shows positive signs of resolving itself without police action, there is a great uplift. If it does not show good signs of solution, suicide may be seen as the only option. It is essential to be sensitive to the caller's need to be caught up in a long-term suicidal state. Many suicidal situations are very transitory, but in this situation you can never be sure of the likely outcome until the material factors, i.e. police enquiries, possible court action, etc., have been determined one way or another. It is not just a question of helping a caller to adopt a more positive and less constricted view, since often loss of status and suicide are so closely linked. The caller may be most grateful for support, but in itself this is not enough in such situations. So there are two essential needs.

1. The provision of a Significant Other or key figure to be able to manage the whole situation. This could be a good mature friend, relative, Samaritan, priest or doctor. This person would need to be able to get the talking therapy going and help the caller face up to confrontation, to reality. This is a time when I feel the key figure will need to be doing, as well as being. You need to be able to mobilize help and communicate with a number of useful contacts. You will need to get into some very heavy talking with the caller giving opportunities for them to express their inner emotional reactions at depth and at the same time to explore quite ruthlessly the possible options. A lot will depend upon how much the key figure can empathize with and be trusted by the caller. If you are able to achieve togetherness then the caller is likely to have confidence in your ways of negotiating. Where sexual problems are involved, some psychiatric backing is essential. Where a person is involved in fraud it may be of use to try and negotiate with the employers, especially in case of theft or misuse of funds etc. A good and trusted lawyer is most important and will need to be constantly consulted. You should also enlist the help of the caller's GP or some competent doctor known to you for monitoring the on-going care and medication which may be necessary. It is best to have the caller's own GP if this is possible, though some people are reluctant to talk about problems involving scandal to a family doctor. You may need to move the caller to another temporary area or organize some private or personal arrangement. All effective crisis suicide agencies should always have easy access to suitable doctors.

Where the situation necessitates the caller giving themselves up to the police, it is most important they do not do so on their own. It is worth discussing which relatives and friends could be contacted. It is quite surprising that although the husband who has run away from his wife and firm, often stealing large sums of his firm's money, initially is adamant about not talking to his wife, after realistic discussion he may allow you to begin some negotiations with her. The likely result is that two people's distress may be greatly reduced and the way opened for much more positive reactions. Nevertheless, a lot of sensitivity and patience is needed with this group, as below the surface there is likely to be a great deal of anger and guilt which may become turned on the caller leading them to kill themselves. It is quite surprising how relieved and co-operative a person can be after some meaningful discussions about their particular problems.

2. It is essential to have on-going twenty-four-hour support available with a contact at least every twelve hours. An emergency telephone service or centre of help is a necessary resource when situations can change so easily. For example, sudden police enquiries or a police search may cause a loss of nerve and intense anxiety to callers. Here the Samaritans can provide an invaluable service with immediate support.

*Do those from other countries and cultures have special problems in a crisis?*
Suicide is no respecter of race or culture, however many Asians and West Indians do live in much closer-knit communities than white people. Therefore there is much more befriending and support within the family. At the same time some special difficulties are beginning to become very apparent.
1. Many young Asians who have been brought up in a Western-style education find it very difficult to cope with the restrictions of their parents. Many live in a state of terrible tension and feel very isolated. Where the parents are very inflexible, the teenager will have to choose between submission or leaving home. These kind of situations are likely to increase in the near future.
2. Although many humanist groups and Christians would support mixed marriages, there is a lot of opposition from parents and society in general. All this causes extra emotional strain and can lead to crisis situations.
3. Racial harassment is always very cruel and deeply upsetting. It is most likely to cause suicidal reactions if the person under attack is already dispirited or in a depression.
4. One of the most serious problems for the helpers is most

likely to be that of communication. By that I do not mean the actual language problems, though of course that has to be managed, rather the ability to identify what the Asian or West Indian caller is feeling, what he or she is really troubled about. It is most unwise to assume that you have tuned into the person's needs just because you have had a lot of experience with troubled white people. A lot depends upon patience and how well you know the caller.

For example, a caller who has recently been bereaved of his wife, asks for help because he says her grave has been interfered with and he must know if she is dead. On the face of it he does seem to have all the symptoms of a serious depression and the worry about the state of the grave could be interpreted as part of his depression. On the other hand, if we get more into his cultures, we find as a West Indian Christian it was very important for him to know that his wife's grave was kept sacred. It is true he is depressed, but he was getting suicidal about his failure to respect his wife's grave.

Determining whether a caller's complaints about persecution are real or imaginary can be complicated by racial attitudes. These can be complex as whites feel persecuted by blacks, and blacks feel persecuted by whites, and there are a number of inter-racial tensions among blacks themselves. Some of the most tragic are to be found among those who know that if they return to their own country because of a political situation they will be imprisoned and maybe tortured. Already some people have killed themselves rather than return to imprisonment.

There is a danger that some black people will be labelled mentally ill because some of their communications are mis-understood. Many over-materialistic Westerners may be con-fused by a West Indian's reliance on the spirits or voices guiding him and so on.

When a caller is very depressed, maybe in need of psychiatric treatment, or is in some complicated emotional relationship, and ashamed to talk to his immediate relatives, this reaction has to be taken very seriously. The stress about offending parents and family plus the other problems could make the person suicidal. Suicide here would be a way of saving face and the honour of the family. It is not always easy for those of a Western culture to appreciate how much the family, which includes all kinds of relatives, uncles, aunts and cousins, controls and influences the person's life. Many also regard admission to psychiatric hospital as a disgrace to the whole family. I have heard husbands say, 'She is not going to that bad place', 'the zoo is no good'.

Many women, often with little English, have to cope on their own when their husbands go away for work or some other reason. Because their husbands are authoritarian, their movements are very restricted and so they suffer from loneliness and isolation.

Although there are a number of important differences and customs between the races, it is essential that we recognize sincerity and that the human response is understood irrespective of colour or culture.

*Do you think it is important that the helpers look after themselves and if so what are the most vulnerable areas?*
I think it is essential for the helpers to be able to look after themselves. This does not imply that helpers should always put their own interests and needs first, but it is important that helpers, professional or voluntary, are able to make their own choices, being mature enough to be in charge of their lives. The helper may decide after careful reflection to put their life at risk for the patient or caller, or to work extra hours for the benefit of some special group in need, but it is their choice. There is always the danger in both the paid and unpaid sectors of workers being exploited by the unmet needs of the community, or because of some personal psychological problems, especially guilt, depressive reactions, or perfectionism driving the person on to become a workaholic. Those helpers who are able to care for themselves and manage their lives with a sense of inner freedom are most likely to care better for those in need than anyone else. We could say this is basic for helpers who are likely to be involved in a lot of very serious crisis work.

There are some special areas of vulnerability.

1. Encountering your own problems, past or present, in the distressed person. Naturally a lot depends upon the nature of the problem and how well you have resolved it. It can be quite a shock if the client suffers from the same sexual problems and difficulties as yourself, or has the same depressive illness. If you still feel very upset then it indicates you are still very vulnerable and it would be better to get someone else to cope with the caller. It is worth mentioning that it is very unlikely for your caller to recognize that you have or have had a similar problem to themselves. People who are in a serious crisis are very self-centred as they are so at risk, and have little or no interest in the possible problems of the helper. It is also most unwise and unhelpful for both of you to open up about your past as you cannot guarantee that your confidentiality will be respected. The situation is obviously quite different in a self-help group, where AA is a classic example.

2. If you are going through some personal relationship crisis or work management crisis, you need to be very cautious, as your judgement and ability to respond positively could be adversely affected.

3. Although we tend to worry more about recognizing our own psychological problems, we also need to attend to our physical health. Even such common place ailments as heavy colds, 'flu, hang-over, or over-tiredness, are likely to reduce our sensitivity and alertness in suicidal assessments. It will be obvious to you that more serious physical disabilities should not be disregarded and consultations are needed.

*If you have a religious faith and are an active member of that faith, are you less likely to become depressed or suicidal?*
How you cope with your daily problems and setbacks will certainly depend upon your quality of life. If you are suffering from clinical depression whether you are religious or not is unlikely to make any difference. It is most important this is clearly understood, since a true depressive illness will play havoc with one's faith and spirituality. If you are in a state of

dispiritment and not endogenously depressed then your religious attitude could make a lot of difference. Durkheim took the view that as common religious beliefs bind people together and give a meaning to life, belonging to such a group would reduce risk of suicide. It is well established that an integrated society will promote a better quality of life, however it should be remembered always that a serious depressive illness may emerge at any time irrespective of whether a person is religious or not. This, as we know, can even happen to those who have close relations with Significant Others, some kinds of severe depression do not seem to be dependent upon a particular philosophy of life. The great religions of the world, Christianity, Judaism, Buddhism, Hinduism, and Muhammadism, all have certain overall patterns in common.

1. There is the seeking to get beyond oneself, to realize and develop the inner self, spirit or soul, through faith and commitment to God or to a theistic theology.
2. The meaning and goal of life is not derived from the pursuit of pleasure and the exploitation of others, but from the spiritual values and ethical codes of the particular faith. In general, these recognize the need for redemption from the human tendencies towards selfishness and destructive behaviour, the respect for each other and promotion of community life.
3. All are especially concerned with teaching about sex, death and future life. At the same time it is essential to acknowledge that these religions are not the same. They include many fundamental differences of belief which often tend to create discord rather than integration.

When we are considering helping the suicidal, surely we may be allowed to see links here between the emerging alienation and disillusionment of men and women not only from religion but also from their Western culture. We could say there never was a time when humanity needed so urgently to discover a more positive and religious way of life in which they may grow in spirituality and feeling.

*What do you see is the role of Christians in their involvement in suicide prevention?*

As an Anglican priest, I would see it as part of my pastoral duties to minister to the suicidal. I am sure there are many Christians working as professionals or volunteers who recognize that suicidal behaviour, depression and despair are very much part of the human condition. In the Samaritans there are a number of Christians including some in religious orders. Sometimes callers become aware of this as the encounters develop. I personally think it is most important for Christians to try and live out the Passionate Christ approach, in so far as our human weaknesses will allow. The following are extracts from a paper on theological comments presented to some interested Samaritan volunteers at an annual conference some years ago by myself.

### Some Theological Comments on the Samaritans

Christians involved in the Samaritans would see the development of their work as a movement of the Spirit in their ministry to those who are suicidal or in despair. They are accepting the Divine Command of Christ to love their neighbour in the spirit of the Parable of the Good Samaritan. At the same time Christians recognize that the activity of the Holy Spirit is not limited to Church People, but 'the wind bloweth where it listeth', and so would be happy to work with, and in some cases under the direction of, those of other faiths or of none. It is not without significance that the key figure in the Parable was a 'Samaritan' – an outcast and one certainly not of the true faith!

The theological significance of Samaritan befriending (day-and-night availability) is to be found in the willingness of one human being offering himself to a brother in acute distress. In this self offering (expressed by being available on the telephone and for face-to-face encounter), there is an expression of love, care and commitment to another human being – the offering of the warmth of love and compassion to the brother who is out in the cold – indeed to the Christ in the cold. The offering must be freely given with no other objective than to give warmth of love to him who is so cold that he may die. What is offered is essentially the human contact and is not a substitute for professional help, and must not be used as a means of conversion. The Samaritan of the Parable acted, i.e. bound up the wounds and arranged lodgement – and our action is to *listen – be available* as another human being. This is not counselling which is specialized work given mainly through priests, pastors, social workers and skilled therapists.

The Christian in his befriending is entering more deeply into the Passion of Christ – he offers himself – he deliberately involves himself in the drama of suffering humanity. Theologically there is a sharing in the Passion of the Son of Man – the living out of the Eucharist, an expression of the Liturgy in the depths of Hell. The carrying on the ministry of Christ committed to his Church. Here is a demonstration of the priesthood of all believers in action.

The presence of the Samaritan befriender is a sacramental expression of the activity of the Divine Compassion in the depths of human misery and despair. The presence is also a Sacramental expression of the power of the Risen Lord – for out of the disfiguration comes the transfiguration as a soul finds it good to be alive.

Some may ask what of the preaching of the Word, the evangelization of the soul who finds no meaning in life – is this not necessary? Surely the theological answer is to be found in the Passion of Christ – the Son of Man who accepted brokenness – here is surely the greatest and most moving of all evangelism. It is true that men need to find a meaning and purpose to life – to reach out and discover that which is beyond themselves. But this transcendence, God Himself, may first need to be found in Hell, in the gutter and cesspool of human misery. It was not for nothing that the Son of Man experienced the agony and isolation of Gethsemane and a Bloody Crucifixion, as the way of expressing the Divine Compassion. Who would dare to suggest the Son of Man would have given his Good News more effectively in theological words rather than in the Silence of the Crucified Christ?

Surely the subtle temptation is to avoid the agony of the Passion through speaking of it rather than sharing in it. This is not surprising – the spirit is willing but the flesh is weak. The man in Hell is beyond pious and profound dialogue, even the sincere theological utterance of the committed Christian, but he may be able to respond to the pure Passion of the Son of Man – even when this Passion touches him through 'the *other* Son of Man' who is but a poor substitue for the Son of Man. Yet the Spirit intercedes for us with sighs too deep for words (Roman 8:26). We cannot pray (live, befriend) as we ought but the Spirit intercedes for us (Romans 8:26).

Dorothee Söelle, in the conclusion of her provocative and inspiring theological book on suffering, writes

Wherever people suffer Christ stands with them. To put it in less mythological terms, as long as Christ lives and is remembered his friends will be with those who suffer. Where no help is possible he appears not as the Superior helper but only as the one who walks with those beyond help. That one bears the burden of the other is the simple and clear call that comes from all suffering. It is possible to help bear the burden, contrary to all talks about a person's final solitude. A society is conceivable in which no person is left totally alone, with no one to think of him and stay with him. Watching and praying are possible.

Everyone who helps another is Gethsemane
Everyone who comforts another is the mouth of Christ

That people suffer and can be disconsolate is taken for granted here. We should forbid ourselves to dream of a person who needs no consolation. We should also stop classifying suffering merely as something out of the past, for this classification is an act of self-contempt. There is a time for weeping and a time for laughing. To need consolation and to console are human, just as human as Christ was.

We can change ourselves and learn in suffering instead of becoming worse. We can gradually beat back and abolish the suffering that still today is produced for the profit of the few. But on all these paths we come against boundaries that cannot be crossed. Death is not the only such barrier. There are also brutalization and insensibility, mutilation and injury that no longer can be reversed. The only way these boundaries can be crossed is by sharing the pain of the sufferers with them, not leaving them alone and making their cry louder[5].

'The only way these boundaries can be crossed is by sharing the pain', Dorothee sums up the role of the Christians in helping the suicidal, 'not leaving them alone and making their cry louder'. We may quite rightly reply it is by no means the prerogative of Christians to support and befriend, as it is indeed exercised by many non-Christians and those of no religious faith.

To return to the question about the role of the Christian in suicide prevention, I would say that the Christians are saying we are not alone in our despair; God participates and shares in our torment. Hans Kung sums it up very well when he writes, 'God's love does not protect us against all suffering, but it protects us *in* all suffering'[6]. Christians believe that victory over suffering, chaos, despair and physical death has already begun here and now in our baptism into the Risen Lord. The transfiguration of our disfigured state has already started. Granted this presupposes faith in the saving power of Christ and a lively participation in the church which is made up of the Baptised – the Gospel of Christ is about 'inviting' men and women into spiritual liberation and so giving some meaning and purpose to their lives. Although so often Christians have failed to proclaim the liberating, reconciling, forgiving and very humanistic message of the Gospel, this does not alter the significance of the Holy Spirit's availability to humanity. The greatest hindrance to the benefits of the Christian Gospel comes from the need for many Christians to protect God and to put more reliance on keeping moral laws, trying to be perfect rather than seeking after wholeness.

Christians, in common with those of other world religions, philosophies or political ways of life, have to grapple with the paradox of the human condition. This is expressed in the potential for positive creativity on the one hand and potential for unlimited destruction on the other; loving and hating, living and dying. Whatever your belief or way of life you have to recognize that suffering and disorder are part of our lives. Some of the pain and suffering is directly attributable to human selfishness and mismanagement. There is also a lot more which cannot be explained away in terms of the human condition. When we cannot get the answer some will succomb to the temptation to create scapegoats or want the security of an all powerful and dictatorial God. I would describe this as immature and unspiritual theology likely to increase the suicide rate because it nourishes the growth of pathological guilt and fear, blocking the benefits of the spirit. Whether we are Christians or not, all of us have to grapple with the inner struggles and life's adversities frequently causing great pain and suffering. The Christians offer that God is the God of powerlessness, who humanizes men and women. He is the God of the Cross. The power of God emerges from his commitment 'to powerlessness' and the power is transfigured into the Risen Power.

If we consider how in counselling, and more so in psychotherapy, the caller only begins to improve when he relinquishes some of his power, he abandons some defensive positions and out of this paradoxical situation healing begins. We recall how Halmos in *The Faith of the Counsellor* suggests that counsellors and therapists have become to rely on faith in the power of love which can be compared to some Christian mysticism. Shneidman reminded us of the need to attend to the 'emotional reactions' rather than the 'rational'. We can only expect to be helped by Christianity if we seek to experience the effects of our life in Christ. The Gospels and the New Testament letters emphasize the union between God and the faithful. The phrase 'in Christ' is constantly repeated and the Christian life is seen as a continuation of the life of Christ. For those who embrace this union are likely to experience a meaning and purpose for their lives which may help them to be much less prone to suicide.

Jesus invites his followers to practise an inner freedom from being controlled by hatred, social status, racialism, competition, power, pollution, sex and aggression. This should not be confused with asceticism or a withdrawal from enjoying the material things of life. The aim is for men and women not to be addicted to their needs but in control of them and so free to be human. However, this cannot be developed without conflict and as we know it is essential for psychological growth to experience and work through conflicts. During the short earthly ministry of Jesus there was tremendous conflict. His disciples were jealous of each other, the most pious religious leaders not only totally misunderstood Him but also actively persecuted Him. They quarrelled about who should be the greatest, Judas killed himself, Peter denied knowing Him. In spite of all these traumas Jesus does not lose his cool or take up a condemning reaction, still common among many Christians today. We recall in Matthew's Gospel,

> Pass no judgement, and you will not be judged. For as you judge others, so you will yourselves be judged, and whatever measure you deal out to others will be dealt back to you. Why do you look at the speck of sawdust in your brother's eye, with never a thought for the great plank in your own? Or how can you say to your brother, 'Let me take the speck out of your eye', when all the time there is that plank in your own? You hypocrite! First take the plank out of your own eye, and then you will see clearly to take the speck out of your brother's[7].

The love and goodness that Jesus is expressing is not in any way sentimental or pious, it is given through passionate encounters and will sometimes seem hard and certainly painful to accept. Passionate relationships are always likely to involve the participants in some suffering and conflict so the results here could be seen as the crisis, the judgement of God. This will often involve forgiving others and hardest of all, oneself – being humble enough to acknowledge one's weakness and need for God and other people. Similarly, there is a significant element of crisis and of judgement in befriending and counselling, as the positive or negative effects are dependent upon the response of the recipient.

*How do you help the grown-up son or daughter who is trying to care for the parent who is suffering from manic-depressive illness?*
Let them unwind and tell you about how they feel. Anyone caring for a near relative who is subject to sharp mood swings is bound to be under a lot of strain. In your encounter, it is likely to be most helpful if you cover the following points.
1. Be sure they have some understanding of the trouble their parent is going through and they recognize it as an illness. It is worth discussing with them the awful experience of the darkness of the depressive mood and the complications of the excitable state. Some may not realize that when their father is unkind, lacking in appreciation and sometimes critical, this is part of the illness.
2. The possible suicide risk should be mentioned as it could be a great source of anxiety.
3. The medical care should be checked and if this is not adequate some additional help should be mentioned, e.g. the community psychiatric nurse would certainly be willing to give support to a relative.
4. There may be a need to try and arrange some special on-going support, because it is especially hard for a son or daughter who have considerable emotional involvement with the parent. They are likely to experience a lot of anger and then guilt. These reactions become more of a burden when it is necessary for the parent to have a spell in hospital, sometimes on a compulsory order for which the son or daughter will be responsible. Check out their possible suicidal feelings and any worries they may have about becoming depressed.
   The following answer was given to me by a Samaritan now in

her thirties in response to my question, 'What is it like to live with a manic depressive in the family?'.

I can only speak for myself and what it was like to live in my family with my father who was manic depressive.

I remember, when I was about eight, that my father would become depressed. Although he and my mother were arguing a lot, the depressions never seemed to stem from these tensions. Rather, they seemed to descend from out of the blue and he would sit, almost immobile, sometimes listening to searingly beautiful classical music, tears often running down his cheeks, isolated in his world of despair. At other times he would play his violin, again in a world of his own. At these times, feeling his fear, I wanted so much to get through to him and it was very painful for me to be ignored or pushed away, filling me with fear and uselessness. When the depression lifted and he became the usual jokey easy-going Daddy that he had been before, I would feel confused and angry and it would take longer and longer each time it happened for him to win back my trust.

Gradually, the depressions grew deeper so that, instead of feeling an atmosphere of fear around him, I felt nothing. It was as if he simply disappeared for the time that he was depressed. In between depressions, he started to be even jollier, even more energetic, even more full of plans than he used to be. The atmosphere in our house altered with his mood swings. When you live closely with a group of people, especially in a family situation, everyone is affected by the way any one member of the group is, but when one member swings from depression to elation, life takes on a strangely unpredictable nature. Coming home from school each day, it was impossible to guess whether there would be a heavy gloom and quietness waiting or whether there would be extreme fun and games for all to join in with in progress. My mother, in the depressed times, would become tenser and tenser, more and more brittle and snappy. In the elated times, she would let go and cry. I felt very much the same, but it was hard to know whether I was reacting to the present situation, a cessation of the previous one or the previous one itself. Always, a change in his behaviour came as relief. Always the relief was short lived as the particular tensions of the new behaviour pattern deepened.

By the time I was twelve, the elated times had become grotesque; a parody of fun, with a somewhat paranoid tinge to the reasoning behind his more and more grandiose schemes. He wrote letters to me almost every day, leaving them by the side of my bed for when I woke up. Sometimes they would run along the lines of he and I being close allies in a cruel and treacherous world, citing my mother and grandmother as chief perpetrators of the treachery. At other times, I was cast as the wicked witch, instigator of all the misery. These differing viewpoints, as with his behaviour, has nothing at all to do with how I, my sister or my mother had been behaving and nothing any of us did had any effect, so, at this point, I felt powerless. I felt that nothing I did, said or thought had any bearing on anything.

It was around this time that he took his first overdose – the first of many suicide attempts. He also left my mother time after time, returning after longer and longer periods away. Day after day would find my mother sitting crying at the kitchen table pouring it all out to my greataunt (her best friend) and sometimes to me. She would rail angrily at one moment, and calmly analyse his character at the next. What seemed curious to me was that she would veer between including me in the conversation as an honorary adult and then directing my greataunt to stop talking about it as I was a child and shouldn't know. Just as my father did, she would often seek my support and, since neither of them ever asked how I was, I gradually came to feel that I had no right to feel anything other than what they felt. So I took their feelings on board, going to whichever one seemed to need me the most at any time, glad, at least, for that attention.

It was not until his first suicide attempt that the professionals were brought on to the scene when he was taken to hospital. Although my mother and I had had long discussions about the fact that he was clearly ill, as he would not hear of this view, rejecting it as ludicrous when he was high and hopeless when low, we had not pursued it. Also, and perhaps more importantly, we had not pursued it because we were all affected and dis-eased by this still undiagnosed manic depression, so that it had become not just his, but all of our illness, just as the affects of any family member's major illness spreads to the entire family, whether that illness is psychological or physiological. We were all suffering from a certain lack in grasping reality.

I am aware that so far I have not said much about my sister. She was not picked on emotionally, and she developed a way of distancing herself from it all (or perhaps it was the other way round!). I stayed very much in the centre of the game, even when I had rare chances to escape for a while, to protect her, as she was younger and less resilient than I, and I loved her very much.

After my mother left him, I became officially responsible for him, taking him back to hospital when he ran away and, puppet like, participating in zany schemes which usually hinged around spending vast amounts of money quickly, not knowing what else to do. Unfortunately, he would not accept that he was ill and had no faith in the psychiatric world, and, like many of his generation and background simply did not believe in mental illness.

I have tried to write about living with a manic depressive family member, almost attempting to separate the illness from the man. At times precious little of the 'real' him was to be found, but there was always something. Through it all, he remained my father; the experience of being his daughter has taught me a lot and I value it highly.

People caring for those who are mentally ill or out of touch with reality are likely to be very vulnerable and often find it very difficult to ask for help. Now that most of those who are mentally disturbed live in the community there will be greater burdens often placed on most unsuitable relatives.

## CO-OPERATION BETWEEN VOLUNTEERS AND PROFESSIONALS

Here we are concerned with how volunteers and professionals working together can best help in suicide prevention. Since suicide is no respecter of persons, it is essential to bear in mind that any one of us can be said to have a responsibility to relieve another human being in acute distress.

One of the most important social issues of today is how effectively volunteers and professionals can work in part-nership. This is especially relevant when in Western society the emergence of community participation in overall mental health care is both wanted and encouraged by laity and professionals alike. These social changes have also brought about a much wider interest and involvement in voluntary work of all kinds. The following comments on volunteers are from the report of a seminar organized by the World Federation for Mental Health, 1982.

### Volunteers

The label volunteers in the context of mental health is deceptive because it is a generic term embracing people of widely differing ages, social groupings, abilities and experi-ence, who perform an infinite range of tasks, from small (though important) practical services to highly skilled work such as counselling.

The old stereotype of volunteers as middle-aged, middle class and usually of the female sex, still persists though it is dying away. Nowadays every section of society – from school-children to elderly people, and from every social class – is represented, though not of course proportionately to the population. The image of the volunteer as a 'do-gooder' – a phrase sufficiently offensive for one person interviewed on television to retort indignantly that he was as much a 'dobadder' as anyone – is also disappearing. We are coming to understand more about the mutuality of helping relationships. At the same time as those with problems are being assisted, a need in human beings to be useful is being satisfied.

It goes without saying that distressed people must be protected from incompetent busybodies, but the old arguments about purity of motivation in volunteers (leaving aside the motivation of professionals) now look rather old fashioned. The point is that the benefits of volunteering are not in one direction only, and helpers and helped can change places at different times in their lives. One British psychiatrist wrote about 'the biological need to help' and said of volunteering, 'it is as blessed and satisfying to give as to receive and it is quite wrong to regard voluntary service as a difficult chore requiring special gifts of saintliness'.

Those giving voluntary help in the UK include many people who have become interested and involved through being directly affected by a particular problem. They also include a substantial number of paid professional workers in the statutory mental health services, who join in the activities of voluntary organisations in their spare time. They do so for many different reasons; because it gives them an opportunity to escape the bureaucratic constraints that hinder them in their daily work; because their commitment to improving the mental health services impels them to give more than the basic hours of work; because as members of a community they want to share in its mental health efforts; and sometimes perhaps because it improves their career prospects. The ways in which these professionally trained volunteers help also vary; often they work on an equal basis alongside other volunteers who have no special training, but sometimes their role is to guide and support them. Unquestionably, their involvement has a significant effect on the way voluntary work as a whole develops.

The settings in which volunteers choose to work also vary, from voluntary organisations where they probably have a voice in shaping their own work programmes, to statutory services like hospitals where their tasks have to be fitted into the requirements of an official body, and avoid conflicting with the interests of paid staff[8].

The usual distinction between volunteers and professionals is that the latter are paid. However, this is by no means true of all voluntary agencies and it is estimated there are 15,000 – 20,000 paid staff in the voluntary organizations. Another distinction, and this is especially relevant in our setting, is that voluntary bodies are independent of the state. There is no doubt that many of the callers coming to the Samaritans do so because of the absolute confidentiality they can offer.

The other long-standing difference is that professionals are trained and therefore specialists in their work. As we have seen from the comments on volunteers, this is no longer so clearly defined as in the past. The motivation of volunteers has received quite a lot of attention and, not surprisingly, is of considerable interest to many of those seeking help. There are some relevant comments in the report *Crossing of Purposes*, in which Giles Darvill, Development Officer at the Volunteer Centre, Berkhamsted, comments on 'Why do people volunteer?'

It isn't always easy to understand why people volunteer. For that matter, it isn't easy to understand why someone becomes a dentist or a teacher in a comprehensive school, let alone a social worker.

I will start a short list that readers can complete. If you are inclined to do so, you might find it interesting to ask how many of these reasons apply to paid staff also. People volunteer:

to make Social Contacts
to get rid of guilt or overcome fear
to earn the right to get help in return
to learn something or to acquire a skill
to get power over other people
to be of use and to effect change
to get status

Clearly, volunteers vary enormously in motivation. Different volunteer opportunities provide for their needs in different proportions. A primary, if unconscious, reason for volunteering may be to be in a position to get help oneself if one wants it. Where volunteers give a service in which there is little expectation that clients will reciprocate, an important sideline of the group activity is likely to be the development of a network of help between the volunteers. In other schemes, for example a good neighbour scheme, volunteers are likely to be quietly examining their contacts with clients to see if there are ways the relationship can become more two-way. For example, when many of the volunteers and recipients are recently retired or are isolated parents.

It is important to understand motives more fully than is the case now in order to be aware of what rewards volunteers are looking for (see Section 13), and it is especially important for Statutory Services to do so if they are trying to make more systematic use of the 'desire to volunteer'. Some motives may not be harnessed as easily as others. A motive that volunteers clearly do not share with paid staff is the need for cash rewards. No one yet knows what impact the introduction of money payments into voluntary workers' rewards will have on the nature of their interaction with recipients[9].

The reference by Darvill to Section 13 refers to his paper on 'Selecting Volunteers and their Activities' in which he points out that the 'Staff in the Social Services department sometimes forget to find out the most important thing about their volunteers; what they expect and what precisely they want to do'[10]. It is not easy to be clear about one's motivation and it may be that more attention is given to the motives of volunteers than to those of some professionals.

The professionals in medicine, social work, nursing, psychotherapy and the Church will all have had to go through some selection procedures in addition to their particular specialized training. Those who are involved in providing psychotherapy will be most likely to have been required to have had their motives and personal attitudes explored in depth. If we are realistic about the whole question of examining motivation for both voluntary and professional helping work, we will have to admit that the results are likely to be very circumspect. It is wise to make some selection procedures, as a safeguard for both the potential workers and consumers, as part of our expression of caring for each other. There is the story of a mature student, who was going to begin therapy training, who was getting anxious about her underlying motivations. Her tutor told her she should go ahead with her course and in her therapy she would discover a lot about her motivations, the tutor felt it would be too much of a shock to be too realistic about them in the beginning.

When we examine volunteers and professionals more closely we begin to discover they have much more in common than may be supposed. Perhaps the common denominator which could consciously, and to some extent unconsciously, bind them together is their desire and need to help people in crisis. Therefore it is most essential for us to consider the most important people in this crisis drama, the callers/patients. Many people, especially those who carry the label of some mental illness, believe that their needs and feelings are not considered in sufficient depth by professionals and volunteers. We all know there has been a long history in the past of neglect, insensitivity and sometimes open persecution of those considered to be out of touch with reality. In Britain Mind has done a great deal about the rights of patients and their needs. Those who are both very mentally and emotionally disturbed, and labelled manic-depressive or schizophrenic, are quite often rejected by would-be helpers. It is still much easier for someone suffering from a physical disability, possibly with the exception of AIDS, to be generally accepted with sensitivity and understanding. Many ex-psychiatric patients have difficulties in getting jobs, because of their psychiatric history, although they are mentally quite recovered.

One of the developments of the 1970s has been the movement towards self-help groups. These are regarded as a growing phenomenon in Western societies and will need to be taken into account by all the medical, social and voluntary services. The fundamental basis of these groups is the coming together of people with a shared disability and problems.

There are, however, many kinds of self-help groups with a wide variety of purpose and organisation. Some groups are closely related to professional services, e.g. CARE, the Cancer Aftercare and Rehabilitation Society in Britain which tries to provide the 'human care' so often found to be lacking in medical services. Some are formed to offer alternative services to the medical model, as for example, some women's health groups. Some seek only to treat themselves as they were once treated by professionals. Some groups are formed by professionals who then withdraw. Some are formed by ex-patients and then manipulated by professionals. Some avoid all contact with professionals.

Judi Chamberlin suggested three models of self-help groups. The *partnership* model where professionals and non-professionals work together to provide a service. Those who receive the service are also partners but, she suggested, in name only. There remains a clear distinction between those who give and those who receive help. Most half-way houses are an example of this model. The *supportive* model allows membership to everyone who wants to use the service, all members are equals since all have problems at some time and all are capable of helping one another. Professionals are only 'bought in' when their expertise is needed for a particular purpose. They are not allowed as members because they draw a distinction between those who give and receive help. In the *separatist* model, membership is open only to 'sufferers' or 'ex-sufferers'. Professionals and volunteers are excluded.

There is, then, a wide variety of self-help groups and the nature of their relationship with professionals varies from group to group. We tried to pinpoint some of the controversial aspects of that relationship which need to be studied in greater depth. The question of *membership* is one such issue.

Membership is the prerogative of the 'sufferers'. The primary focus of the group will be the mutual support to be gained by the members themselves. Both professionals and volunteers will be, to a greater or lesser extent, outside the membership yet their role may be crucial to the way a group develops[11].

Groups are also developing for the mutual support of those who have been bereaved by suicide. It is encouraging to know that interaction between the consumers and the helpers is alive and that discussions and critical appraisals are possible.

Now to take a look at some of the practical ways of co-operation. It will be useful to examine some common experiences. The following quotation is from my paper given at IASP Congress in Paris in 1981.

*Fourth Section*
*Areas of co-operation between Volunteers and Professionals*
As a professional counsellor I think it would be helpful for us to recognise some of the common experiences we already share here. Most of us know what it is like to have been a patient. Those of us who have had the experience of therapy will be able to accept our mixed motivation for involvement in helping agencies, professional or voluntary. Some of us may have been callers, we are all potential callers and psychiatric patients.

The callers and volunteers will have their fantasies of what they need and what they can offer or should offer.

It may be easier for doctors to be more realistic since volunteers offer support, befriending and doctors, whilst they are not unfriendly and supportive, are primarily offering treatment.

In Table 8 we have a demonstration of a failure of volunteers to recognise an over-demanding caller who is not in need of treatment. Volunteers become over-anxious to help the caller and arrange referral to professionals, this leads to the volunteer feeling rejected and the caller becomes more demanding. Result is tension on both sides, volunteers frustrated and professionals have a loss of confidence in volunteers.

This is a very vulnerable area for volunteers, especially in emergency telephone help services. It is possible for over-demanding or manipulative callers to more or less control an emergency service, unless volunteers work under the direction of an experienced leadership. It is in this area that professionals can be of great help in providing training and on-going support.

In Table 9 we have a failure on the part of professionals to recognise the wisdom of trusting the volunteer's judgement about the need for the caller to have a psychiatric diagnosis and possible treatment. This demonstrates the dangers of professional inflexibility. This causes loss of confidence not only from voluntary helping agencies but from the community as a whole, and hinders the effectiveness of developing community psychiatry. Brian Barraclough (1972) has pointed out the great importance of getting clinically depressed people on the right anti-depressant drug therapy[12]. Many depressed callers are reticent, guilty and afraid to trouble the doctors.

Richard Fox (1978) draws attention to co-operation between professionals and volunteers in Ed Shneidman's 'Taxonomy of Suicide' or 'Four Phases of Suicide'[13]. You will see from Table 10 that there can be an inter-relationship between the support befriending, psychiatric treatment and psychotherapy. A great deal will of course depend upon the sensitivity of the volunteers and their ability to quickly pick up at what stage they are encountering the caller. Support by a volunteer in stage one and an ability to maintain the contact is probably the most helpful. This could also help some callers in emotional turmoil to feel secure enough to have treatment. In stage three volunteer support may make the difference between moving over into death in the final stage, as the volunteer becomes the Significant Other during this time of crisis.

In Table 11 we have the positive results of a good assess-

**Table 8**
**FAILURE OF CO-OPERATION BETWEEN VOLUNTEERS AND PROFESSIONALS — 1**
**Negative reaction of volunteers**

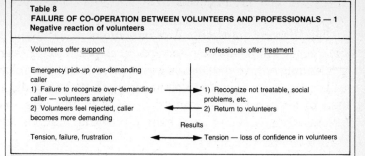

Volunteers offer <u>support</u>                    Professionals offer <u>treatment</u>

Emergency pick-up over-demanding
caller
1) Failure to recognize over-demanding  ⟶  1) Recognize not treatable, social
caller — volunteers anxiety                     problems, etc.
2) Volunteers feel rejected, caller  ⟵  2) Return to volunteers
becomes more demanding
                                        Results

Tension, failure, frustration  ⟷  Tension — loss of confidence in volunteers

---

**Table 9**
**FAILURE OF CO-OPERATION BETWEEN VOLUNTEERS AND PROFESSIONALS — 2**
**Negative reaction of professionals**

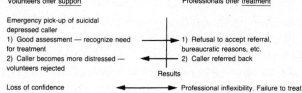

Volunteers offer <u>support</u>                    Professionals offer <u>treatment</u>

Emergency pick-up of suicidal
depressed caller
1) Good assessment — recognize need  ⟶  1) Refusal to accept referral,
for treatment                                   bureaucratic reasons, etc.
2) Caller becomes more distressed —  ⟵  2) Caller referred back
volunteers rejected
                                        Results

Loss of confidence  ⟷  Professional inflexibility. Failure to treat

---

**Table 10**
**TAXONOMY OF SUICIDE — Four Phases of Suicide (Ed Shneidman, May 1977)**

| **Callers State** | **Help Available** |
|---|---|
| 1) Inimicality, out of step, lonely | Volunteer support — befriending |
| 2) Perturbation, emotional turmoil | Psychiatric Aid |
| 3) Constriction, human contacts progressively reduced (cf Ringel's concept of the narrowing-in syndrome) | Volunteer support/befriending |
| 4) Desire for cessation, eternal tranquility, death | ? |

---

**Table 11**
**POSITIVE WAYS OF CO-OPERATION BETWEEN VOLUNTEERS**
**AND PROFESSIONALS — 3**

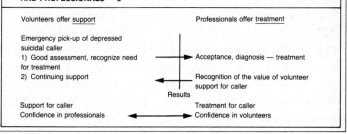

Volunteers offer <u>support</u>                    Professionals offer <u>treatment</u>

Emergency pick-up of depressed
suicidal caller
1) Good assessment, recognize need  ⟶  Acceptance, diagnosis — treatment
for treatment
2) Continuing support  ⟵  Recognition of the value of volunteer
                                        support for caller
                                        Results

Support for caller                       Treatment for caller
Confidence in professionals  ⟷  Confidence in volunteers

ment and support on the part of the volunteers leading into professional acceptance of diagnosis and treatment. This is based on the professionals' willingness to recognise the intrinsic value of carefully selected and prepared volunteers. This results in continued support, befriending plus treatment for a depressive, suicidal or mentally ill person. Good volunteer support has a vital role in caring for those in psychiatric treatment, especially outside the hospital.

At the same time many callers who are in a crisis situation may be suicidal, but not suffering from endogenous depression. If they are depressed it is a reaction to an external situation and suicide may be a logical answer to their problems, or an urgent cry for help. George Day (1980) psychiatric consultant to the Samaritans, prefers to describe this state as one of 'dispiritment'[14]. Herman Pohlmeier (1980) examines the thesis that suicide is not only a problem of depression, but exists in other connections[15]. For many suicidal callers who are not in Psychotic depression, but are in acute crisis situations, the 'listening volunteer' can be of vital significance and on many occasions sufficient. George Spaul (1970) when speaking on crisis pointed out that the volunteer gives the caller the opportunity to have an immediate encounter with a volunteer giving support, befriending and time to discover their own solutions[16].

There are other situations where the caller may suffer from what Erwin Ringel terms neurotic disfigurement of life which often ends in suicide and he draws attention to the type of neurotic behaviour pattern which moves towards suicide[17]. Such callers, when contacting our service are not likely to be dramatic or demanding, but in my experience can benefit from gentle support, befriending given by volunteers who are sensitive enough and emotionally strong enough to empathise with such depths of human isolation! This, hopefully may begin to open the doors to much needed psychotherapy. However, we need to give much more study to our reactions to this kind of caller, if we are to respond with sufficient sensitivity and competence[18].

Here is a practical example of volunteer and professional co-operation.

The Central London Branch of the Samaritans (CLB) has always provided considerable extra resources and back-up in befriending the suicidal. This takes the form of a special interview system, established since the branch began in 1953. The branch has always had the help and expertise of two or three priest counsellors or a psychiatric social worker, working within the branch. This is assisted by a strong outside back-up organized by the branch, from psychiatric consultants, general physicians, psychotherapists, clinical psychologists and psychiatric social workers.

The presence of the two full-time workers now supported by twenty-four experienced Samaritans operating in a Deputy Director's role, enables the branch to provide assessments at considerable depth through the special interview. This means that the CLB services have some of the ingredients of a crisis intervention model and a counselling model.

*The crisis intervention ingredients*
1.  The very early on-the-spot provision of professional assessments by the full-time worker or voluntary leaders working under his/her supervision.
2.  The setting-up of immediate befriending support from the volunteers on duty at the centre and the provision of protected accommodation at the centre for a day or so.
3.  The accompanying of a caller to hospital, etc. and provision of befriending support until the caller is admitted to hospital or some other suitable arrangements are made for their care. This could involve the on-going befriending support of one or more volunteers, as they may need to interchange over a possible twelve-hour period.
4.  After the assessment, the special interviewers may initiate some psychological or psychotherapeutic help and will monitor the results of the arrangements over a period of several weeks.
5.  In situations involving a pending court case, especially those

related to depression and suicidal risk when the caller is charged with shop-lifting or some sexual offence, the special interviewer initiates legal, medical/psychiatric help as well as continuous befriending support from volunteers during the crisis period.

6. In an acute marital or similar relationship crisis, the special interviewer is able to offer some immediate help to both parties if required, in addition to on-going befriending support from the centre.

7. Callers with serious sexual problems can be greatly helped by the informal atmosphere of a Samaritan special interview and for the first time may be willing to seek some much needed expert help.

8. Third-party calls are frequently referred to the Branch from gatekeepers and professionals.

*The counselling model*
The Samaritans do not consider themselves as counsellors or as running a counselling service. However as we have discussed earlier, in recent years, the terms counselling and befriending cannot be so easily distinguished. Here we are briefly noting some of the ingredients of the counselling we find in Central London Branch.

1. When a special interviewer feels it would be helpful to see the caller at the Centre for a number of encounters, over and above an initial assessment, there are elements of both befriending and counselling present.

2. The caller may be mentally ill, with or without some medication, and may need special support – fortnightly special interviews for some months can be helpful. This will always apply to some very demanding callers who need to have limits set for them within a befriending situation.

3. Some callers may benefit greatly from a weekly encounter on a special interview basis. For some callers, the structured special interview encounter is less threatening than outside on-going befriending which is bound to be more informal.

FIGURE 16: DATA ON THE SUICIDE-AT-RISK GROUP PREPARED FOR THE PARIS ISAP INTERNATIONAL CONGRESS IN 1980, FROM CLB ANNUAL FIGURES

| | |
|---|---|
| 1. New Callers | 12,744 |
| 2. Total Calls | 60,000 |
| 3. Suicide thoughts/ideas | 39% |
| 4. Suicide plans | 14% |
| 5. History of suicide attempts | 26% |
| 6. History of depression and mental illness | 36% |
| 7. Depressed in treatment | 28% |
| 8. Alcoholic | 28% |

INFORMATION ON THE SERVICE PROVIDED BY THE CLB IN 1984

*First encounters*
The majority of callers make initial contact by emergency telephones, 6 per cent by referral of a third-party, 1.5 per cent by letter or visit. The outcome of calls will depend upon the needs and motivation of the callers. The volunteer will befriend by telephone following special guidelines. Some callers will benefit from a one-off call. Some will need befriending on the telephone before they are confident enough for face-to-face encounters. A number of callers will use telephone calls as a way of acting out their psychological needs and problems.

*Centre befriending*
At the centre the callers are befriended and helped to clarify some of their needs. An essential part of the befriending by the volunteer is to help lower the emotional temperature and to make sure the caller has the benefit of the resources of the family; Samaritan and professional help, etc. For many, the Samaritans become for a time the Significant Other.

Good assessments are essential both for the good of the caller and to prevent the Branch becoming overpowered with de-manding callers. Therefore special daily attention is given to on-going notes. Interaction between volunteers, callers and professionals is quite common, especially in crisis situations and when psychiatric treatment is needed.

Emergency admissions to hospital for overdosing, psychiatric emergencies, etc average about twelve a week. There is close co-operation with many GPs, especially with callers suffering from clinical depression. Overnight emergency accommodation is provided for an average of 150 callers annually at the centre when there is an acute risk of suicide.

*Special interview encounters*
Here the callers are likely to be more at suicide risk requiring intensive befriending and professional help. It is important to note that where outside befrienders are assigned or professional help is sought there is two way traffic, i.e. the Samaritans engaged in befriending are supported and supervised by the Samaritan who did the special interview; the caller getting professional help is likely to maintain close links with the Samaritans and many of the callers will be among the 300 in assigned befriending.

*Assigned outside befriending*
Assigned befriending which takes place outside the centre and may involve home visits lasts an average of three to six months, although there are exceptions, and sometimes a new Samaritan will take over. Special interviews are frequently arranged in addition to the assigned befriending.

*Professional help*
Some of the professional help is provided directly by permanent staff and branch consultants. The rest is provided by a bank of professional resources built up over the years. These include National Health medical and psychiatric services, psychotherapists, counsellors, social workers, lawyers, etc.

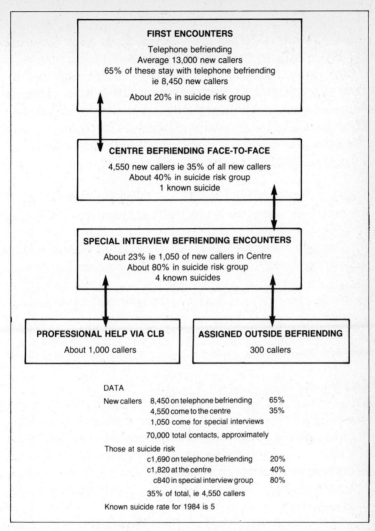

Figure 17: Information on the service provided by Central London Branch in 1984

BENEFITS OF THE VOLUNTEER – PROFESSIONAL – CALLER INTERACTIONS

1. Many young callers have been befriended and introduced into psychotherapy with very positive results.
2. A number of alcoholics have been befriended and introduced into suitable means of treatment with good results.
3. A number of callers with clinical depression and some with manic-depression rely a great deal on the befriending and arranged professional resources.
4. A number of callers have had their personality problems contained, gaining support for themselves whilst being prevented wreaking havoc with Samaritans and other helping resources.
5. A number of callers with sexual problems benefit greatly from the mixture of befriending and professional assistance.

Here we have an example of volunteer and professional co-operation where the needs and the wishes of the caller are given priority. At the same time the independence of the voluntary organization is preserved and the integrity of professionalism is maintained as their expertise is used for the caller's benefit.

Some comments from an active volunteer in the Samaritans in response to the question, 'How do you feel in your role as a Samaritan in relation to the professionals?'

I have been a Samaritan volunteer for six years. From the word go, I was told that we are not experts, and this was reassuring, as I *knew* I was no expert, and it was comforting to know that I was not expected to have any such expertise. So, from the start, I always regarded Samaritans as an 'as well as' organisation, rather than an 'instead of' one. Some callers present themselves, on the phone or face-to-face, neither receiving, nor requiring professional help. Others may already be getting help, perhaps from a psychiatrist or doctor, maybe from a psychotherapist, or from any other professional, but, at that time, they may feel that they also need what Samaritans can offer. On such occasions, there may be some reason for a Samaritan to liaise between the caller and his professional, for instance, when a caller is referred to Samaritans as a source of extra support by social services, or a solicitor or whoever the caller is involved with. At other times a caller may ask Samaritans specifically to speak to someone, perhaps to explain something on their behalf or to clarify a certain point. We may be involved with supporting someone through a legal case, in which instance, while going to court or to the solicitor's meetings, the volunteer and professional are bound to meet.

There are also those callers who are in need of some form of professional help but who are not, at the time of their contact with Samaritans, receiving it, and have no easy way of finding it themselves. In such circumstances, having discussed it thoroughly with the caller, an experienced volunteer may refer the caller to the correct form of help. This could involve arranging a meeting, probably having spoken to the professional in question about the caller first. If, however, it is an emergency situation, a volunteer may, for instance, accompany the caller to hospital, or wherever is appropriate.

Dealing with professionals can sometimes be a little like skating on thin ice. Most are pleased to hear from us, but it is imperative during these contacts to remember very clearly the message we started out with. No matter how well we feel we know the caller, and whatever views we may have formulated about the situation, we certainly are *not* experts and they are.

The caller is not being 'passed over' to the professionals, but rather is free to maintain contact with us or not, as he chooses. When, as frequently happens, a psychiatrist asks us about a caller, with the caller's permission, we should give as concise, articulate and intelligent picture as possible, from our lay position – i.e. neither hazarding what can only be uninformed guesses as to our opinion of this caller's diagnosis, nor exclusively babbling about what an incredibly nice person the caller is and please please will you do something.

As in every situation, in every relationship between individuals or between groups, respect is a mutual affair.

Patrick, not his real name, who is a Samaritan caller, wanted his story to be used as an illustration of the benefits of close co-operation between volunteers and professionals. In his fifties and single, Patrick has suffered from severe depression for most of his life. He started training for the Catholic priesthood in his teens, but had to give up because of his health. He has had a number of jobs in the past and is now unemployed, but heavily involved in voluntary work in several hospitals. Patrick has had three overdoses, the most serious ten years ago. He has been in psychiatric hospital four times, generally for short periods, for the last five years he has suffered very severe periods of depression keeping in touch regularly with the Samaritans. He would state that he has not killed himself because of the Samaritans and his doctors.

Patrick has a very good GP and psychiatrist and is on a heavy dose of anti-depressants. He has always been happy for Samaritans to co-operate with his doctors and they have been pleased with this arrangement. This has had the effect of creating a certain amount of security around Patrick, who is without close friends or near relatives. The Samaritans became very much the substitute for absent relatives. His psychiatrist has often said 'as long as he can have and manage with Samaritan befriending he is better than in hospital, in spite of his very low periods'. Like other callers Patrick stays overnight at the Centre when he is very much at risk. He points out that he, like many people with a depressive illness, often feels very lonely in a crowd. He does not have much confidence and feeling for people outside, as they talk about him and cause embarrassment. The Samaritans can be quite firm and set limits, yet they can accept him in a depressive mood. Three years ago he nearly killed himself with weed killer and feels it was through talking to a Samaritan quite frankly about his suicidal feelings and plans that he was able to change his mind.

Patrick reads a lot and does some good work in the voluntary sector, but feels guilty about being unemployed. He feels the Samaritan befrienders have helped him to be less guilty and more open. Although his depression has not lifted completely in recent months, he feels it would be worse without the medication. When asked about his Christian faith, for he is still an active Church member, he says, 'when the depression is fully upon me I feel cut off from God and being a Christian does not make any difference'. When he is less depressed, he feels different and is able to be uplifted spiritually. He has not found many clergy, young or old, who have much understanding of depression. What seems to be helping Patrick to cope with his serious depression is the combination of Samaritan and psychiatric help. The combined nature of the support is important; if he had only Samaritan or only psychiatric help this would be insufficient. The Samaritan befriending itself needs to be individual, shared and well supervised.

ON-GOING PREVENTION AND EDUCATION

We are living in an age of cultural and scientific revolution. The process of these fundamental changes is bound to have a profound psychological effect on how people cope with their lives. Therefore, those of us concerned with suicide prevention have to address ourselves to the immediate needs and to education in the long-term improvement in the quality of social conditions.

In the first place, the co-operation between volunteers and professionals and the increasing awareness of society is of great significance. The emergence of the Samaritans, IASP and suicide prevention centres similar to those in Los Angeles are likely to reduce the number of suicides. It is extremely difficult to evaluate the effectiveness of these agencies with proven facts. If a drop in the suicide rate is attributed to the presence of a large number of Samaritans, is a rise in the suicide rate also due to the Samaritans? Similarly it is no easier for professionals to evaluate their effectiveness. As we know, surveys on suicides are constantly highlighting how the patients who killed themselves had recently seen their GP or psychiatrist.

In a similar study on the Samaritans, Barraclough noted how many of their callers made contact prior to actual suicide. It was

Stengel, who whilst very much a professional, was open to working with volunteers and the community, who reminded the Samaritans to give more attention to the quality of their service than to statistics. This applies also to the professionals; knowing how many people killed themselves within a week or so of seeing their doctors does not give us any precise information on the affectiveness of their treatment. It is most unwise to jump to quick conclusions about such a complex problem as suicidal behaviour. Many of those who turn to their GP for help in a crisis are not suffering from any treatable psychiatric condition.

'Social isolation cannot be treated by doctors alone or remedied by experts in Social science'[19]. Even when the patient is suffering from a depressive illness and is suicidal it is quite unrealistic to expect a doctor to allocate more time for the depressed at the expense of a patient with cancer or some other serious physical illness. The relatives and members of the community have to take responsibility for each other and not try to use 'experts' or the professionals as the scapegoats. Stengel also pointed out

Suicide prevention agencies can reach only a small minority in need of help. They are unlikely to reduce drastically the suicide rates. This can be expected only from suicide prophylaxis which begins at birth and even earlier. Its aim is to eliminate or reduce all factors which tend to increase the incidence of suicidal acts and to strengthen all those which tend to reduce it. The preservation of the family, active membership of a religious community or some other social group, the fight against alcoholism, good mental and physical health, good medical services, full employment, are all powerful factors against suicide. Divorce of the parents, physical and mental illness, alcohol abuse, widowhood make suicide more likely. Some desirable advances may indirectly lead to an increase in the suicide rate. The triumphs of scientific medicine have benefited mainly the younger age-groups and enabled more people to grow old and sick and thus more liable to suicide. Improvement of medical and social care for the old would make a noticeable impact on the suicide rate[20].

He goes on to remind us how aggressive tendencies play an important part in suicidal acts and how the progressive reduction of the working hours is likely to release an increasing amount of aggressive forces. Since Stengel wrote, the working time has not only greatly decreased with automation, but there has also been a massive increase in unemployment.

On the positive side, the Samaritans are now beginning to fulfill, to some appreciable extent, the need Stengel predicted in 1964. 'What is needed is a mobilization of the latent resources for helping and healing in our Society'[21]. Through the emergence and growth of the Samaritans and IASP with a number of other helping agencies, many more people and resources are available to those in a suicidal crisis.

It is obvious to all of us who are involved in the immediate care of the suicidal, how this is so closely related and dependent upon education and positive social change. 'We must match the scientific and technological revolution with as revolutionary change in social living'[22]. This is indeed strong language and recognizes that the floodgates will be opened by the force of our despair and aggression, releasing the waters of self-destruction. Suicide is a very personal act, but as we have seen, it is not unrelated to the environment. Improvement in the quality, as well as the value, of life, is an essential part of prevention. Political involvement needs to be concerned about the provision of an efficient health and welfare service, to include housing, and to give special attention to human values and the quality of relationships within society. This raises important questions about how society uses its resources, manages the economy and administers the legal system. Inevitably, there will be controls and laws which have to be obeyed. Sometimes these will be exercised in a moderately democratic manner, sometimes in a more totalitarian way. No society will be perfect and each one will have overall control, either directly or indirectly. In any society, much will depend upon how people behave towards each other. We can so easily become the victims of our own scientific and technological inventions. The classic example here is nuclear weapons, others include pollution of the environment and the total dependence on and enslavement to machines. If we are to have a moderately healthy mental and emotional life, we need to experience an identity, both as individuals and as groups. It is most important to realize that many of our disorders and situations leading to despair and suicide are brought about by the life-styles in society.

When very involved in suicide prevention, we may be tempted to believe that the provision of the right kind of helpers, volunteers and professionals will give the answers, but they too can be victims of the system.

Surely the pragmatist would be in favour of any political party which promotes a better quality of life, both mentally and emotionally. The actual cost to the economy of thousands of parasuicides, the considerable amount of absenteeism through depressed and despairing reactions among workers and the marked increase in violent behaviour, is of tremendous importance to any budget. It would seem that many aspects of our Western society need to be changed or improved if we are to have a better quality of living.

In our very limited approach here the nerve centre most related to suicide prevention is the improvement of our education. We are constantly reminded by all the schools of psychology and sociology of the importance of our formative years. It is still possible, however, for children to pass through some of the most highly respected schools both in the state and private sectors and later through the most esteemed universities with hardly any preparation for coping with the essentials of their emotional life. It would certainly be grossly unfair to suggest that teachers and university staff can be held ultimately responsible for the psychological state of their students. The parents or the Significant Others in the child's early environment will always set the pace. However, the teachers can provide several very beneficial contributions through being sensitive and understanding of how children and young people express their depression and giving them permission to verbalize their suicidal feelings and thoughts. There is a need to be alert to the extremes of high achievers and the so-called rebels. It would be ridiculous to imply that all high achievers are suicidal or disturbed, yet at the same time the sensitive tutor needs to discover how such students are feeling, relating and coping outside their intellectual performances. This could prevent the suicide of a very talented and potentially able young man or woman. The rebel or trouble-maker should not be dismissed as beyond help. It may be that a particular school or educational establishment is unable to help him or her for perfectly valid reasons, yet special care and help should be provided. The underlying reasons of the so-called 'rebellious behaviour' or 'inability to conform' should be explored with sensitivity and openness to listen to what the student is trying to communicate. There are many sensitive and wise teachers who are prepared to recognize that not all are able to conform to preconceived patterns of behaviour, because of severe emotional wounding in early childhood or the beginning of a mental illness or neurological disturbance. This reaction will result not infrequently in improving the quality of a life rather than promoting suicidal or anti-social behaviour. Teachers can also help parents to have a greater affinity with their children and adolescents. It is a fallacy to assume that parents have any speical in-built abilities to care for their children. Many mothers, who are most responsible, are quite unprepared for the constant need for care and the emotional demands of the under fives. Here the sphere of education is pre-school and outside the domain of teachers, yet what has happened in these early years will have a marked effect on behaviour in the primary school. It is surely in the interests of teachers and parents alike to work closely together.

There is a need for active education to be in process at the nursery or pre-school age. Charlotte Ross, Vice-President of IASP and responsible for promoting an education programme on suicide prevention for schools in America, stresses the need for co-operation between teachers and parents. She makes these very important comments when addressing the needs for educating both students and teachers.

Perhaps the most difficult task facing the suicide prevention education is that of finding ways to help those seeking to understand the dynamics of depression to do so in a way that is both cognitive and effective.

Wordsworth has described poetry as 'emotion recollected in tranquility', and these words seem as well as any to describe one approach to this task, which was to lead both students and staff through a recollection of a time when they had experienced a period of depression. This approach contains implicit suggestions that depressive episodes have endings as well as beginnings, and therefore serves to remind the participants that they have survived past depression and learned from them. Also, by demonstrating that many feelings and reactions to depression are similarly experienced, this approach can serve to reduce feelings of fear, shame or guilt, and help to replace judgemental attitudes with feelings of empathy[23].

REFERENCES

1. Diekstra, René, 'Renée or the complex psychodynamics of adolescent suicide', in *Suicide in Adolescence*, ed. Diekstra and Hawton. Martinus Nijhoff, 1987, p. 44
2. Murgatroyd, Stephen, *Counselling and Helping*, British Psychological Society and Methuen, 1985, p. 42
3. Ibid., p. 5
4. Dryden, Windy, *Therapists' Dilemmas*, Harper & Row, 1985, p. 135
5. Söelle, Dorothee, *Suffering*, Darton, Longman & Todd, 1973, pp. 177–8. Poem from the Russian liturgy, cited by Gottfried Benn, 'St Petersburg mitte der Jahshuderts', *Gesammelte Werke*, Vol. 3, Limes Verlag, 1960, p. 219
6. Kung, Hans, *On being a Christian*, Collins, 1978, p. 436

7. Matthew 7:1–5, *New English Bible*, 1961
8. Morgan, Edith, 'The development of the voluntary movement in the UK – questions for the future' in *Professionals and Volunteers – Partners or Rivals?*, ed. Gordon, Pat, Kings Fund, 1982, p. 12
9. Darvill, Giles, 'Crossing of Purposes' in *Professionals and Volunteers – Partners or Rivals?*, ed. Gordon, Pat, Kings Fund, 1982, Section 2, pp. 18–19
10. Darvill, Giles, 'Selecting volunteers and their activities' in *Professionals and Volunteers – Partners or Rivals?*, ed. Gordon, Pat, Kings Fund, 1982, Section 13, p. 3
11. Gordon, Pat, 'Self-help groups', in *Professionals and Volunteers – Partners or Rivals?*, ed. Gordon, Pat, Kings Fund, 1982, p. 12
12. Barraclough, Brian, *Social Science and Medicine*, Pergamon Journals, 1972, pp. 661–7
13. Fox, Richard, 'What are the arguments for and against the claim that the Samaritans are largely responsible for the falling suicide rate?' in *Answers to Suicide*, ed. the Samaritans, Constable, 1978, pp. 113–24
14. Day, George, 'Potential suicides' in *The Samaritans in the '80s*, ed. Varah, Chad, Constable, 1980, pp. 82–5
15. Pohlmeier, Herman, 'Suicide as a psychodynamic problem of depression' in *Crisis, International Journal of Suicide and Crisis Studies*, Vol. 1, No. 1, pp. 27–34
16. Spaul, George, 'Crisis' in *The Samaritans in the '80s*, ed. Varah, Chad, Constable, 1980, pp. 82–5
17. Ringel, Erwin, 'What kinds of patient profit most from psychiatry or psychotherapy, with befriending used only to break down resistance to these?' in *Answers to Suicide*, ed. the Samaritans, Constable, 1978, pp. 43–58
18. Eldrid, John in *Co-operation of Volunteers and Professionals*, ed. Soubrier, J. P. and Vedrinne, J., Pergamon Press, 1981, pp. 686–8
19. Stengel, Erwin, *Suicide and Attempted Suicide*, Penguin, 1964, p. 125
20. Ibid., p. 124
21. Ibid., p. 125
22. Ibid., p. 128
23. Ross, Charlotte, P., 'School and suicide: education for life and death' in *Suicide in Adolescence*, ed. Diekstra and Hawton, Martinus Nijhoff, 1987, pp. 164–5

# – 7 –

# Caring for those bereaved by suicide

When encountering those who have been bereaved by suicide we will be getting the full impact of the sting in the tail caused by suicide of a partner, near relative or caller. When sudden death comes to a loved one through an accident or unexpected illness, the loss is much greater to bear than when there has been some opportunity to prepare for death. Even when someone has been ill for some time and there was no hope of recovery, the actual death still comes as a shock. In the suicide of a loved one the emotional pain is made much more severe by their traumatic sudden departure. It is most important for the helper to realize that with sudden death the caller will be left with a feeling of inner numbness and sorrow too deep to express. They will feel caught up in some kind of nightmare experience, an awful mistake, they want to scream out that it is not true, yet the words cannot be uttered. Edwin Shneidman sums up the psychological effects of the emotional enormity of the event when he says,

> I believe that the person who commits suicide puts his psychological skeletons in the survivor's emotional closet – he sentences the survivors to deal with many negative feelings, and, more, to become obsessed with thoughts regarding their own actual or possible role in having precipitated the suicidal act or having failed to abort it. It can be a heavy load[1].

It is bad enough if sudden death is caused by a road accident or a coronary, but when the cause is suicide then the burdens to be borne by the bereaved are even greater. Although thousands of people kill themselves annually in Britain, there is much more guilt, stigma and hostility about suicide than about any other cause of death. The helper will have three immediate needs to consider.

1. The degree of shock and what immediate resources of support are available to the caller.

If the suicide has just taken place in the last day or so, then the bereaved should not be on their own. They should have, at the least, twice-daily contact with appropriate help. Where the crisis has developed out of delayed reaction, which is not uncommon after several months or even years, the helper will need to arrange on-the-spot support. The bereaved person may need some on-going professional help, but it would be most unwise not to meet the immediate needs in terms of emergency befriending. In both situations medical help may be needed to cope with the shock and in a delayed reaction with anxiety and deep-rooted depression.

2. The particular effects of the suicide on the bereaved. The majority will experience shock, but for many, there may also be feelings of guilt and responsibility for the death.

It is obvious these reactions need to be worked through gradually during on-going help, but the helper needs to give special attention to the severity of these reactions. It may be that the bereaved has been passing through some very traumatic emotional times just prior to the suicide. The result may be emotional and physical exhaustion.

3. The need to assess the possible suicidal feelings, thoughts and plans of the bereaved.

This is most essential, as it is quite likely the bereaved person may have been suffering from a depressive illness quite independent of the deceased. They may now feel, because of their sense of guilt and failure, that suicide is the answer for them. If they were part of some direct or indirect suicidal pact, the risk of their suicide at the first opportunity is very high. If this is the situation they are going to need all the care and arrangements required for those at serious risk.

A survivor can also exhibit manifest agitation. The stress of sudden death can trigger off a flight or fight response in a person and lead to a very agitated depression. A sudden increase in levels of adrenalin usually is associated with this agitation[2].

Those who are left often feel that in some way it was their fault, or think they should have done more. In many ways, it is not surprising that a suicide causes this reaction of failure, because someone has chosen to leave those around them. The person who makes this choice may be seen to be rejecting the immediate family and the society in which they lived. The bereaved have to face up to the terrible truth in suicide, that it was a deliberate act by their loved one. The suicide says, 'I need no more people to love outside of myself, therefore I reject you'.

This rejection will trigger off a whole catalogue of failures and memories of harsh exchanges with the person who died. Many of these are likely to be exaggerated out of proportion, yet the profound questions will keep arising. How could he do it? Why, why was I not more sensitive? He knew he was loved, surely he knew we cared? As one wife said, 'That we loved each other so much, that he had to suffer alone or so horribly, that there was nothing I could do. I will never get over it. It breaks my heart'[3].

This kind of experience puts the bereaved caller into a state of helplessness. The lover, partner, with whom they have lived and slept for over twenty years, just goes away. There is a feeling of bewilderment and frustration – could it be that they just did not know what was going on all this time? This understandable reaction is likely to cause anger and bitterness against the person who could be so destructive.

If all these awful feelings are not bad enough, for some there may be added that of shame. This may be picked up from those around them because, no matter how permissive society may have become, most people are not very accepting of those who kill themselves or of their relatives. It is probably because, if we are honest, most of us know any of us could be suicidal, yet we want to deny it.

Those near to the deceased will experience a fair amount of the stigma and fear associated with death by suicide. They may feel ashamed to say how he or she died. Added to all the other troubles, they will be exposed to police enquiries and legal formalities with an inquest in a coroner's court. The situation will be made more grotesque if there is public interest and the Press are involved. It could be that a survivor may be travelling on the Underground, or a bus, and the passenger next to him is reading about what happened, and he suddenly becomes associated with a public figure – his man or woman found dead.

In addition to all the grief for the loss of a loved one, the bereaved person experiences deep feelings of failure, guilt, rejection, helplessness, anger and shame. It will be difficult for him to describe what is happening to those around him. It is rather like being plunged into a nightmare; he was carrying on with the daily round, trying to cope, and then it happened. Someone said, gently and trying to be kind, that he was dead – he had killed himself. The nightmare begins and the fog of unreality comes down and there is extreme emotional pain which can border on the unbearable.

The helper's job, together with the bereaved person, is to try to find some positive directions out of the fog of unreality and to free him or her from the emotional nightmare maze. We cannot presume to imply that we know how the caller feels because of our close association with suicidal people. Their sufferings and experiences are the result of deep emotional relationships, often of very long standing, and are unique and sacred to those involved. Hopefully, together we may become more sensitive to, and aware of, some of their emotional reactions and also those of the person who died. It is most important to discover whether the feelings and interpretations of the caller were the same as those of the person they have lost and also how they may have differed.

When responding to those bereaved in this way it is necessary for the helpers to try to discover if the feelings and interpretations of the callers are a realistic conception of why the suicide happened. In spite of all the complexities of such an encounter, it is possible to clarify some of the situations, especially when the deceased is suffering from a recognized psychiatric illness. Let us consider the person who has clinical depression and kills himself because he considers he is unworthy to love, hopeless and emotionally dead, because of the effects of the illness. He kills himself because, for him, this is the only solution. He also would think this is best for his partner, as he is bad for everyone. Now the partner without sufficient knowledge and insight into some of the recognized causes of suicide directly related to depression, will interpret his suicide as rejection or failure.

It does help the bereaved to recognize that severe depression takes people over and isolates them in a cloud of blackness so they think by staying alive they will contaminate their partners. There is a real sense in which the one-time Significant Other loses their significance; they are no longer a reason for living, because the depressed person can no longer feel or relate to anyone. A similar situation is likely to occur with those suffering from schizophrenia where quite unexpectedly a person kills himself in front of a train or in some other violent manner. The partner or relatives are often quite unprepared for such an event, even those who knew the deceased was suffering from a mental illness. As helpers, we cannot assume the bereaved caller had been well briefed about suicide risks by those in charge of the case.

When you have helped the bereaved to recognize that the suicide was directly related to an illness and not a failure on their part, it will still be necessary to work through with them their feelings of loss, guilt and anger. When seeing callers who are related to a deceased who was in depression or schizophrenia, we should be sensitive to their own anxiety about whether they are heading the same way. It is well established that relatives or partners of suicides are in greater danger that the average person of getting into suicidal behaviour. The following response by Ann to the question about her father's suicide well illustrates the sense of confusion, shock and anger she felt, even when she recognized that he was mentally ill.

Ann, in her early thirties, has been a Samaritan volunteer for several years now and was pleased to offer some of her feelings and thoughts, as a possible source of help to others. Her father killed himself twelve years ago.

*How did you feel about the suicide of your father?*
As each of his suicide attempts were like deaths in themselves, and as his depression had been so painful over the years for everyone concerned, when he eventually died I had already done a lot of the grieving. His death, therefore, came not so much as a shock, but as an inevitable end to what had always seemed a serious and potentially fatal illness. He had 'phoned me the night before, asking if he could come over, feeling depressed. I had said no for the first time, knowing what the consequence might be. I also knew that if I said yes that time, there would be another time in the future when I couldn't – even more than I couldn't this time – and that would be the time that he would attempt suicide again. I had bailed him out so many times before, at vast emotional cost to myself and, try as I might, we never found the permanent solution, simply staving off what seemed more and more inevitable.

The next morning, when my mother 'phoned to say that she was on her way round, I knew what had happened. I told myself very firmly that I did not need to feel guilty – that I had genuinely tried as hard as I could over the years, and luckily I believed myself. None the less, a blanket of shock enveloped me. Because of the strong undercurrents of anger and confusion, built up over the years, none of which either my mother or I could talk about, we sat in my kitchen with her friend and my boyfriend of the moment, drinking tea and talking, as if we were discussing the price of margarine. We went through the events of the morning, when she had found him in their shop and had dialled 999, and of the previous night and his phone call to me. My mother said that, when people asked, we should be honest and unashamed of the way he died. After all, when someone dies of a physiological illness, there is not usually any reason to hide the cause of death, so why not be straight forward about his depression leading to his suicide? All well and good, but, although this was helpful to a degree, it conveniently buried our involvement with my father and his illness's manifestations and ramifications over the years. A casualty of all this is the relationship between my mother and myself. We still cannot look one another in the eye, and, though we mention Daddy from time to time, we will never bring the past, present and on-going emotional pains and entanglements out into the open.

For many years, I felt angry at my father and violently hated him. This started as his depression grew worse and intensified with each suicide attempt. When he asked for my help, I would give it though. Sometimes, knowing how much he wanted to be told 'I love you' and have a cuddle, I would steel myself to tell him and hold him, really wanting to shout and hit him. At other times, I ignored his requests, unable to show any love or affection to someone who seemed to be trying his utmost to destroy me. When it happened, it felt as if his actual suicide occurred in the centre of an emotional whirlpool in which the currents were most strongly felt on the way in and, later, on the way out. When he died, I felt, to some degree, set free. Little by little, I allowed the feelings to surface again, to sort through the confusion and to begin to see how and what I could learn from it all. It was a slow, painful process and I sometimes wondered whether a tendency toward suicide was hereditary. It was not until the first time I could allow myself to remember some happy times with him that I began to feel and know that I was OK.

Following these discussions with me Ann felt moved to express her feelings.

It was a couple of weeks ago I got to thinking about my father, and felt moved to write down what I was feeling in the form of a letter to him. This is what I wrote.

Dear Daddy,

I thought: I've done a lot of travelling. I wish you could have. Well, you could have done really, but you didn't. I know now why you didn't. It wasn't as important as the rut you inched then miled into, or the creeping then galloping lethargy, and the love you bore my mother, 'your mother' as you would habitually call her, or even the mistaken direction your love for us took. God knows I only wanted you to be happy. And far, on reflection, too. Well, I have done a lot of travelling. It has been for myself, primarily, but you are welcome to share it, if you can do so unobtrusively. I would like you to do that, but, as I say, only if you can manage it without making your presence known, if you want to.

I married a travelling man seven years ago. A reluctant traveller though, he is. With him I have been to India, the West Indies, Kenya, America and all around Europe. Without me he has covered much of the rest of the world and we have not finished yet. Even before I met him I had had a lot more adventures than most. I understand the great itching you always had but it was always up to you and no-one else to scratch it, and somehow you could never quite reach. Mind willing, spirit weak. I hope you are happy now, wherever you are. The more you travel, the sharper focused becomes the suffering of people it seems to me. Maybe you had enough to contend with at home. I want to thank you for showing me how to love a tree, and through that tree how to look for love in everything around. I am not so good at it now, but its memory is sustenance. Through that lesson I find that I can honestly forgive you for everything I dared to presume I could blame you for. It is easier to forgive the hazy memory of the dead. I really wish, though, that you could have stayed alive long enough to have met my husband, or do I mean long enough for him to have met you. These days, quite rightly, it is his interests I have at heart far more than yours, and, of course, my own. I did hate you and dislike you, but I do not remember feeling disrespect toward you.

I also loved you intermittently and, luckily, love survives over hate. I do not want you back and I do not know why I am writing this, but I would like to send out wishes for your happiness and, what you always wanted, in your own words – 'peace of mind' (or 'peace of spirit' now maybe), and love.
Ann

In Ann's situation, and that of many people who have had a similar experience, there is a serious build-up of inner stress when coping over a period of years. So that helpers need to recognize there is not only the shock and grief to bear, but also the effects of frequently long-drawn-out psychological struggles. Even when it is obvious the person who died was suffering from a mental illness and the caller is able to recognize this as the primary cause of death, he may still have a lot of ambivalent feelings, because he is caught up in a mixture of reactions which do not follow logical patterns.

When the caller is bereaved by someone who kills himself as a reaction to loss, broken relationship, criminal offence, etc. the burdens are even greater to bear. They can expect to have to experience prolonged periods of uncertainty. They will not, at least at first, be able to identify any of the underlying causes of the suicide. They are likely to feel trapped in a whirlpool of emotional frustrations, guilt and anger.

When writing about some of his impressions while helping the survivors of suicide, Allen O. Battle says,

They are so utterly perplexed by the event that they feel a strong need to understand, not only suicide, but also how the mind functions and how to unlock the mind's secret recesses. They clearly feel trapped by the event, their memories and their lack of comprehension. They seem to be certain that their surcease of sufferings can be achieved by the following dictum – 'Know the truth and the truth shall make you free'[4].

As we look at some of the emotions and problems that callers are likely to encounter, we will begin to see that their loss from suicide will cause them many difficulties in coping with their grief.

Richard McGee, director of a large suicide prevention centre in Florida, believes that '. . . suicide is the most difficult bereavement crisis for any family to face and resolve in an effective manner'[5].

John Hinton, a British professor of psychiatry, who has made a special study of the rational and irrational emotions associated with death, says about the effects of suicide,

> the unexpected death from suicide brings great distress to the bereaved. Besides its tragic, shocking quality, it leaves others with a greater sense of failure than that which follows a natural death[6].

It is just because it is so hard to bear this kind of loss that they will need to share their pain with others. It is because of this need to relate to each other and to share that we experience such anguish when a loved one dies. It seems particularly important to remind ourselves that if you have not personally experienced bereavement by suicide, it is essential to explore their painful reactions. It is agreed by those experienced in bereavement counselling that the loss by suicide is the worst kind of bereavement anyone can experience.

As helpers, it will be enlightening for us to consider what may be described, as the classical reactions to loss, such as shock, sadness, anger, guilt, anxiety and pining. We will also need to add the extra burdens caused by loss from suicide.

SHOCK

The first experience of the bereaved will be one of shock and sadness which will be intense when the cause is suicide. The degree of emotional and physical effects will vary according to the depth of the relationship with the one who has died, and the personality of the one who is bereaved. For the majority of those who were very closely involved with the deceased, the trauma of loss will be very great. People tend to underestimate the severity of their feelings of profound sadness, isolation and, sometimes panic. This is so especially if there was a great degree of dependence on the dead person. Even when the death was not unexpected, and came after a long illness, the actual time of departure will cause emotional shock. Apart from the pains of sadness and loneliness, there will be some marked physical effects.

People seen for grief counselling often experience the following sensations – these are the most commonly reported,

Hollowness in the stomach.
Tightness in the chest.
Constriction in the throat.
Oversensitivity to noise.
Feeling of depersonalization – 'I walk down the street and nothing seems real including myself'.
Breathlessness, feeling short of breath.
Weakness in the muscles.
Lack of energy.
Dry mouth.[7]

There may also be disturbances in eating and drinking habits such as loss of interest in food and an increase in the intake of alcohol. Many will complain of sleeplessness and restlessness. All these reactions are quite normal and are the human response to loss. They are not going to disappear within a short period. We have to give ourselves permission to grieve, to experience the effects of a period of mourning. It may seem strange to suggest that we need to give ourselves this permission, but there are many bereaved people especially men who have problems in appreciating that it is normal to express their emotions. This is partly due to the belief that it is a sign of weakness to show your feelings.

SADNESS

Many bereaved people get a lot of sympathetic support in the first days or weeks. Then those around them begin to withdraw, sometimes of necessity; the caring relative or friend who gave close support during the funeral and stayed for a while, has to return to their own family and work commitments. The bereaved person then senses the expectation that they should now begin to 'get themselves together' on their own. Others who have had little or no demonstration of affection and feelings in their family background may feel ashamed or embarrassed to show grief, even if the relationship was the most significant in their life. Friends and neighbours do not always show a lot of patience. They too may be embarrassed by tears and mistakenly think it is best to forget as, 'it is all over now'. In fact, the mourning process is just beginning. We may ask, how long is mourning going to last? To quote from J. Bowlby and C. M. Parkes,

> Asking when mourning is finished is a little like asking 'how high up?' There is no ready answer. Mourning finishes when a person completes the final mourning phase of restitution. In my view mourning is finished when the tasks of mourning are accomplished. It is impossible to set a definitive date for this, yet within bereavement literature, there are all sorts of attempts to set dates – four months, one year, two years, never. In the loss of a close relationship I would be suspicious of any full resolution that takes place under a year and, for many, two years is not too long[8].

Many callers will need assistance to help them to give themselves permission to mourn. It is not easy but it is essential if they are to be true to themselves and their loved ones both departed and living. Failure to allow yourself to grieve can result in quite serious psychological disturbance later on. Grief is not an illness, but a deep human expression of love and affection for the departed and for yourself as the griever. The Christian injunction by Jesus to love your neighbour as yourself implies a responsibility to love, and to care for yourself.

After a person has died, those who knew and loved him continue to suffer. Even if death has been anticipated for a long time, when it finally comes there is a resurgence of grief. The immediate reactions of the bereaved will not be limited to those of straightforward sorrow. The death will arouse a great turmoil of emotions and give rise to wide varieties in behaviour in different people[9].

This 'great turmoil of emotions' needs to be recognized and worked through – and the additional inner emotional tearing apart caused by suicide will need very special sensitivity. In this initial period for the caller just to be held and allowed to weep can be most healing.

ANGER

When some of the shock has subsided and the sadness seems to be less acute yet, in a way, worse as it grows into dispiritment, feelings of anger begin. The dispiritment and anger are closely related. It is generally agreed that behind most depression there is unexpressed anger. For the bereaved, anger will be perhaps a rather surprising reaction. It is not easy to accept that you are angry because your wife, husband, gay partner has died. If he or she had not drunk so much, had taken the anti-depressants, worked less, gone to the doctor sooner – there is an unbearable feeling of frustration. 'Why did I not act differently?'

It is not unusual for anger to be directed against doctors, the hospital and, not least, against God. We all look for, and at times need, a scapegoat. This is made much more difficult by the suicide of a loved one, as it frequently sets off intense reactions of anger. This adds an extra dimension to the depths of anger felt by the bereaved, because the deceased caused his own death. It is so often said 'How could he do this to me!' In this situation, blame may be centred on the deceased, at least for a while. The bereaved may later turn it onto themselves. As with all bereaved people when a loved one has gone, the separation may trigger off deep feelings of anger and resentment.

As has been said before and bears repeating, we have anger and confusion within the cloud of dispiritment and can so easily get lost in the maze of emotional conflicts. The bereaved need to realize that the anger is really against the person who has died. They are angry with them for dying because they loved them, their anger can be seen as a mark of their affection. Insight into this is needed if they are to resolve the anger. It will be more difficult if there was a very ambivalent relationship with the deceased, the anger may then be combined with guilt feelings. Tensions will be reduced if they can talk about some of the love-hate reactions between them and their partner. Once they can recognize that they did have angry feelings towards him or her, and sometimes they were justified and that both of them could be unreasonable, they will begin to see that, far from damaging their memories, they are moving into a more reconciled and loving memory.

GUILT

Shame, guilt and a feeling of failing your loved one are very common reactions. Within the setting of dispiritment one loses confidence and it is easy to question the validity of your past actions. J. Hinton says,

> The bereaved frequently blame themselves for not having done enough for the deceased, even if they have, in fact, performed wonders of care during the past illness. Although it may be clear they have made the correct choices when faced with the different decisions involved in the care of the dying person, after death they often question the standard of their conduct. Should they have got the patient into hospital earlier or insisted upon some different plan of treatment? Should they have taken the dying person from hospital to end his days at home even though it was patently clear that he could have been looked after adequately only in hospital? . . . It is not uncommon for the bereaved even to accuse themselves of having contributed towards the death by their neglect or the demands they had made on the deceased[10].

Many bereaved who are closely involved with a loved one's illness find it very hard to get to grips with a rational reaction. The emotional hurt is often so great and the belief that you have let him or her down can be very strong. When you are involved in sudden death caused by suicide the emotional stinging is going to be even more severe. It may be helpful to remind the caller that in their most agonizing hours of isolation they are still part of that great family of the bereaved, who experience similar responses of guilt, anger and shame. These feelings however will be fierce and testing when related to the trauma caused by suicide.

After counselling people in despair over many years, I feel that we have to guard against suggesting that those who have experienced the acute despair of the suicide of a Significant Other are in a different group to those in the everyday drama of bereavement. Their sense of loss and guilt will be paramount, but they are not freaks, just deeply-hurt human beings. We have seen that even uncomplicated situations can produce serious problems of shame and guilt, so they are inevitable when there is a suicidal death; guilt is part of the reaction to loss.

ANXIETY

Another common reaction of the bereaved is anxiety, the level of which will vary according to the dependency of the relationship and the personality of the bereaved. C. M. Parkes says,

> The most characteristic feature of grief is not prolonged depression but acute and episodic 'pangs'. A pang of grief is an episode of severe anxiety and psychological pain. At such a time the lost person is strongly missed and the survivor sobs and cries aloud for him[11].

When there has been a very close emotional relationship, a special togetherness, the feelings of deep hurt and loss will be felt as anxiety. There has been a cutting off of the close daily ties

and a plunging into separation. For some people the togetherness, included not only emotional needs but the sharing of
practical and material things. This applies not only to the
traditional concept of the married partners' dependence on each
other but is found in any relationship and in business and
professional partnerships.

> People left behind after a death often feel very anxious and
> fearful. Much of the anxiety stems from feelings of helpless-
> ness, feeling that they cannot get along by themselves or
> survive alone. This is a regressive experience which usually
> eases with time and the realisation that, even though it is
> difficult, they can manage[12].

Another cause for anxiety is that the death of a loved one or
friend is a reminder of the inevitability of your own death. Your
bereavement greatly heightens your awareness of your own
mortality. This can cause quite a shock. In spite of extensive
media coverage of accidents, terrorism, crimes of violence and
the threat of a nuclear holocaust, death is not openly talked
about. When bereaved by suicide the caller may also become
suicidal to justly punish themselves for the partner's death. On
the other hand, the caller may have been in a serious depression
before the partner's suicide, therefore the risk of another
suicide is very likely.

PINING

Lastly, pining or yearning for the deceased person is very
common. There is a biological need to search for a lost partner
in many of the lower species. Young children will also seek out
the parent or parent substitute if they are missing. This is
because the child is totally dependent on the person who cares
for him and becomes very attached to the parent-figure. This
need for an attachment figure continues in adult life. The more
stable a person's psychological background the more they will
recognize the benefits of emotional well-being created by a

healthy and normal relationship. When it is taken away, there will be a pining for the loved one. The constant thinking about the dead person and recalling detailed memories of him or her, is very natural. It is likely to be made harder by suicide, as there may have been many emotional tensions before and now there is rejection.

> Preoccupation with thoughts of the lost person and with events leading up to the loss is a common feature of bereaved people. 'I never stop missing him', said one widow. The tendency to return again and again to thoughts of the lost person was still present in most of the London widows a year after bereavement[13].

Many people find a lot of comfort in recalling the loving and happy times they experienced together. Others may be disturbed by memories of bad and difficult periods and will become morbid, possibly feeling the loss as a punishment. They may feel there is a lot of unfinished business, things they would have liked to have said and explained but now it is too late. They have a strong urge to find the lost person, although rationally they know this is not possible, the need to join them may take hold. If they are depressed or there was some traumatic emotional experience previously associated with the departed, there is a risk they too may become suicidal in the hope of being reunited with their loved one.

Now we need to explore more deeply the special on-going problems for the person bereaved by suicide, who is likely to have more pains than anyone else. There will be some barriers and difficulties which it will be necessary for the helper to work through with the bereaved.

A very helpful study has been carried out in the USA by Dr Allen O. Battle,

> One of the most valuable outcomes of the experience has been the opportunity it provides to observe indirectly the psychodynamics of people who commit suicide as those dynamics reflect themselves in the survivors[14].

He goes on to say,

As I listened to the survivors of suicide, it was possible to delineate conclusions which the survivors had reached, often at an unconscious level, about their relationships with each other. These implicit recognitions were accompanied by the most bitter and heart rending emotions.

Hopefully, the pain which gave the following insights birth will be justified by the assistance which the insights may be to professionals who work with other survivors and suicidal people themselves. The insights are not listed in any particular order of importance or date of emergence.

1. The successful suicidal person puts his loved ones in the same predicament as the one from which he has escaped – helplessness.
2. When the suicide says, 'I can't handle the problem', he is also saying to his loved ones, 'You can't handle the problem either'.
3. Insofar as suicide is an attempt at mastery and control, however ineffectual or ill-advised it may be objectively, the suicide is saying, 'My death is preferable to my trying to work out my problems with you or through you; therefore, you and I are terribly distant'.
4. The suicide is saying by his act that the hated situation or person is more important to him than his loved ones or the affection and dependency that he had upon them.
5. The suicide says, 'I need no more people to love outside of myself; therefore, I reject you'.
6. The suicide says, 'I, by my act, save you, my beloved from hurt'.
7. The survivor feels, 'I was passive (certainly *too* passive) while my beloved faced defeat and finally was beaten'.
8. Surviving parents and others who knew the victim as a child have a kind of proof positive that the child rejected any identification that he or she may have had with them or that their child was not close to them in the first place.

Somehow these last two implications seem to be the most poignant factors with which the survivors must struggle, although all of them are gall to swallow.

None of the survivors of suicide is able to state in words any profound insights as such, yet they know in their inmost hearts these eight unstated understandings. The survivors have revealed them time and again in statements they made without fully recognising what they have said. The survivors, in their confusion and consternation, do not 'know' what they know, but their inability to verbalize certainly does not negate the fact of their knowledge. It is in fact because of the implications of the suicide's death that survivors of suicide face an utterly unique problem in dealing with the death of their loved one.

In working with the survivors of suicide, we have a kind of Alice-through-the-looking-glass phenomenon vis a vis suicide. The survivors' situation is a kind of mirror image of the suicide's predicament. Just as the suicide needs to confront his problems head-on without escape from reality so the survivor must be helped to face the fact that self-destruction can appear very alluring indeed to a person in crisis who does not have the capacity to cope. The survivors must understand that the suicidal 'solution' is not the survivor's fault.

If we look at the survivors only demographically, they are like a random sample taken from any street, and it is that fact which makes it so easy to identify with them. They are 'Everyman'. I commend them to colleagues who have not worked with people in this type of situation before and assure you that in addition to helping some of them, you will also learn more about victims of suicide, their loved ones, and yourself than you imagined possible.

The implication, in point number seven, that many survivors felt they had been too passive in relation to helping their loved ones is a quite common experience among those helping the bereaved through suicide. This creates another barrier as the bereaved feel they are not entitled to any help. Why should their sufferings be relieved when the loved one suffered so much and had to die because of it? Although this is a common reaction it is unrealistic and it will not help the bereaved to keep the special relationship they had, as it is likely to increase bitterness. If the survivor can persevere and get some insight into what has been happening, they are not only helping themselves but also showing a deep respect for their loved one who has died. When we experience deep personal relationships, especially where there are strong sexual attractions and involvement, surely we are caught up in a 'passionate encounter'. The media and advertising want us to believe that passionate relationships are all about sexual pleasure, having a good time and not being lonely. Hopefully a lot of the time the passionate encounters will give us a lot of sexual satisfaction and happiness. However it is very immature and unrealistic to imagine this is the whole story. Those in deep relationships are likely to experience a lot of loving and not infrequently, emotional conflicts. Allen O. Battle's findings are very much concerned with emotions, and passionate reactions, of love, anger and rejection. This is what makes it so hard to grasp what is happening and why many survivors are left in a state of confusion and dispiritment.

Now let us look at some of the reflections of Barbara, herself a Cruse Counsellor and former Director of Reading Samaritans. Barbara's views are very significant as she is pioneering some of the survivor group work in Great Britain.

SURVIVOR GROUPS

*As a pioneer for running a group for the survivors of suicide in the UK, would you say how you got it going?*
Working as a Samaritan volunteer, I suddenly began to come across a number of people who had been bereaved by suicide, and they all seemed to want one thing – to talk with others who had experienced the same kind of loss. At a Cruse conference I led a group concerned with this topic, and became aware of the extra pain and difficulties faced by those who have lost someone

close by suicide. I made enquiries and could find no support group in existence, so finally decided I would have to do something. I spoke to my Samaritan director, then to the chairman of our local Cruse branch, because it seemed sensible to see if they had any plans in that direction. She put me on to a very experienced Cruse counsellor whom I already knew slightly, and the two of us talked things through. We both had training and experience in working with groups as well as in counselling, and we decided to further underpin the venture by asking a local GP to act as our consultant/supervisor. Having agreed with both Samaritans and Cruse that we were not an official part of either organization, but that we had the support of both, we planned our structure. We would meet once a fortnight, in the evening for one and a half hours (in a smallish comfortable office with easy chairs). The group would be an open one, that is, open over an indefinite period to anyone who had been bereaved by suicide and expressed a wish to join, but subject to a preliminary interview with one of the leaders, and also subject to a meeting's notice to any existing group members. In the event during the first year several potential members backed off after interview, and a few after one group meeting. We began with five members, all of whom were referred by personal contact. One member left, and we remained at four for some months. Gradually others heard of us, mainly through Cruse and Samaritans, though we did try to make the group's existence known to local GPs and churches. It took over two years between first realizing the need and the first meeting. Now, eighteen months later, we are looking at the possible need to split the group or start a second one because of pressure of numbers, as we feel eight should be the maximum (and six is really preferable). The leaders are over and above this number, and have not themselves experienced this particular kind of bereavement. We feel that this is important in giving some stability to what is often a very emotion-loaded group. The members share experiences and feelings from the inside and I think get a further support from the leaders being, in one sense, on the outside.

*In what special ways have you discovered survivor groups help?*
The sharing of similar experiences and feelings – different stories, but the same desolation and despair, guilt and anger – all this seems greatly valued. There is enormous relief in finding that feelings previously thought to be wrong and selfish are shared by others. As time goes on, the world outside no longer gives openings for grief to be expressed (if, indeed, it ever did) and survivors have frequently said that the group is the only place where they can still talk about the suicide and go on working through their feelings, perhaps into the second and third or more years after the death.

*Do you feel all survivors need some individual help?*
I would not like to make such a definite judgement, but certainly there may come a time, either before or at the same time as belonging to a group, when any survivor may feel the need of individual help. If this happens, it is something to be encouraged rather than something to be ashamed of.

*When do you think survivors are most likely to ask for help?*
We have not been going long enough to know! But I think that individual help is likely to be needed very early on – it may not be asked for, but could be gently offered by anyone in touch with the survivor suggesting some likely source of help. I think a group is probably of most help a few months on, when some of the real problems and worries have already been experienced.

*What are some of the most common worries you have identified among survivors?*
All the usual worries experienced after a bereavement are intensified, it seems. Shock, disbelief, guilt, anger, nobody liking to talk about it – all these occur after any death, but are understandably greater after a suicide. In addition, feelings of rejection and helplessness can be strong, and there is often an intense feeling of isolation – society's stigmatisation is felt, causing both shame and intense anger. On a practical level, the inquest and local press reports often cause much anxiety and distress.

Those who have lost a spouse have a particular anxiety about their children's position. If they are young, when and how should they be told of the suicide, and will they be at risk of suicide themselves as they get older, are questions often raised.

Now, I would like to answer some questions from my own personal experience in counselling a number of survivors.

*Do you feel this is a special kind of bereavement to bear?*
Yes, I think death by suicide is one of the hardest losses to bear. There are two particular reasons for this.

1. As we have seen, the partner or parent feels very rejected. This is understandable as the suicide, for whatever reason, is turning his or her back on everyone, whether near or distant.

2. I think because of these very rejecting and frequently aggressive attitudes, society regards suicide with anger and suspicion. The bereaved have to bear a certain amount of the stigma, as if they were in some way in collusion with this opting out from society. These two factors are not present in other bereavements.

*Do you think the bereaved have extra problems about confidentiality?*
Yes, there are several areas where helpers will find they may have special problems.

1. The bereaved may feel very embarrassed to talk about their very personal life and feel it could be a betrayal of the person they loved. This is especially so if what they disclose seems to be critical or damning of the deceased. They need to be assured to talking within a seal of confidentiality provided by a counselling or Samaritan context. In this very real personal encounter, the helper with the bereaved is trying to discover a way forward so that they, with their loved one (who may have been husband, wife, partner, son or daughter) may gather up what is still special, unique and positive out of the catastrophic aftermath of suicide. Even when this is fully discovered, the helper may have to give a lot more reassurance about keeping confidentiality about some of the complexities of their situation.

2. Many will be very anxious about the stigma attached to suicide. It is not unusual for parents not to tell their children, because they feel it could injure their future in some way.

> The child who survives a suicide of a parent may have special difficulties. There is the shame and stigma of the death and the mystery that often surrounds it . . . The child senses mystery and guilt, yet does not know the reason . . . A careful study of responses in children carried out by Shepherd and Barraclough (1976) found that 50% of parents in their study failed to tell their children anything about the suicide and the remainder gave varying amounts of information, despite their good intentions. The mean age of the children told of the suicides was 10, and of those told something about the death was 8, and of those told nothing was 4[15].

*Do you think parents and others should be open with children about suicide?*
The immediate answer is yes without a doubt. It is very confusing for children to be left in doubt and this may create a lot of anxiety and guilt. Quite often before a suicide there are a lot of rows, emotional disturbances and the child may sometimes have been told he is the cause of the trouble, therefore when one of the parents kills himself, he may feel it is his fault. Children are much more aware and sensitive to atmosphere than many adults realize. It is not going to help their satisfactory psychological development to try and protect them by withholding information.

*Is it possible to live with the feeling you have failed your partner, son or daughter?*
As helpers, this is the question with which we will constantly have to grapple when we are with the bereaved and there are no answers. Many will need individual counselling over a period of weeks. Much depends upon whether their bereavement is within the last few weeks, or months or even years. I think a lot

depends upon whether the bereaved person wants or has a need to start some on-going counselling in the early stages. Some certainly will need support, but may not feel motivated to go down to exploring the emotional depths until some time later. There will also be some bereaved callers who have been blocking out most of their feelings for several years and something has triggered off a crisis.

I am convinced the helper needs to accept each caller as unique, with their special problems and needs. At the same time there are some common emotional reactions and problems we all may experience from time to time. When people ask for help it is often related to some kind of crisis which may result in their beginning to discover ways out of the nightmarish situation created by anger, rejection and guilt. Then the violence done to their togetherness by suicide decreases as they are able to embrace the conflicts and rediscover what was very positive in their togetherness.

No human being is perfect and none of us can expect to have a perfect togetherness. We can try to liberate ourselves from anger, bitterness and guilt so that we can keep loving in spite of our failures and human weaknesses. As we become more able to recognize what Jung called 'the darker side' of ourselves, and our loved ones, we will begin to discover greater understanding and new depths of positive feelings and be less disillusioned about what has happened. There is a need somehow to get beyond reacting in terms of failure or success. We need to forgive those who died and ourselves.

*Do you think it is possible for the bereaved to cope positively with some of the awful skeletons left in their emotional closet?*
Yes, I think for a number of people it will be possible. When two people are deeply attached to each other there will be considerable emotional involvement which will not suddenly end with the suicide of a partner. If the survivor wants to work through some of these emotional skeletons they have to tackle some of their inner feelings. This is not easy, as all of us from time to time resist discovering too much. There is an urgent

need to accept that emotional conflicts, negative and positive reactions are common to all human relationships. The bereaved are naturally very upset because of the traumatic experience of sudden death by suicide, and will tend to question all aspects of their relationship far too critically. Before the suicide took place, it is likely that the deceased had serious psychological, and perhaps environmental and social, problems. These difficulties may have been mainly for the person who has died or experienced in their relationship with others. We help the bereaved person to face the fact that emotional conflicts are part of deep personal relationships. He or she may respond by saying – 'but not all relationships end in suicide!' Of course, this is true, but at the same time many people do kill themselves for reasons not caused in any way by those close to them.

It is not easy always to be aware of the deeper feelings of a partner and it is frequently common for us not to understand what is really happening. This is not because either or both parties are being selfish or indifferent – the reasons are generally much more subtle. Two people come together for all kinds of different causes and motives, some they are aware of and others are hidden. Your attachment to another person will affect your behaviour in many ways. There will be feelings of affection, love, sexual attraction, sharing and dependency – all these will help to cement the bonds of togetherness. In addition, there are likely to be some negative and, sometimes, destructive attitudes. There may well be a mixture of masochistic and sadistic behaviour in sexual relations. These reactions can be harmful or disruptive when they are used to exploit or harm a partner.

Many people, married or living together, are very much more dependent upon each other than either may realize or wish to accept. It is not unusual for couples to get into a psychological collusion which may promote healthy positive emotional growth or the union may be used to feed on their mutual negative reactions. Some may not want to acknowledge that anything like this is possible or that it should be dismissed as psychological claptrap, therefore the helper will need to take on the role of 'the reality tester'.

To quote from some of Shneidman's tentative conclusions in his work with survivors of suicide.

> Remarkably little resistance is met from survivor-victims; most are willing to talk to a professional person, especially one who has no axe to grind and no pitch to make. The role of negative emotions toward the deceased – irritation, anger, envy, guilt – needs to be explored, but not at the very beginning. The professional plays the important role of reality tester. He is not so much the echo of conscience as the quiet voice of reason[16].

As helpers we need to enable the bereaved to discover what has been deposited in their 'emotional closet' and to talk freely about how they feel responsible for their partner's or child's suicide. Each encounter is going to be different, yet here we are considering some of the basic emotional reactions which we can expect to find in most human relationships. However, there is one fundamental difference, that is the introduction of suicidal behaviour which tends to make the bereaved acutely vulnerable to self-criticism. They need to be helped to take a realistic look at their relationship with the deceased. Many will want to see this in idealized terms. They need to experience a deeper awareness of how the quality of loving and respect is nourished by realistically recognizing our emotional conflicts and weaknesses; therefore, the best way we can express our love, respect, tribute and even criticism of a loved one is to acknowledge objectively their positive and negative reactions. Human togetherness is about loving, friendship, mutual attractions, anger, hate, guilt, ambivalence, dependence and unspoken needs. When a person does the right thing or the wrong thing, indulges in wild behaviour, loses patience, becomes over-anxious and withdraws, this is surely an expression of profound togetherness with the loved one. That is why even suicide can be an expression of love and togetherness.

We may find it difficult to understand how this apparently ultimate act of rejection can be linked in any way with togetherness. Here we are not only thinking of those who have killed themselves in the grip of the black despair of clinical depression; we are thinking of those who were prepared to get deeply involved with, and share, the emotional conflicts of their partner. Because of this readiness to express their togetherness in this way, much of their partner's negative and destructive reactions will be projected on to them as a part of their psychological collusion. This means that, before the partner's suicide, they were likely to have been carrying a lot of responsibility for his or her well-being. This will be very true if they were the more secure personality and, because of sensitivity, had become accustomed to try to absorb his or her unresolved emotional conflicts. They were in partnership with someone who was very much a suicide risk. They may readily recognize all this and see it as evidence of their failure – they should have loved more, been stronger or more sensitive. As in the initial reaction to shock, this interpretation could be valid but it is not when viewed from the depths of their togetherness. Even in the worst emotional struggles, there must be room for some individual freedom since one cannot express love in terms of control and domination. It is possible that the partner lived so long just because they did not try to dominate. It is not possible, or morally right, for anyone to have complete control of another person therefore, in the last resort, you cannot be responsible for a suicide.

It is important to point out that there is a danger that those who have been over-exposed emotionally to the traumas resulting from suicidal behaviour, might become obsessed with guilt. Those who have had a close relationship, an emotional togetherness, will be more vulnerable. They will need to avoid their awareness of guilt becoming out of proportion, to be realistic, and not to distort the truth.

*Do you not think that all this 'reality testing' will cause the bereaved a lot more emotional pain?*
Yes, I think it will cause a lot of pain and it is important for the helper to be very sensitive to how the bereaved is coping. I am assuming that in these encounters the helper is an experienced

volunteer or professional in bereavement work. It will be good if the bereaved also belongs to a support group or is being befriended outside. There are three things we have to consider.

1. If the bereaved is becoming more upset and dispirited then some medical care will be needed in addition to your help.

2. There is a need for the helper to be realistic; many survivors of suicide are very much in need of urgent help and there is no reason to believe they will be harmed by being helped slowly and gently to face up to reality. It should be remembered that the closet in which the bad feelings are stored is an emotional one and so the destructive feelings are likely to have harmful effects anyway. I have seen people who were survivors of a suicide of several years past, who, at the time, did not seek help. Suddenly a crisis developed and apparently without warning they became very anxious, depressed and confused about the past. For them the reality testing through counselling sessions causes a kind of liberation and they begin to experience a new attitude to the deceased.

3. We have to try and help the bereaved to recognize that they are responsible for embracing a togetherness which was precarious and full of emotional traumas. They know people come together for many known and unknown feelings and reasons. The bereaved feel the need to judge the hallmark of their togetherness and surely it is the emotional quality of their relationship which is so important. Those who carry the awful effects of a suicide should not allow this to undervalue the special quality of their togetherness, in spite of the suffering. If they doubt this, they should recall how ambivalence and inconclusiveness are part of most relationships. In psychodynamic terminology, they are embracing the emotions, the positive and negative reactions, the known and the unknown – they are sailing on the uncharted waters which is surely the lot of all lovers.

Beverley Raphael reminds us,

Each person must make his way through life encompassing two important facts. If he loves, there will be the great rewards of human intimacy, in its broadest sense; and yet when he does so, he becomes vulnerable to the exquisite agony of loss. And one day – he knows not when or how – he will die[17].

*How do helpers cope with the actual suicides of callers and patients?* All of us who have had the privilege of trying to care for suicidal people, and have had a number of our callers kill themselves, will feel great sympathy for the bereaved. At times, we too will have experienced deep feelings of failure, guilt, anger and helplessness. For anyone counselling, supporting and treating a suicidal person for some time, professionally or as a Samaritan, the emotional involvement will not be as deep as that of a lover or relative, but for many it will be very close.

During the last twenty-nine years, I have been involved with twenty-four actual suicides, ten of these directly so, and countless parasuicides. Out of the ten actual suicides, I could still feel upset and very dispirited about four of them, two of which occurred some years ago. I mention this because it does seem that the effects of the losses of caller or patient by suicide can be very intense and last for a long time. It is important to realize that coping with death and bereavement situations is emotionally draining for all the helpers. When there is a suicide this will make the helpers feel a failure in much the same way as the relatives or partners felt in our earlier discussions. In some ways, the feelings of failure and responsibility may be greater for the helpers, as they are there to prevent suicide and were asked to help or give treatment. Helpers of the suicidal are likely to get into a close relationship. Whether befriending or giving on-going counselling, much of their time with the helper is spent talking of intimate and distressing matters. A number of general practitioners, contrary to what sometimes is suggested, give a great deal of extra time to their suicidal patients. Many doctors also spend quite a lot of time outside surgery hours talking on the telephone. Psychiatrists have to face the effects of a considerable number of suicides and live with the constant risk. Many therapists would say that an essential part of helping is empathizing with the caller, so emotional ties and togetherness need to develop.

One of the very significant impressions I have is that ninety per cent of those suicides personally known to me made little or no demands on the helpers. They were always most grateful for any support and attention they received. As a matter of interest, ten out of the twenty-four were suffering from serious depression. Helpers then, are likely to become very fond of them and have a lot of compassion for them. This does not mean that other people involved with them will share this degree of empathy. I feel that, because we have a therapeutic relationship, there is a certain uniqueness about our togetherness, therefore we too will feel especially rejected and hurt when they kill themselves. I think we need to acknowledge that our special relationship does not mean we had control over them. As volunteers or doctors we must not act as though we were God or the ultimate controller of human life. We need always to discuss the loss with colleagues and be allowed to have the opportunity to express our worries about how we coped with the person who died.

There are also the heightened attachment and closeness that crises of loss and disaster involved. There are also, in some instances, very strong identifications with those for whom the caring person cares. To retain his compassion, the caring person in the field may need considerable support from others, both his family and his colleagues. He needs, for instance, to share the burden of cases in supervisory sessions. He needs back-up and relief for the cases he finds hard to bear. He needs to take clean breaks from such work, which are officially sanctioned, and indeed required, by his system of work. He needs, in short, care and consolation from others to bear the enormity of much of the pain and loss and death he helps others encompass. If this is not available for him, he may develop defensive pathology in the form of dehumanisation, distancing of interpersonal relationships or isolation of effect, so that cold mechanical relating and care is all he can give (Raphael 1981)[18].

All of us involved in suicidal crisis work have to bear emotional pains and feelings of failure, loss or guilt as part of the costs of providing aid for people who are feeling so desperate. Yet out of these struggles seems to emerge the uniqueness of these passionate relationships. We have to learn to accept that each person has a need sometimes to express their dignity even in suicide.

## REFERENCES

1. Quoted by Cain, A. C., in Worden, William J., *Grief Counselling and Grief Therapy*, Tavistock, 1983, p. 79
2. Ibid., p. 85
3. Battle, Allen O., 'Group therapy for survivors of suicide' in *Crisis, International Journal of Suicide and Crisis Studies*, Vol. 5, No. 1, p. 153
4. Ibid., p. 52
5. Worden, William J., *Grief Counselling and Grief Therapy*, Tavistock, 1983, pp. 79–80
6. Hinton, J., *Dying*, Pelican, 1967, p. 167
7. Worden, William J., *Grief Counselling and Grief Therapy*, Tavistock, 1983, p. 23
8. Ibid., p. 16
9. Hinton, J., *Dying*, Pelican, 1967, p. 167
10. Ibid., p. 168
11. Parkes, C. M., *Bereavement*, Penguin, 1983, p. 57
12. Worden, William J., *Grief Counselling and Grief Therapy*, Tavistock, 1983, p. 43
13. Parkes, C. M., *Bereavement*, Penguin, 1983 p. 66
14. Battle, Allen O., 'Group therapy for survivors of suicide' in *Crisis, International Journal of Suicide and Crisis Studies*, Vol. 5, No. 1, pp. 52–4
15. Raphael, Beverley, *Anatomy of Bereavement*, Hutchinson, 1984, p. 120
16. Shneidman, Edwin S., *Deaths of Man*, Quadrangle, The New York Times Book Co., 1973, p. 41
17. Raphael, Beverley, *Anatomy of Bereavement*, Hutchinson, 1984, p. 402
18. Ibid., pp. 404–5

# Conclusion

Being involved in helping those who are suicidal constantly reminds us of the despair and sadness of so many people. The outcome of the majority of our encounters will be uncertain, which means we have to cope with our anxieties and to bear with the inconclusiveness. We will soon discover, if we have not done so already, how much we have in common with many of our callers. We will share the deep emotional feelings of love, power, loss, selfishness and weakness as part of our human response. Suicide, like war, can be given romantic, glorious and even honourable descriptions, when in reality both are about untimely death and destruction. We should have no illusions about how attractive the solution through death may become to any one of us. It is only when we touch the ultimate that we come, as it were, to the brink and then often we experience inner stirrings of hope.

Often we will not know the outcome, of our meetings yet sometimes, just through even one intense encounter, the caller's pain will be reduced. Those of us who have had the privilege of seeing many suicidal callers over a large number of years, have learnt from them how much they have been helped. Because of the intensity of our task and the emotional stress of many of our encounters, we need to relax and build up our confidence as an essential part of the helping process. So many people in their desperate hours need to be gently embraced with human warmth, confidence and hope.